Also available at all good book stores

9781785316357

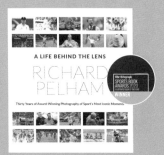

9781785315466

9781785317767

9781785318443

9781785313837

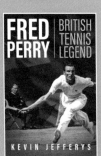

9781785312908

9781785313868

9781785313608

The
GOLDEN
BOY of
Centre Court

For Bill Condon,

the finest tennis player never to

appear at Wimbledon

(or so he's always told me)

The
GOLDEN
BOY of
Centre Court
How **Bjorn Borg**
Conquered Wimbledon

Graham Denton

First published by Pitch Publishing, 2021

Pitch Publishing
A2 Yeoman Gate
Yeoman Way
Worthing
Sussex
BN13 3QZ

www.pitchpublishing.co.uk
info@pitchpublishing.co.uk

ISBN 978 1 78531 777 4

Typesetting and origination by Pitch Publishing

Printed and bound in India by Replika Press Pvt. Ltd.

Contents

The Iceman Cometh

THE SPIRE of St Mary's Church rose up in the distance like a pencil point sketching a sky over south-west London. Standing on the roof of the competitors' tearoom at the All England Club, home of the Wimbledon Championships, the oldest tennis tournament in the world, a 16-year-old Swedish boy was gazing out over the expanse of outside courts towards it. It was early July 1972, and the youngster had not long claimed the title of Wimbledon junior champion, emerging from the final of the invitation event victorious against Britain's Christopher 'Buster' Mottram. Beside him, John Barrett, a former Davis Cup player and captain, asked the boy what his ambition was in the game. 'To be the best player in the world,' came the quiet reply. It was, Barrett later recorded in his book, *100 Wimbledon Championships: A Celebration*, 'spoken without a trace of conceit, stated as a fact'.

It's perhaps appropriate that Bjorn Borg, born in 1956, came into the world on 6 June. For it was a national holiday celebrating Swedish Flag Day, a day that marked the crowning of the country's first monarch, King Gustav Vasa, in 1523 – in effect signifying the end of the Danish-ruled Kalmar Union, and the birth of Swedish autonomy – as well as commemorating Sweden adopting its constitution on the same day in 1809. Appropriate because, the only child of Margarethe and Rune – he was given his father's name for a middle name – Bjorn Borg grew up a spirited, strong-willed and thoroughly independent individual determined to plough his own furrow.

He was born and brought up in Sodertalje, an industrial manufacturing town of then around 40,000 people, 30 minutes' drive south-west of the country's capital, Stockholm. A predominantly working-class town, it was most notable for producing Volkswagen car parts. And ice hockey stars. Borg, like most Swedish schoolboys, was raised on the game, reared on a rink, slapping a puck back and forth. He was a highly promising player. Even at the age of five he showed signs of outstanding talent. At nine years old, he became the centre-forward for his town's junior team. The game was almost an addiction for him and for those first nine years of his life, the young athlete had no greater aim than to wear the jersey bearing the emblem of the 'Three Crowns', the shirt of 'Tre Kronor', the men's national outfit. There were many who considered him more than capable of achieving it.

Call it fate, providence, a happy accident, what you will, but, in the summertime of 1965, everything changed. Although an article by Shirley Brasher in *The Observer*, 3 June 1973, would state that had it not been for a lucky raffle ticket and a winning draw at his father's local table tennis club, Borg might never have played tennis at all, while English sports journalist Frank Keating had it that Mr Borg actually made his son his first wooden racket, the generally accepted story is slightly different: that Rune, 33 at the time and employed as a clothing salesman, was a very fine table tennis player – one of the country's best – and when he collected, as first prize in the town's annual championship, a golden, adult tennis racket, not interested in the game himself, he bestowed it to his son to simply, as Borg later recorded, 'play around with'. 'And that's how I started playing,' Borg would confirm time and again over the years as the tale became the stuff of legend.

Initially fascinated by its frame, once Borg took possession of the racket, tennis took hold of him. Starting playing, however, wasn't that straightforward. The racket too heavy for him to hold, the right-handed Borg gripped it with both hands, playing all his shots, forehand and backhand, in what was a distinctive two-fisted fashion, the way he'd learned to swing an ice hockey stick. To begin with, even hitting the ball he found almost impossible. But Borg was undeterred. Launching fanatically into his new obsession, practice morning and night – soon a daily ritual – brought brisk improvement.

Smacking a ball against the grey garage door at his family's home in a large modern complex – they lived in a first-floor apartment – Borg spent every spare moment, long, solitary hours, competing with himself, but pretending in his fair-haired head he was Sweden facing a formidable foe in a Davis Cup rubber. 'If I hit the ball five times against the door, I got the point,' he would recall. 'If less than five, the United States got the point.' And though the repetitive thudding sometimes drove his mother to beg him to stop and certain neighbours to complain, the youngster ploughed on regardless.

Having at first been turned away from the overcrowded beginners' course at the Sodertalje tennis club, when a vacancy opened, Borg spent the remainder of his summer there, honing his new skills from 7am until dusk, constantly pleading for someone to hit with, never willingly leaving the court until his parents collected him. Mrs Borg even asked if her nine-year-old son could enter the neighbouring village tournament's doubles to give him more match practice.

A placid, pleasantly modest child, Borg was, nonetheless, also one who possessed a vigorous urge to succeed; he strove to excel at whatever he did. Both Margarethe and Rune viewed his drive as a positive and necessary quality. In any field in life, they believed, you had to fight to achieve. It was something they'd always fostered. Weekends were spent organising games for him. On family boat rides to a close-by island, for instance, they'd tack a target to a tree and defeat the young Bjorn at darts. He was a boy who hated to lose. At anything. 'I cried and cried when I lost,' Borg recalled. 'They would let me win then, and I would get confidence back.' It was his parents, he would later acknowledge, that 'taught me to be competitive and persistent'.

He was extremely stubborn as well. 'If his mind was set,' his mother told ITV's Brian Moore during the making of a 1980 ITV documentary, 'it was impossible to change.' That quickly became obvious at the tennis club. While Borg's homespun groundstrokes made him a laughing stock with some, they had others tearing out their hair. Told by older members to alter his two-handed grip, that what he was doing was 'wrong', the youngster resisted, sticking steadfastly with what worked best, what felt right. 'The members got angry with me,' he recorded in his 1980 book, *My Life and Game*, 'because I obstinately refused to listen.'

It was at the club the following summer after enrolling on a course that he met Percy Rosberg. Sweden's leading tennis coach of the day, Rosberg was a teacher employed by the national federation to scout budding talent and prepare any discoveries for international play. In Sodertalje to observe the skills of two 13-year-olds, Peter Abrink and Leif Johansson, thought to be the country's rising stars, Rosberg instead had his practised eye caught by the skinny little novice about three years their junior. The ten-year-old Borg played what Rosberg termed 'working tennis', without much style; he didn't know how to serve (he had no timing); his grip of the racket was highly unusual; gangly and somewhat awkward, when he scurried around retrieving balls, he reminded his young opponents of a 'bull, charging'.

Yet Rosberg, knocking up with Borg for about 20 minutes each session, noted the young player's ability to return the ball consistently, accurately –

'he could put the ball where he wanted it' – and with great power. 'I had to run well even then to get it back,' Rosberg reflected some years afterwards. He was already remarkably quick about the court. 'His footwork was fantastic,' Rosberg said. The youngster also impressed the coach with his desire to learn – 'he kept bothering [me] with questions' – and his fighting spirit. There was something – 'this look in his eyes' – that told Rosberg that Borg was special.

Receiving both praise and criticism, Borg appreciated Rosberg's coaching methods. So, when the boy was invited to train with him at the Salk Club in Stockholm, he jumped at the opportunity. Soon, Borg embarked on a rigorous everyday routine of commuting by train to the capital after school, playing, coming home late, studying, bed, getting up to go to school, then getting on the train again. At school, his mother said, 'he read his home lessons very well', but it was in sport – soccer as well as ice hockey and now tennis – that his physical and mental energies had always been truly invested. And even though his devotion to tennis inevitably saw Borg's education suffer, far from interfering, Margarethe and Rune fully supported their son's pursuit.

Such was their backing that when, in July 1967, Borg heard brand-new Wimbledon champion John Newcombe say on the wireless that he had originally learned to play the game by reading a 50-year-old instructional book, *Match Play and the Spin of the Ball* by former American great, 'Big Bill' Tilden, Mr Borg selflessly scoured Sweden's bookshops for a translation so that his son could stay up nights reading and learning by heart Tilden's '13 Points for Young Players to Remember'. Among those the youngster committed to memory were: Tennis should be played defensively with an offensive attitude; Never ever blow an easy shot; Start a match with one alternative strategy up your sleeve – but never change a winning game; Have a killer instinct but also be a sportsman.

Borg had a strong advocate in Rosberg too. While the federation also wanted the youngster to ditch the two-handed grip, Rosberg, resisting any attempt to destroy Borg's unorthodox but effective groundstrokes, concentrated instead on improving his comparatively weaker serve-and-volley. Rather than rush the net, though, Borg preferred to stay back pounding away with metronomic rhythm and regularity. 'I feel good at the baseline,' he told the coach. And he was good. 'Even then he would hit one more ball back against the opponent,' Rosberg said.

His style was still questioned; it was 'too jerky' and unreliable according to all the teaching pros. 'No champion,' Borg was told, 'used that grip.' 'Change to a more accepted approach,' came the counsel. He still wasn't listening. Tennis, he felt, was a highly personalised game, one, he would later write, 'of instinct and common sense, rather than proper grips and tedious tips'. Despite what he was instructed and custom dictated, it called for innovation and originality. Playing in his own fashion, refusing to be trapped by the rules of technique, Borg confounded decades of coaching tradition; it was the unexpected, he later held, that gave him an edge over those that followed more predictable patterns.

As it turned out, whilst developing his game, Borg discovered that it was easier to hit the ball with topspin if he adopted a one-handed forehand, using a western grip with a closed racket face, holding the heel of the racket inside his palm and whipping the ball over the net. 'All wrist, like a ping-pong shot,' Rosberg called it. It gave the ball an exaggerated spin. Borg made the stroke with his shoulders open and his feet out of position according to the book. But like a table tennis player walloping the little celluloid ball, Borg now packed a forehand drive with a killer punch behind it. He was quickly snuffing out opposition.

Only 11 when tennis's Open era started in April 1968, he didn't need too much time to make a name for himself. In 1967, Borg had won his first tournament, beating Lars Goran Nyman in the Sormland County Championships, and over the next four years, he swept every junior championship in his age division. In 1968, he won the Swedish National School title; the following year, the National Junior Championships for 13- and 14-year-olds. By the time he was 13 he was beating the best of Sweden's under-18 players like a drum.

In 1970, the same year that he committed himself completely to tennis, Borg was selected to represent Sweden in his first international tournament, a junior championship in Berlin, the then East German capital. He won it. There were other impressive successes in tournaments in Barcelona, Milan and at the prestigious Orange Bowl in Miami on his first trip to the US in 1971 (a championship for boys 18 and under he would win again in December 1972 after a straight-sets victory in the final over a young American named Vitas Gerulaitis). On home territory he would serve notice with victories over some far more seasoned opponents – the Puerto Rican Charlie Pasarell at the Swedish Pro Tennis Championships in Gothenburg in October 1972 and Spain's Andrés Gimeno the following month at the Stockholm Open.

Borg possessed a fiery capacity for the game. He was a player of immense athleticism and endurance. One day, aged 13, after travelling down to Malen in the southern part of the country where tournaments in all age groups were taking place, he stayed on the court for 11 hours: a mammoth stint during which he completed nine matches, reached the finals of five different classes and won the 14-and-under event. 'I'm glad Bjorn didn't play in the women's doubles,' his mother was heard to say. 'We wouldn't have had time for lunch.'

That capacity, though, often manifested itself in much darker forms – and led the youngster into all sorts of bother. So fierce was his will to do well, Borg was, to use his own words, 'crazy', 'a real nut case', completely unable to keep hold of his temper on court. 'When I was young,' he recalled in a 1978 interview, 'between the ages of maybe 9 and 12, I would throw my racket, I screamed, I cheated.' He was, he said, 'hitting balls over the fence – everything'. The player's young friends might call him 'Nalle' for teddy bear (Bjorn means 'bear' in Swedish) but at times he was anything but cuddly.

Such antics left his parents so ashamed eventually they refused to attend any more of their son's matches. They'd done what they could to hand him some important lessons. Once when Borg pulled a tantrum in a match, his mother took care of the situation immediately. 'She took my racket away from me and locked it up for a month,' Borg remembered in 1981. 'She told me, unless I learned to control myself, I couldn't use it again.' The deprivation hurt. But still he struggled to stifle his anger.

He paid a price. The day following another outbreak of abuse – and racket hurling as he lost a quarter-final match at his club – someone called at the Borgs' residence to inform Margarethe that her son was being punished for his behaviour – the Swedish Tennis Association was suspending him for approximately three months. Borg was distraught when he heard. Living in such a small town, the news spread rapidly. 'People whispered behind my back about my being the "bad boy" of Swedish tennis,' he wrote in his book. In Sodertalje itself, they forbade him from practising at the club. They'd even wanted him thrown out for good. It was 'a devastating experience,' Borg said, that stung deeply.

It was events in 1972 that really provided the launching pad from which the youngster's life lifted off. In April, with the Swedish authorities' agreement and his parents' consent, Borg took his leave from Blomback school – quitting in the ninth grade, one semester short of the required period – to participate in the Madrid Grand Prix. The 15-year-old's decision made headlines around Sweden. Irrespective of the fact that he'd begun to hate studying, Borg was dedicated to making a success of his tennis career.

Earning fortunes was never a motivating factor, but even at 15 Borg was well aware of how lucrative the sport had become, that riches followed wherever success went. He was said to have pleaded with his parents, 'If you let me leave school this term, I promise to make you both a million before I'm 20.' Borg desperately wanted to repay them for the sacrifices they'd made. (Much of Borg's first earnings from tennis – of more than $60,000 in 1973 – went to buy a small local grocery store in their Sodertalje neighbourhood for Rune and Margarethe. They had always wanted to run their own business.)

The tournament was a decisive moment. After beating Italy's Antonio Zugarelli in the first round, Borg's victory over Jan Erik Lundquist, a Swedish tennis legend nearing the end of his career, qualified him for the Davis Cup team, which would face New Zealand in May. In Spain, Borg was knocked out in the next round by the Czech, Jan Kodes, but now had the chance to fulfil a dream he'd held for so long. The following month, in Bastad, a tiny seaside resort village of, at the time, around 2,000, on Sweden's south-western coast, and known as the Little Wimbledon of Scandinavia, Borg made his Davis Cup debut. Just shy of his 16th birthday and eight months past the age of the youngest-ever to compete in the cup, Haroon Rahim of Pakistan, Borg became the youngest player ever to win a match in the competition, triumphing over the experienced Onny Parun.

Two sets down to New Zealand's top player, Borg came back tenaciously to record a memorable upset. Under severe pressure, he'd held his nerve, displaying a remarkable calm for one so tender in years. In the decisive set, a bad call that he might well have questioned he simply let pass. He then beat Jeff Simpson in straight sets on the final day. At the end of the tie, the Swedish press hailed the youngster's display, declaring that he had '*is i magen*' ('ice in the stomach'). No one had thought he would win either match. Now, in a land where Davis Cup was everything, Borg was arguably the biggest Swedish sports hero since the one-time heavyweight boxing champion Ingemar Johansson.

Borg regarded representing his country as 'a great honour'. His captain's advice to switch to a lighter racket mid-match had also played its part in his victory. That captain was a man 31 years his senior. A native of Alingsas, a city in Sweden's Vastra Gotaland County, Lennart Bergelin was an elegant, accomplished tennis player in his day, outstanding at doubles. Winner of 20 national championships (nine singles and 11 doubles), in 1948 he became the first Swede ever to win a grand slam crown, partnering the exiled Czechoslovakian Jaroslav Drobny to the French doubles title. In 1951, Bergelin won the German championships. His career saw appearances in three Wimbledon quarter-finals too. For eight straight years from 1946 to 1955 he was a mainstay of Sweden's Davis Cup team, winning 62 of his 88 rubbers, at one time leading his country to a famous upset of Australia in 1950.

Upon retirement in 1959, after a spell selling Lambrettas and Vespas in a Stockholm suburb, Bergelin turned to coaching. Taciturn, somewhat strict but also good-natured, the tall, balding Bergelin was an extremely shrewd figure who brought a wealth of knowledge to his tennis tuition. It was little surprise when, in 1971, the national federation invited him to become Davis Cup captain. He agreed, on one condition: that he could take the country's best young players around the world for six months of the year to gain expertise playing in international competition. One of his first recruits was the 14-year-old Borg, a player he'd originally encountered when the youngster, then 13, was losing the final of a tournament for which Bergelin was handing out the prizes.

Bergelin was another who'd recognised Borg's exceptional quality early on. He'd 'never seen such magnificent groundstrokes, or anyone who moved so fast,' he said. Borg 'was dancing on the court, all the time'. Yet, at the Davis Cup training sessions, his relationship with the youngster might have been broken irreparably before it had even fully formed; what became a memorable weekend at Bastad was nearly ruined by one more Borg flare-up. During the try-outs for the team, Borg, losing a set in a match with Ove Bengtson, questioned three calls made by Bergelin who was officiating as the umpire. 'I even called him a cheat,' Borg admitted in *My Life and Game*, 'at which point Bergelin went berserk, pushing me over the courtside benches and hurling a racket at my head.'

From his chair, an infuriated Bergelin had first of all thrown down a box of tennis balls at Borg before the pair engaged in a vicious row. Borg quit the match in tears and refused to practise for two days. Man and boy did not speak to one another. It was Bergelin who took the flak, the press criticising him over what was deemed 'harsh discipline' and 'bullying' of his players. When Borg was named to face New Zealand, however, any complaints disappeared. The always pragmatic and rational Bergelin never fretted over the choice. 'Despite his young age, I simply didn't have anyone else,' Bergelin wrote some years later. 'He was already the best in the team.'

There were still times when the tiger got loose. 'I guess the 15th and 16th years are rough periods for succumbing to tantrums for many players,' Borg reasoned in his book. A month later, in the Championship Cup against Leif Johansson, Borg's rival neighbour from Sodertalje, Borg queried a call by stomping over to Johansson's side of the court and circling the mark on the clay where his ball had hit. It was captured by national television cameras. He lost the decision and the match, and his own reputation suffered again.

The press who'd lauded him for his coolness against Parun now wondered whether this was, in fact, Borg's true character surfacing. A genuine turning point had occurred, though. Not only had Borg been instantly embarrassed by his conduct but, afterwards, he rued bitterly that it had so upset his concentration that it cost him the match. It was to be, as Borg later referred to it, 'the last real display of poor sportsmanship of my career'.

Their set-to all but forgotten, Bergelin effectively took Borg under his wing and took over as the youngster's full-time coach. It was an invaluable association. In the fullness of time, as their bond cemented, he would not just be Borg's trainer and physio but a friend, mentor, father-figure, confidant and constant companion, accompanying him to all the major tournaments, acting as a de facto agent, taking care of everything from Borg's travel arrangements to planning meals to sourcing practice partners (more often than not fulfilling that function himself). Most importantly, perhaps, he would perform the role of shield to Borg against an intruding world, providing a protective cocoon that allowed the player to concentrate on nothing else but showing up for his matches fit and ready.

Bergelin's influence was felt almost immediately. 'Early on,' Borg said of him, 'he taught me three rules: first, play tennis; second, eat well; third, live cheaply.' They were rules by which Borg tried to live from then on. Bergelin believed in old-fashioned values, like hard work and proper preparation. He instilled this into his young prodigy. A double dose of daily practice was demanded from Borg. A sensible lifestyle was encouraged. There would be no drinking, smoking, gambling. No special girlfriends. The youngster accepted that it was necessary. He didn't feel he was missing out. Tennis was his 'fun'. Gaining victories gave him the highs others found in less healthy activities.

His tennis improved and so did his temperament. What Bergelin did was set about channelling Borg's passion into winning instead of allowing him to waste it fighting a turn of fortune or against an opponent. Borg sought to mirror the manner of his childhood idol, the great Australian Rod

Laver. 'Rocket Rod', the little red-haired left-hander from Rockhampton, Queensland, had followed in the illustrious footsteps of countrymen Ken Rosewall and Lew Hoad to dominate tennis in the 1960s, with 11 grand slam successes just in that decade. Soon after he won Wimbledon in 1962, for the second year running, Laver joined the professional ranks, so the tournament was a no-go for the next five years. When he returned in 1968, in the first Championships of the Open era, he captured the men's singles title again, many regarding it an even greater achievement as he had to better all the pros this time. A fourth Wimbledon crown followed in 1969.

Laver played with a humility that made him eminently likeable. Though just 5ft 8in tall, the Australian was immensely strong with a bulging left forearm, and was a real fighter. But one of his greatest attributes was that he always focussed on the game. 'The next point – that's all you must think about,' he once said. 'I admired his concentration and straight face,' Borg would say. 'He never got upset.' So, under Bergelin's watchful eye, Borg set about adopting a similar attitude, above all cultivating the cold countenance that he'd endeavour to wear on court whatever fate may throw his way. Even if a stormy sea was raging within, on the outside only a glacial calm would show.

Like Drobny and Romania's Ion Tiriac, who had both started out on ice too – the latter representing his national team at the 1964 Winter Olympics – Borg had made the transition from ice hockey to tennis fairly easily. Strength and quickness of the eye were important in both sports. It was ice hockey, Bergelin reckoned, that toughened up Borg and made him such a strong figure on court. Borg's inner (rather than outer) aggression is what had first appealed to Bergelin. It was a quality the former Davis Cup player regarded as the most important – it controlled everything else in the game – but was one, Bergelin believed, that 'cannot be learned'. Borg had what Bergelin termed 'the right kind of courage'.

That courage was never more evident than during the two weeks from 26 June – 9 July 1972, when Wimbledon got its first glimpse of Borg's precious talent. Competing for what was officially termed the Boys' Singles tennis title, Borg eased through four rounds of three-set matches to make the final, where he met Christopher 'Buster' Mottram (who'd squeezed past Vitas Gerulaitis in his semi-final).

The son of Tony Mottram, who represented England between 1947 and 1955, and later coached the national team, Buster was tall, powerful and fast on his feet, a stylish player with great technical control. He was rated by those in the know as his country's finest young prospect since three-times Wimbledon winner Fred Perry. Against Borg, 14 months his junior, after losing the first set 3-6 then taking the second 6-4, Mottram led 5-2 in the third and looked destined for victory on home soil. But the young Swede, again exhibiting traits that had been evident in Bastad, recovered from the deficit, winning five games on the bounce to dash the Briton's hopes.

Borg's name was posted on a winners' board at Wimbledon for the first time. The boy who, unlike many top players, hadn't been given a tennis racket as a substitute rattle had learned fast and matured swiftly. For someone who'd only been playing since the age of nine, he'd made astonishing strides in the game. But the craving for taking more was voracious. And after his success on that rather cool July day, his thoughts were already elsewhere. As the 16-year-old stared out from the staid old stadium on the outskirts of England's capital there was no limit to the horizons he had in his mind's eye.

25 June – 8 July 1973

ON SATURDAY, 23 June 1973, two days before the action commenced at the 87th All England Lawn Tennis Championships, a BBC Two preview show starting at 9.50 that evening saw bespectacled presenter Harry Carpenter and veteran tennis commentator Dan Maskell 'assess the form and the prospects of the favourites' heading into Wimbledon and also 'look back at some of the great champions of recent years'. As part of the one-hour-and-five-minutes long programme they recalled, too, the previous year's memorable final between Stan Smith of the USA and Ilie Nastase of Romania – 'and who doesn't want to see that again?' asked *Radio Times* in its new issue.

However many might have wanted to, no one would be seeing it. Earlier that day, in brilliant sunshine, a sell-out crowd had jammed the Queen's Club in West Kensington, London, to watch Nastase face Britain's Roger Taylor, anticipating what they thought might well be the line-up for the Wimbledon men's singles final a fortnight hence. The Romanian won 9–8, 6–3. Taylor, under normal circumstances, would have been far from favoured to reach the last two of the world's most celebrated tournament. But normality was a ball that had long been slammed out of the court, perhaps never to be found again, because in the early hours of the morning that Saturday, despite hopes that it still might be called off, a boycott of Wimbledon by 81 members of the Association of Tennis Professionals (ATP) had been confirmed – the climax to weeks of bitter wrangling between the nascent players' union and the International Lawn Tennis Federation (ILTF).

Its catalyst was a 33-year-old Yugoslavian named Nikola 'Niki' Pilic. The month before, Pilic, a muscular, lissom athlete whose best year at Wimbledon was 1967 when he lost a semi-final to Australia's John Newcombe, the eventual champion, had allegedly refused to represent his native country in a Davis Cup tie against New Zealand, opting instead to play a well-paid doubles tournament in Montreal. Though Pilic denied the charge, the Yugoslav Tennis Association suspended the player from all international competition for nine months, a suspension upheld by the ILTF. He was also handed a lifetime ban from the Yugoslavia Davis Cup team. Although the barring from competition was then decreased to one month, until 30 June that year, it still prevented Pilic from playing at Wimbledon, due to commence on the 25th. The ATP, of whom Pilic was a member, contested the ILTF's right to exclude a player without due process. Pilic, they claimed, had been unfairly treated. Ban the player, they said, and you ban the entire group.

The advent of tennis's Open era in 1968, when grand slam tournaments agreed to allow professional players to rub shoulders and compete with amateurs, had spawned a period of great change and much turmoil. The emergence of rival circuits caused clashes of interest, the chief conflict taking place between World Championship Tennis (WCT), the Dallas-based promotion organisation set up by Dave Dixon (later succeeded by Lamar Hunt), to whom many of the top players were contracted, and the ILTF, which approved the Jack Kramer-conceived Grand Prix circuit.

With the national associations around the world (within the ILTF), along with commercial promoters, really making all of the decisions regarding who played where and when and for how much money, players were left straining for their rights. Nobody represented the male professionals as a group, so the ATP – essentially a union to protect players' interests – was formed in September 1972 at the US Open by former Davis Cup captain Donald Dell its lawyer, the ex-Wimbledon champion Kramer its executive director, and South African Cliff Drysdale its first president. The American player Arthur Ashe was installed as treasurer.

The ATP welcomed the spread of the game; what they wanted was for players to have a bigger share in its control. They proposed a new international council on which representatives of the ILTF, tournament directors, the players as well as sponsors would all be included and all have a say in how tennis was run. For too long, in their view, the existing national and international bodies had attempted to run the game along dictatorial lines; they were too autocratic, virtually ordering players to play at their whim. The basic grievance was that, while professionalism was accepted, the system was not geared to administer it. A more updated administration was needed to cope. The ATP considered the ILTF rules to be out of tune with the modern game – many had been written ten years prior during tennis's amateur days and were no longer relevant – including the one that compelled a man to appear for his country in the Davis Cup if he was selected: the rule that led to Pilic's ban.

The ATP's fight wasn't with Wimbledon. It just so happened that The Championships found itself slap bang in the middle of the acrimonious dispute. All England Club chairman Herman David was, if anything, sympathetic to the players who were standing behind one of their union members. On the Tuesday evening, in the week preceding Wimbledon, in protest at Pilic's exclusion, the ATP players decided to withdraw from the tournament. A few days of intense efforts at mediation and wrestling with consciences followed but no settlement was reached, and a burgeoning crisis quickly came to a head.

Despite much debate and even the attempted intervention of Sports Minister Eldon Griffiths, after a conference at the Gloucester Hotel between ATP officials and many of the game's leading lights that lasted most of Friday night, any flickering hopes that a peace formula still might be forthcoming were finally snuffed out. At 3 o'clock on the Saturday morning, just seven hours before All England Club officials would sit down to study the entry list and make the draw, the ATP executive board, including Stan Smith, voted 6-2 for the walkout, confirming that 81 out of 84 of its members had signed a declaration not to participate. Their position was final and irrevocable.

Having originally accepted 112 players for the men's singles with 16 more places left open for the winners of the qualifying tournament going on between rain showers since Monday of the previous week, an alternative list of 128 was made up of the non-boycotters plus the hopefuls who entered the qualifying event. Dozens of lower-ranked players filled the vacated places; many who would not normally have got there in a lifetime of trying were now unexpectedly bidding for a sudden chance at fame, thrown into the hunt for a share of the £10,275 total prize money on offer. As one familiar name followed another out of the hat, it gave the tournament an unrealistic look.

Unsurprisingly, the Wimbledon organisers maintained a stiff upper lip. Despite the defections, they confidently expected the tournament to prove itself once again greater than the players. The previous year Wimbledon had managed without many of the big stars – the likes of top Australians, Newcombe, Laver and Rosewall – because of a dispute with WCT promoter Lamar Hunt, and attendances were the second highest in The Championships' history.

From the original seeding list – consisting of 16 seeds, instead of the customary eight, for the first time since 1970 – Stan Smith, John Newcombe, Arthur Ashe, Ken Rosewall, Tom Okker, Marty Riessen, Roy Emerson, Tom Gorman, Cliff Richey, Adriano Panatta, Manuel Orantes, and Bob Lutz were all now missing. Just four – Nastase, Taylor, Jan Kodes of Czechoslovakia, and the Soviet Alex Metreveli – were left in a revised draw of only eight seeds.

Nastase, according to the *Evening Times*, had 'elected to stay with tradition' and 'let his fellow professionals in the ATP seek their own salvation'. The truth, however, was a little more complicated. Nastase, as an ATP member, had firstly responded to the group's strike call by withdrawing from the Wimbledon competition, but his decision to compete had been forced upon him – a letter from the Romanian tennis association in Bucharest brought an about-face; his government made it clear to Nastase that, while he was able to enjoy a home in Belgium (he had a flat in Brussels) and to play tennis all around the world, he was still a citizen of a communist country and he shouldn't forget it.

Taylor, too, initially told the ATP that he would join the boycott but delayed signing the declaration form and confessed he was in an agony of indecision before finally, just as the draw was about to start, phoning tournament referee, Captain Mike Gibson, to say he would honour his entry. Taylor put his loyalty to his national association first. British tennis officials were jubilant over the decision. His playing colleagues not so. Taylor, in the company of his lawyer, had already been informed by ATP officials that should he defy the ban he would not be allowed to play in any of their tournaments again. Despite denials by Arthur Ashe of any attempts at coercion, the pressure on both Taylor and Nastase to not participate had been strong. Jack Kramer told the press that Taylor would have 'nowhere to hide'. Nastase, Taylor and Australian Ray Keldie – the other ATP member who'd defied the group's wishes – all faced disciplinary action following The Championships. (They were each later fined.)

Cliff Drysdale called it 'an all-or-nothing fight'. But the ATP soon came under criticism because of the strong-arm methods used by some players to persuade their fellow pros to join the walkout. There were reports of threats against those who refused. Inferences were made to younger players that, unless they withdrew, the ATP could make it extremely difficult for them to get to America and play under the group's umbrella. The following week, John Barrett would announce his resignation from the association because, while he agreed with all the ATP was fighting for, he didn't agree with how they were fighting. He was particularly incensed about alleged attempts to intimidate 18-year-old British player John Lloyd (which Kramer denied had taken place). Nastase, staying with his wife, Dominique, in a hotel occupied entirely by ATP players, had to check out, and moved elsewhere. The atmosphere, he said, was 'very unpleasant'.

Feeling in tennis circles and in the press was running high, with public sympathy against the ATP. Accepting 'it would have been embarrassing in the circumstances' to carry on, Kramer, unsurprisingly, gave up his job as a BBC television commentator, a role that had made him a popular figure for a decade. One London newspaper publicly invited him to 'go home' to the States, and the *Daily Express*, on the tournament's opening day, suggested he resign his All England Club membership, which he had held since taking the men's singles title in 1947. Writing in the paper, columnist Frank Rostron described the ATP 'militants' as 'flannelled fools who left school too early and have learned little from their world travels but the rotation of the tennis courts and the banks'. The *Sunday Times* called the ATP an undisciplined rabble. Kramer, they wrote, was a bully.

However, one journalist, the Australian Peter Thomson, sympathised with the boycotters, criticising 'an astonishing blindness on the part of the amateur tennis officialdom, lawn tennis scribes and the public generally'. Statements, he wrote in *The Age*, 'carried the unfair inference that money is involved, and only money'. That wasn't at all what was at stake in Thomson's view. 'Just plain old-fashioned mutual respect and acceptance is what they asked for,' he believed. The pros who threatened 'one of the cherished institutions of the English summer … have a wider view of the game and its progress or lack of it' than the 'people whose life centres around one London suburb.' Thomson wrote 'They have already left for other places. Wimbledon from thousands of miles away falls into its proper perspective.'

For one player, perhaps, the boycott couldn't have been more fortuitous. Less than three weeks after his 17th birthday, Bjorn Borg was not only playing in the senior event at Wimbledon for the first time but suddenly found himself seeded No.6, observers reckoning he must be the youngest-ever male seed since the idea of seeding was introduced in 1927. Already a household name in his native Sweden, Borg had fast established himself as one of the tennis personalities of Europe. After playing well on the Riviera early in 1973, reaching the final at Monte Carlo before losing to Nastase, the following month he'd taken another step nearer maturity and astonished experts by leaving in his wake an impressive list of victims at the French Open, the first grand slam tournament in which Borg had competed. On the way to the last eight the unseeded 16-year-old completely demolished Cliff Richey, a former US Davis Cup player, came from behind to upset French hero Pierre Barthes, and then outlasted another US Davis Cup star, Dick Stockton, before losing a rain-interrupted quarter-final to eighth-seeded Italian Adriano Panatta. The youngster had faltered at the Italian Open earlier in June only because he had to go to the dentist (handing a walkover to Jamaican opponent Richard Russell).

Generally accepted as the best junior tennis player in the world, Borg was now demonstrating he could hold his own in much older company.

Many of the world's leading tennis coaches described him as being more talented than either Lew Hoad (in 1953, the youngest player to be ranked world No.1, at age 19 years 38 days) or Ken Rosewall (only 18 when, also in 1953, he won his first singles title at a grand slam event, the Australian championships) were at the same age. Wimbledon, Borg had long stated, was the title he would like to win most. At 16-1, he was obviously a long shot but he wasn't without confidence – 'I play important matches very well,' he said. 'I play the big points well.' An outside chance or not, it was felt by many that Borg could turn out to be the main attraction of the fortnight.

With defending champion Stan Smith among the absent rebels, it was Nastase, the man whom the American beat in the previous year's final, who was immediately installed as a runaway favourite. The supremely talented but tempestuous Romanian was odds-on to become the first European in seven years to secure the title. That 1972 encounter, described by Dan Maskell as 'a see-saw struggle of complete opposites' – Smith, the lanky, 6ft 4in Californian from Pasadena, with the neatly trimmed fair hair and moustache, a quiet, calm man in complete control of his emotions, versus the short, swarthy-featured Nastase with his unruly mop of black locks and an explosive temperament – was hailed as the greatest final for 40 years, going the full distance before Nastase's artistic wizardry eventually succumbed to Smith's power-play.

Since his defeat, though, the Romanian's precise, lively tennis had secured him a first grand slam title, the US Open at Forest Hills when defeating Arthur Ashe; then successes in Paris (beating Pilic in the final) and Rome had solidified Nastase's reputation as the world's best on clay. Shot for shot there wasn't a more stylish player anywhere. On form and concentrating hard, he was almost unbeatable. Nastase, wrote Bill Brown in the *Evening Times* in 1972, 'has the sort of genius that can suddenly blossom like an orchid'.

Unfortunately, he also possessed a persona that often withered, whatever gifts he had. Russell Miller, in a *Radio Times* Wimbledon preview, described Nastase as 'completely unable to treat the tennis court with the required degree of holy reverence'. He was 'an incorrigible joker, a gentleman prepared to use every trick in the book'. Those 'tricks' – patently questionable forms of gamesmanship that he freely admitted he employed to needle opponents and break their advantage – were always unpredictable and invariably infuriating. Constantly falling, or turning his back and shouting, 'Stop, I'm not ready' precisely at the moment an adversary was about to serve, or outrageously mimicking his opponent's stance, were just some in the irrepressible Romanian's bag.

Off the court, Nastase was so nice and polite, butter wouldn't melt in his mouth. On it, that mouth was often expletive-filled; sudden and vicious outbursts were common. He'd bicker with linesmen and umpires over what he felt were incorrect decisions, engage in loud and vociferous arguments with cameramen, even direct insults (and sometimes tennis balls) at spectators. His nickname 'Nasty', though affectionately given him by his fellow pros, wasn't just a derivation of his surname – it was apt. Not for nothing was he also labelled 'the Beast from Bucharest' and 'Ilie the Terrible'. Nastase said often that he had no time for losers but, all too frequently, if the player's opponents were not good enough to beat him, he did it himself. His volatility continuously put him in the bad books of the tennis establishment and, the feeling was, it was preventing him from realising his full potential.

With such a weakened field at Wimbledon, it was considered the golden chance of a lifetime for Nastase to underline his tennis supremacy. For all the talent that was missing, once the tarpaulins were rolled back, the tournament still got underway in what the *Glasgow Herald* termed 'the spacious, flower-decked precincts of the All England Club' with all of the ritual that made it so unique. The blue-and-crimson hydrangeas were potted in window boxes, the cucumber sandwiches neatly cut, the strawberries and cream paired up again for their annual outing as a doubles team. With seats for Centre Court and No.1 Court sold out in February, months before Pilic's ban, both courts were packed well before the first ball was struck.

When Nastase took to the immaculate new turf for the opening contest, baking sunshine – with a cooling breeze – and a standing ovation from a capacity confetti-coloured crowd greeted him, the applause led by the Duke and Duchess of Kent who, in a rare exhibition of regal solidarity, stood up in the Royal Box as he entered (though, post-match, the player confessed 'I was too shy to look up', so missed the gesture). And, after the poisonous atmosphere of the previous few days, the match provided a successful antidote. The grass was slick and so, for the most part, was Nastase. Though perhaps apprehensive about his future, he produced some sparkling tennis, hitting winners when he most needed to and quickly seeing off Hans-Joachim Plotz, 6-3, 7-5, 6-2.

Plotz, an energetic little West German, had opened the previous year on Centre Court, too, against Stan Smith, from whom he got just five games. He fared a bit better this time, but was no match for the Romanian who graced the sunlit afternoon with a show of delicate strokes – precise cross-court shots, deft lobs and wickedly top-spun backhand volleys. A fitting repayment for the ovation accorded him. 'It was as if I were winning Wimbledon,' Nastase said afterwards of the marvellous reception.

If anything, Roger Taylor's welcome as he entered the arena was even more rousing – 'positively celestial' wrote the *Daily Mirror*'s man – the royal duo rising once again for an ovation that lasted several minutes as what the *Glasgow Herald* called 'a wave of defiant patriotism' swept through Wimbledon. Hailed in the press as a national hero, Taylor, who'd borne the brunt of the ATP's disapproval, rewarded the rapturous support by beating Jean-Louis Haillet, the 19-year-old son of former France Davis Cup player and winner of the 1975 French championships, Robert Haillet, without any bother.

The player who truly caught the gallery's imagination, though, was Borg. The filling in the Nastase-Taylor sandwich, the Swede's first senior big-time appearance at Wimbledon and his Centre Court debut was against Premjit Lall of India. On paper, the 32-year-old was a much more daunting opponent than Borg might have wanted. One of the best of India's post-war players, Lall was a well-versed Wimbledon competitor. In the second round at the 1969 Championships, the right-hander had come closer than anyone else to spoiling Rod Laver's bid for a second Grand Slam; he'd led the top seed and world No.1 by two sets to love and 3-1 in the third, the Australian ultimately denying Lall a significant upset then going on to win the title. Four years on, the Indian No.2 (behind Vijay Amritraj) was still no 'stiff'.

Yet, clearly unruffled by the occasion, Borg showed few nerves, and, as *The Times's* Geoffrey Green recorded in his match report, this 'new face, swift and precocious beyond his tender years … challenged the conventions with withering speed against the adroit, Oriental calm of Lall'. The 17-year-old made a sensational start. Serving four straight aces, he took the opening game to love and, while misjudgements threatened briefly to make a nightmare of his dream beginning, at 2-2 the youngster was jolted back to reality. Once he gained confidence the 'infant prodigy' (as Green called him) reeled off winners like an old hand, winning two successive games without dropping a point. The stately Lall might have had the experience but 'this Swede knows his lawn tennis onions,' observed the *Daily Mirror's* Peter Wilson. In the first set, won 6-3 in only 17 minutes, Borg surrendered just two points on his service. In the 22-minute second set, won 6-4, he lost a mere four.

Already the hallmarks of Borg's style were catching the eye: aside from his booming service, the 'forehand topspin driving ... provided a whirlwind of instant action,' Green noted. 'Rallies became of secondary importance as he tried to knock the cover off the ball.' His two-fisted backhand, in which the left hand was snatched away quickly after the ball had been hit 'as though the racket has become red hot' wrote Wilson, was like a hammer.

Borg's timing allowed him to generate much more power than his physique suggested. All hair and slightly hunched shoulders atop a slim build, with exceptionally long legs, the Swede seemed to have very little torso. On court, he strode with a rolling walk, 'a puzzling side-to-side rocking action,' Sports Illustrated's Curry Kirkpatrick called it, 'that is nearly Chaplinesque'. But if he appeared ungainly, it was deceptive. About his baseline he bounded lithely from one side to the other. Feline metaphors would recur in reports on Borg's matches. To Geoffrey Green, he was 'leonine'. Another journalist described him as 'thin, cat-quick, long-haired', while others said he ran 'with the speed of a puma' and was 'nimble as a panther'.

In the third set, though, as Green recorded, 'Lall's cunning put a brake on the runaway success.' Tiring a little, and with the strongly built Indian more in touch, judging better his opponent's groundstrokes and beginning to counterattack, Borg was fully extended. At 8-7, he had a match point but spurned it, netting a forehand drive. When Lall levelled for 8-8, the tiebreak was introduced. 'And like all good artistes,' reported Peter Wilson, 'Borg saved the best and most exciting for the climax.'

The tiebreak, described by Geoffrey Green as 'pure Russian roulette, as first one and then the other avoided the bullet,' took an agonising 20 minutes to complete, Borg, belying his youth, refusing to crack despite Lall dominating from the net, finally winning it 20-18 on his eighth match point after surviving six set points. The 38 points eclipsed the previous highest total of 19-17 set at the WCT finals in Dallas two years earlier by Britain's Mark Cox and the Australian Roy Emerson, winner of the Wimbledon singles title in 1964 and 1965. The raw young Swede was already breaking records.

He was also capturing hearts. Lall's mishit volley from another tremendous Borg forehand ended the 100-minute drama, but a love affair had long before started. A delighted crowd had taken to Borg almost immediately, warming to his go-for-broke attitude, with the schoolgirls who always flocked to SW19 particularly smitten. Tall, tanned and blue-eyed, with handsome, clean-cut good looks, and blond hair fashionably flopping around his broad shoulders, Borg was a flame bound to draw in his fair share of moths. Cheered and applauded throughout by his young supporters, at the end of the match Wimbledon's brand-new pin-up was almost mobbed as teenagers rushed on to the court. 'I've never seen this before in my life,' declared Dan Maskell from the BBC TV commentary box. Nastase was a huge favourite with his own set of fervent female followers who surrounded him in small clusters as his matches concluded, scrambling just to touch his sweat-saturated shirt. But this was quite unprecedented.

Borg's exciting debut lit up the opening day. Thrust into the spotlight, he'd shone. In the wake of his win, the punning headlines were inevitable – 'A STAR IS BJORN!' cried the *Daily Mirror* in bold capitals. The Swede didn't lose a single service game, hitting a stream of aces – 19 in all – and double-faulting only once. 'The pace of Borg's serving, the boldness of his volleying and the accuracy of some of his passing shots – all those spectacular weapons helped to turn him into an instant hero,' enthused *The Guardian*'s David Gray. 'Who is going to miss Cliff Richey or Charlie Pasarell when there are players of this quality to take their places in the centre of the stage?'

A host of little-known names or not, the first-day crowds still flooded in – nearly 23,000 – overflowing the stands, sipping tea and promenading in the annual fashion show that made Wimbledon as much a social occasion as a sporting one. The players may not have been the same, but the atmosphere was. At least to some. On a noisy, emotional day, proceedings on Centre Court 'seemed more like a celebration than competition' wrote Gray. *The Times's* Rex Bellamy, despite 'a great many worthy amateur talents on view', was less impressed, describing the scene as 'a lovely, familiar old painting in which the central subject had suddenly faded'. Wimbledon's inimitable appeal was there but around the outside courts the 'public looked blank and vaguely puzzled as if they had turned up at the wrong party'. 'There are about 80 players out there I don't even know,' one veteran umpire had reportedly said, 'and I get around.'

The *Daily Mirror's* Frank McGhee took an even dimmer view. He wasn't convinced by 'those Wimbledon diehards who cling with stubborn optimism to the theory that whatever happens their tournament will be successful because it is quite simply the best'. The fare was pedestrian. The men's singles had 'meagre appeal' and it would be a 'tragedy' should either of the 'folk heroes', Nastase and Taylor, exit before the semi-finals, at least. Borg's hit performance was greeted with delight but, to McGhee, 'the enthusiasm of the Wimbledon "establishment" for the youngster's success ... smacked of clutching at straws'. He continued, 'The boy isn't yet big enough to rescue a tournament the size of this one on his own. Still, the organisers must now be praying almost as hard for the survival of this blond athlete' as they were for the longevity of Nastase and Taylor.

If they were, their prayers were answered. Two days later, on an afternoon of leaden skies and unsettled weather, with play halted early when what Rex Bellamy called 'the kind of rain that seemed to hang round like mist over marshes' turned heavy, Borg followed up his first-round triumph by scoring a second straight-sets victory, this time breezing past Belgium's Patrick Hombergen, 6-4, 6-2, 6-4. In another dynamic display, the youngster seized the initiative, clipping the back corners of Hombergen's court with his ferocious forehand drives and hitting backhand strokes that the Belgian seldom got near. Borg lapsed temporarily in the third set and lost a service game for the first time in the tournament, but he hastily reasserted his authority to earn a well-deserved win.

The legion of adolescent fans turned out in force once more. Wedged shoulder to shoulder around No.2 Court – latecomers couldn't get near – they'd chatted to their new idol throughout the match; and at its conclusion, as a sea of teenagers swished beneath him, the umpire, reported the *Sydney Morning Herald*, 'was marooned in his wildly rocking high chair', while two policemen were swept off their feet by the girls trying to reach the 17-year-old Swede. Rex Bellamy observed their adulation later on. 'When he [Borg] was driven away last evening it sounded like some pop festival, with his admirers screaming and Borg waving shyly (as if modestly aware that something was expected from him) as the car inched its way through the mob.'

According to some papers, Borg was keeping his mixed doubles partner by his side as a buffer against any over-enthusiastic fanatics. Helena Anliot, the 16-year-old Swedish junior champion, who lived in a village near Stockholm only ten miles from Borg, was someone with whom he'd often been seen. Borg wore her initials on a chain around his neck and talked warmly of their relationship, which Helena described as 'very happy'. Hugging her for the cameras, he told reporters: 'She is my shield. This is my way of frightening off all those girls.'

But his hope of warding off amorous attention was forlorn. On a thundery Thursday afternoon against West German Karl Meiler, Borg was once again the chief exhibit, cheered on by a shrieking gallery as thousands of young girls packed the standing room around Centre Court.

Reporting on the match, Peter Wilson, a veteran of 37 Wimbledons at the time, claimed it was the first time 'the green cathedral … has been transformed into a top-of-the-pops session for teeny-boppers'. Wilson studied the west side of the court, 'And of the 1,250 or so places, I swear that only the odd 50 were occupied by men – and that scarcely a girl there was out of her teens.' *The Guardian*'s David Gray concurred. Every girl 'looked as though she belonged to the fourth form,' he observed. 'Straw hats, blazers, satchels – young middle-class England letting its hair down.'

After successive wins against what Rex Bellamy termed 'respectable, if not intimidating opposition', in his third opponent Borg faced a much tougher proposition. Meiler – a large, introspective man 'who gives the impression that, even if he has nothing to worry about, he will soon think of something' wrote Bellamy – was a powerful player with a range of fluent groundstrokes – all of them hit uncompromisingly. On the circuit they called him a 'clubber'. He could be either brilliant or appalling.

At the start of the year Meiler had beaten Ken Rosewall (claiming the notable scalp of the top seed on his way to reaching the semi-finals of the Australian Open), and also enjoyed recent victories over both Nastase and Taylor (blasting the Sheffield man to defeat when architect of Germany's Davis Cup quarter-final humbling of Britain in May). Possibly the best non-seeded player at Wimbledon, Meiler had come through against America's Greg Peebles then dealt firmly with another teenage wonder boy, 16-year-old Billy Martin, who, the previous August, had become the youngest player ever to compete in the US Open.

In an opening week when the tennis was often interesting, often entertaining, but rarely touched any great heights, Borg's clash with Meiler was the first real sizzler – though for two sets looked a foregone conclusion. Hampered by a heavily bandaged right wrist and a misguided obsession for drop shots and stop volleys, which either stopped too soon on Meiler's side of the net or the fleet-footed Swede flicked back time and again, the German to begin with could do little to stop his 17-year-old opponent.

Speeding deer-like about the court, Borg, 'lightly and quickly mobile and discreetly adventurous in his panache' wrote Bellamy, dominated. With a flurry of aces and service winners, he dropped only one point in his first three service games. A succession of winning forehands – sharp, brave shots that were never far from the lines – gave him a break at 3-2 and when he went on to seal the first set and then the second after a single service break again, it looked to be plain sailing.

But Meiler then began to put together all the wayward pieces of his game. As he discovered his touch, Borg lost his rhythm. In an extremely long sixth game of the third set, leading 40-30 on service, Borg double-faulted twice to go 4-2 behind. It was the first sign of his faltering. After Meiler hung on to take the set 6-3, he retained the upper hand in the fourth set. Borg started badly, dropping his service in the opening game and Meiler was now not only getting his service in but thumping Borg's as well. 'The Swede's attack, which had been like a Viking's battle-axe,' wrote Peter Wilson, 'was now a rubber sword.' Despite his pressing, Borg appeared tired, Meiler running up a 5-1 lead, losing only five points in the process, before wrapping up the set 6-2 to level the match.

Borg's supporters – 'Bjorn's Battalion' David Gray called them – had endured an hour of tormented doubt. When Borg played a game full of errors and was broken at the start of the decisive fifth set, their heart-throb looked all washed up, his maiden Wimbledon voyage nearing its end. Not yet. Borg, though still erratic, suddenly stormed back. With a double fault, a net-cord dribbler and one of Borg's flashing backhands that caught him flat-footed, Meiler dropped his service to love and the Swede, his confidence restored, soon regained his early mastery. 'The scalpels of his groundstrokes were honed to perfection,' reported Wilson.

Borg won four games in a row. As he counterattacked, 'St Trinian's exploded into the noisiest of ecstasies,' noted David Gray, 'and the moppets began to squeal and clap again,' said Wilson. A rattled Meiler started the fourth game with another double fault and when, on his second break point, Borg hit a perfect lob that Meiler chased before falling over near the baseline, the loud cheer from Borg's partisan following that greeted Meiler's topple triggered the German into an angry rebuke for what he obviously thought very unsporting conduct: he 'raised his racket to the crowd in a gesture more familiar in Italy,' stated American journalist Robert Musel. Although he recovered, twice holding service, Meiler couldn't make up the lost ground. The crucial argument had been settled. Borg held to love to seal his 6-4, 6-4, 3-6, 2-6, 6-3 victory and, Bellamy wrote, 'the terraces erupted in a bedlam of teenage delight'.

'Wimbledon's hallowed Centre Court may have seen better tennis but it has never heard more disturbing – or high-pitched – cheering,' wrote a UPI journalist. Peter Wilson reported that 'the squealing and the oohing and the aahing reached such a high pitch that they were almost inaudible to the human ear'. It was relentless. Besieged afterwards and needing a police guard outside his dressing room, Borg described the hero worship as 'unbelievable'. He was still finding his voluble fans hard to get used to. 'Girls here talk to me all through matches,' he said. 'It's not so bad on Centre Court. They are a bit removed. But on other courts it can be upsetting. They call to me during games, and when I change ends. They will say, "Oh, look at me", "You're so sweet" and "You're lovely." It's nice but not all the time.' The shy, self-effacing Swede found such comments 'embarrassing'.

It was the violence of their support that the German took exception to – they'd shouted encouragement for Borg even when Meiler made mistakes. At the end of the match, Meiler, refusing to walk off with his opponent, had almost sprinted from the court. Borg's fans even forced a change of schedule later that day. With the Swede's evening doubles match due on No.4 Court, scores of school-age girls either patrolled all possible routes from the dressing rooms or took up station courtside, separated only by a waist-high canvas from the playing surface. Meanwhile, 'in the referee's room a historic decision was being taken' reported Musel. 'Matches have been switched from one court to another practically since the famous tournament started 96 years ago. But never for the reason of possible danger to life and limb of a player. And no one who has seen the teeny-boppers in action here has any doubt Borg ran the risk of affectionate injury from his over-stimulated fans.'

Borg's doubles match was moved to the fully enclosed No.1 Court where admission was by ticket only, save for a few standing-room places. The news of the switch drew gasps of disappointment. Even then Borg had to be smuggled on to the court via a catwalk to avoid an ambush and, after the match, sneaked off the premises via the women's changing rooms. 'Was Wimbledon ever like this?' asked Rex Bellamy.

It was an odd first week all round. The crowds milled about in their thousands, but memorable play was at a premium. All eight seeds, no doubt to the joy of tournament officials, made the last 16. The other idol of the crowds, Nastase, had been celebrating his top seeding by clowning it up off court. He appeared on the first day dressed in a wig, a drooping moustache and a floppy hat. Then, on another day, went skylarking into the stands of No.3 Court made up as an ice-cream vendor. On court, though, he wasn't so chipper. The mercurial Romanian, after beating Plotz, gave his supporters and All England Club committee members a scare, dropping the second set to 27-year-old Colombian Ivan Molina, before donning a pullover and getting down to business to register his 50th win in his last 51 matches. But during the second-round victory, Nastase, his moods swinging between jocular and morose, kept feeling his back tenderly and generally created the impression of a man in grave pain; kidney trouble had bothered him for years, and the discomfort had apparently resurfaced in the match.

Nastase consulted a medical specialist and, after receiving a clean bill of health, returned to top form, coasting past Toshiro Sakai of Japan and into the fourth round. There he faced unseeded Alex 'Sandy' Mayer, a law student from Wayne, New Jersey, who hadn't even practised on grass until he arrived in England the weekend before The Championships, a day after winning the American inter-collegiate clay-court title. The bright and breezy 21-year-old was only at Wimbledon, he'd declared, 'for fun' but his smashing serve and hard volleys had seen off Britain's Richard Lewis, Roberto Chavez of Mexico and Czech Vladimir Zednik. 'I can't hope to overpower or out-finesse him, so I've got to play solidly and wait for his bad streak,' said Mayer ahead of the clash with Nastase. He did just that – and more. In arguably the biggest upset for years, Mayer confounded himself and everyone else, beating the bookies' 2-1 favourite in four sensational sets. Nastase had played three matches the day before – a singles and two doubles – and maybe it was that, maybe his mystery back injury was troubling him, but he never looked to be on his toes. At times, he was limp and listless, playing as though he wanted to be beaten. (Ironically, after his opening match, Nastase claimed that some ATP players had asked him to deliberately 'throw' the game. 'Not me,' Nastase told reporters. 'I play to win. There is no way to make me throw a match. Wimbledon – that's the big one.')

He was slammed out without even the benefit of a Centre Court execution. On No.2 Court, the noisiest at Wimbledon, where the fans pressed in on the players, and one he particularly disliked, Nastase lost his rag on several occasions, even taking a verbal swipe at his schoolgirl fans. 'If I needed girls to scream at me, I would have brought my wife,' he cried out to a group at one stage. It was these same girls who shed a tear for him when he lost. Nastase's wife, Dominique, wasn't crying any, however. 'In a way I'm glad it's all over,' she said. 'Ilie had been under a great deal of pressure for the past week or so. Now we can relax, and enjoy ourselves.'

With Nastase's surprise departure, an already rather dim firmament lost its brightest star, and left the singles wide open. 'They called it the poor man's Wimbledon and that's just what it's becoming,' scoffed Australian writer Peter Stone. Another star was still on the rise, though. Borg reached the quarter-finals but with police protection once more required off court, again lived dangerously on it. Against Szabolcs Baranyi, history was nearly quick to repeat itself. Having taken the first two sets easily from the Hungarian No.1, Borg, as he had versus Meiler, lapsed. He suddenly seemed to lack confidence in his volleying and, as Baranyi charged back into contention, Borg boldly rushed the net and was passed frequently. Baranyi took both the third and fourth sets, and Borg once more had to go the full distance. But calling on all his reserves, he came roaring back. With cannonball services, convincing volleys and cunningly placed backhands, the youngster ran up a 3-0 lead in the final set, before going on to secure a 6-3, 6-2, 6-8, 5-7, 6-1 success.

Borg's reward was a tie against Britain's last hope, Roger Taylor. His odds shortened to 7-1, the Swede now faced his severest test. Taylor, the burly left-hander, who'd recently moved to a new home just half a mile from the Wimbledon headquarters, had 'suffered the death of a thousand mental cuts', according to Peter Wilson. The decision – whether to keep faith with his colleagues (Taylor was an ATP founder) or with the Wimbledon crowds – had bothered him a lot and occasionally he looked to be feeling the strain. Never at his best throughout the tournament, he'd nevertheless negotiated a reasonably safe passage to the last eight, past West Germany's Harald Elschenbroich (easily) and Czech Jiri Hrebec (less so), before labouring to a four-set victory against 22-year-old American Bob McKinley, the younger brother of 'Chuck' McKinley, Wimbledon champion in 1963.

Wide-shouldered and dark-haired, with film-star looks, Taylor had a brooding presence. For such a strong player he was blessed with a very deft touch. Borg claimed that the prospect of facing the man 14 years his senior was a happy one. 'I like playing left-handers,' said the youngster. 'It suits my game. I serve to his backhand.' But on a scorching Centre Court, under hot sun, it was the older man that started more assuredly.

While Borg seemed a little inhibited, the 31-year-old played beautifully, his fine tactical game overwhelming his youthful opponent. The Englishman's big serve was thundering past Borg 'who, at times', wrote Bill Brown, 'looked like the precocious youngster he is'. Hitting penetrating volleys and passing shots and lobbing effectively throughout, Taylor seemed to have Borg on the run. All the Swede's aggressive instincts were curbed or punished. Taylor swept through the first set for the loss of only the fourth game in just 16 minutes.

In the second set, though, after breaking Borg early, Taylor's service betrayed him. Its power, rhythm and timing went astray. Knowing Borg's talent for full-blooded returns, the third seed – determined not to offer 'a sacrificially short second service which the Swede could have murdered' wrote Peter Wilson – served fast and deep, but too often tried too hard. Less confident in his service, Taylor moved more slowly around the court.

In the fourth game, the 17-year-old broke back. 'The machinery of Borg's game had been lubricated by adversity,' wrote Bellamy, and the energetic Swede, with all the courage and enthusiasm of youth, attacked, hitting Taylor with a pacy topspin bombardment. 'It was all joyously spectacular,' reported David Gray. While 'the Yorkshireman merely smouldered', by comparison 'Borg blazed'. After breaking again, at 5-3 he served for the set. In vain. Taylor got back on terms and took the score to 6-6, yet he couldn't assert his old command. At 7-6 in Borg's favour, Taylor served and found Borg's cross-court volleying and return of service too much. A dramatic second set had lasted 44 minutes.

A rampaging Borg was now in the ascendency. With the schoolgirls urging him on, he surged into a 4-1 lead, eventually taking the third set 6-3, and Taylor was looking distinctly disgruntled. Drawing on all his experience, however, he steadied himself. Although Borg was still smacking brilliant winners, Taylor took control. At 2-3 in the fourth set, Borg lost concentration – fatally. Taylor broke service to love and, dismantling Borg's serve-and-volley game with cleverly placed lobs and stop volleys, went on to tie the match at two sets apiece.

Borg, brought forward to repeatedly chase drop shots and acutely angled volleys, all of a sudden seemed burnt-out. From 1-1 in the final set, he slid to 1-5 and, reported Wilson, 'The shrill trebles of Borg's "Boppers" were drowned by the bass note of old England.' Borg and his following appeared downcast and defeated. Two of the Swede's only four points in that spell had come via Taylor double faults.

In the seventh game, he faced two match points against him, but saved them both, with first a smash, then an ace. He was clearly encouraged. Borg, 'precociously mature in his competitive resilience' wrote Reg Bellamy, slowly crept back into the frame. With a stream of fierce, perfectly timed shots, he took four games on the trot to level at 5-5. Taylor had no answer to the young Swede's short drops, cunning cross-court shots and cannonballs down the line. He began to snatch at his volleys. He was now rocking on his heels.

In the next game, serving at 40-30, Borg held a point for 6-5 and seemed in sight of a vital advantage – only for fortunes to shift again. Borg was foot-faulted. And when Taylor, whose lead had melted away in the sun, hit two passing winners, the Englishman broke to forge ahead once more. Serving again for the match, Taylor went 40-15 up. A wayward delivery produced a 20th double fault but at 40-30 he still had a fourth match point. Taylor served to the left-hand court, fast and wide to Borg's backhand. It looked long, but the linesman, his view perhaps obscured by Borg's body, remained silent and the crowd erupted as the umpire declared Taylor the victor.

But Borg wasn't happy. Dropping his Slazenger racket, he spun round desperately to query the decision, only for the linesman, a Mr Alf Fulston, to indicate it was good. Taylor, though, surprisingly supported the Swede's plea. 'I could see that nobody was going to call the serve out,' Taylor said later, 'so I raised my arm to the umpire – who had already awarded me the match – to show him that my serve was a fault.' Taylor voluntarily offered to replay the point. 'I didn't want to win a match on a ball that was three inches out.' Questioned by the umpire as to whether he wished to reconsider, the linesman did alter his decision; the umpire requested that a 'let' be played.

It was a remarkable act of sportsmanship on Taylor's part, and one that immediately came back to bite him. When the point was replayed, Borg won it with a driven backhand return, and the score was now deuce. The bite, however, didn't prove lethal. Another serve, slower, was netted by Borg to hand the British No.1 a fifth match point. His first delivery hit the top of the net but fell into court 'to twist the knife of suspense yet again', wrote David Gray. Taylor's second service was bold and good and this time there was no argument; the Swede stretched wide and chopped his return into the net – the drama and his first Wimbledon was over. Taylor had won a stirring, always absorbing, often tense tussle 6-1, 6-8, 3-6, 6-3, 7-5 in two hours 35 minutes.

'At the end, the crowd applauded as though it had been a final,' reported Gray. For Taylor's staunch public it was a popular victory. For Borg's adoring mob, a heartbreaking loss. Several young girls rushed on to the sacred turf to commiserate with their thwarted hero before police drove them away. But the youngster remained the centre of attention; Taylor stood by as press photographers clustered around the loser.

'The only time I thought I could win was when I had that point for 6-5,' Borg told a packed news conference later. 'I think that if I had had a little luck, I would have won.' Nonetheless, he wasn't too downhearted in defeat. Playing on the famed Centre Court 'before large crowds and hearing the murmur from the stands' was a fantastic experience, he said. He was 'thrilled and exhilarated by the atmosphere'. Expecting to only win a round or two, Borg was, he declared, 'fairly pleased' to have made the last eight.

Given the perception of some that the boycott was about bank balances, it was one of sport's little ironies that four of the players competing for a semi-final spot weren't eligible for any of the prize money. Borg and Sandy Mayer were both amateurs, while neither of the two players from Communist Eastern Europe, Alex Metreveli (who preferred to be called a Georgian rather than a Russian) and Jan Kodes, could collect any financial reward – any money they won would go to their national tennis associations.

Of those playing for glory rather than gold, only Borg didn't make the final four. After his stunning victory over Nastase, Mayer showed it was no fluke and, demonstrating his fine match temperament, recovered from two sets down to beat the eighth-seeded West German No.1 Jurgen Fassbender. In his quarter-final, Metreveli faced Jimmy Connors, at No.5 the one prominent American player in the seeded ranks. America's great white hope, a 20-year-old left-hander with a swinging service and a walloping forehand, Connors had impressed on his first appearance at The Championships the previous year when making the last eight before losing to Nastase (though perhaps hadn't announced himself loudly enough – this year Rex Bellamy was still addressing the youngster as 'James Connors' in his match reports).

In declining to tour on the more prestigious WCT circuit after he'd first turned professional, preferring instead to be the unchallenged star of an under-publicised series of smaller but still lucrative wintertime tournaments operated by his manager, the freewheeling Bill Riordan (a former boxing promoter), the player had acquired a reputation as something of a maverick, a self-interested loner who refused to be one of the boys. His refusal to join the ATP only cemented that. Arthur Ashe bitingly labelled Connors 'the only American dissident' when he didn't embrace the walkout.

At Wimbledon, Connors had beaten two Brits, Mark Farrell then David Lloyd (in a robust Centre Court match of errors, Connors dropping his only set thus far), before wins against New Zealand's Russell Simpson and South African Bernie Mitton. After the exit of Nastase, with whom Connors had formed a doubles partnership and what would be a lasting friendship, the American – 'a happy-go-lucky player' according to the *Nashua Telegraph* – was made the new favourite for the title.

Whether or not carrying this burden on his sturdy shoulders affected him, Connors seemed overawed and never lived up to the occasion against Metreveli, serving 12 double faults and failing to find his rhythm. The Georgian, too, was on edge, snapping at suspect decisions, throwing his racket on the ground and a ball into the air. But Metreveli, who'd lost to Stan Smith in the quarter-finals in 1972, was much improved after joining the WCT circuit – and playing, Rex Bellamy reported, 'like a wise angler dealing with a strong young fish', he eventually overcame Connors in a dour battle.

Jan Kodes became the other semi-finalist. Unseeded 19-year-old Vijay Amritraj was the man he beat. Amritraj, who'd reached the last 16 by beating John Lloyd, the blond youngster described by Rex Bellamy as

'Britain's long-haired antidote to the Borg craze', and then caused an upset by nosing out seventh-seeded Australian Owen Davidson, was a tall, slender Indian who glided about the court, and stroked the ball with feeling and touch. But in a marathon five-setter, Kodes's extra know-how and doggedness saw him through to the last four for the second successive year. At the same stage a year earlier, the former economics major at the University of Prague had bowed out to Smith.

Nicknamed 'the Iron Man of Prague', Kodes was a moustached, middle-sized and muscular player renowned as a cagey fox, a real tough nut to crack. Although seeded second, the wiry Czech, twice winner of the French title, had looked a little ill at ease on the fast grass throughout the tournament. Alongside the brilliant flashes of players like Borg, his disciplined, functional game appeared far more unattractive. Rex Bellamy likened him to a miniature steamroller who 'tends to start slowly but subsequently crush everything in his path'. Next in his way was Roger Taylor.

A two-times Wimbledon men's semi-finalist already – losing to eventual runners-up, Wilhelm Bungert in 1967 and Ken Rosewall in 1970 (when the British No.1 had caused a major upset by putting out Laver in the fourth round), Taylor went into his clash with Kodes looking to be the first Briton to reach a Wimbledon final since Bunny Austin was beaten by Don Budge in 1938. The Centre Court crowd was rooting for him.

It was a match that assumed epic proportions. At two sets all and 5-4 to Taylor with Kodes to serve, a possibly pivotal decision was made. Blessed with fine weather throughout the fortnight, Wimbledon suddenly went awry in the rain stakes. Drizzle had been falling for three games or so and the light was poor. So, at the most dramatic moment, the referee, Captain Mike Gibson, decided to call a temporary halt. 'I am sorry about this,' he told the crowd in true British fashion. 'I am sure you wouldn't want either of these players to suffer an injury on these quite slippery courts – at this stage anyway.' Both players admitted later they would have preferred to proceed.

The break debatably cost Taylor the match. During the 42-minute interval, he stiffened up. The pair reappeared on court at 8.05pm but three games and eight minutes later, it was all over. The Czech won all three and a place in the final. A fascinating struggle had lasted four and a half hours. Taylor, who'd saved two match points but to no avail, was philosophical in defeat. 'You get used to this sort of thing,' he said. 'I played well and I lost. That's life. I'm a professional tennis player.'

By contrast, 28-year-old Metreveli had a much easier time of it versus Mayer. Appearing flustered and out of his depth, the American – his father, Alex Snr, one of Hungary's pre-war greats – lost his magic touch, double-faulting 12 times, regularly missing chances with volleys and smashes, and unable to cope with Metreveli's cross-court backhands. Metreveli, 'who looks and acts more like an Italian tenor than a Russian', one UPI journalist pointed out, indulged in a spot of arm-waving and shouting through which the watching Princess Anne, her cousin Princess Alexandra, and other members of British high society remained diplomatically silent. But his unspectacular tennis was enough to put a stop to Mayer's giant-killing as he became the first player from the Soviet Union to reach the final. The trophy was certain to go behind the Iron Curtain.

It was a first-ever men's singles final contested by two Eastern Europeans. Since 1936, not one Championship had passed without either an American or an Australian making the last two. But much in keeping with what had gone before, it was a largely uninspiring meeting. At Wimbledon in 1970 – the only time the two had met on grass – Metreveli had beaten Kodes in five sets, but the Czech had triumphed twice against the same opponent on indoor courts in America earlier in 1973. And it was Kodes, showing greater manoeuvrability, returning strongly and rallying well, who made it a hat-trick of victories, deservedly defeating a deflated-looking Metreveli to become the second Czech to win the title since Drobny beat Rosewall in 1954 (although Drobny was living in exile in Egypt then), and the first European to triumph since Spain's Manuel Santana in 1966.

After Kodes ran away with the first set, a tighter second reached eight games all, meaning the first-ever tiebreak came into operation in a Wimbledon singles final. But with Metreveli off his game, much as he had been throughout, Kodes capitalised on the Georgian's errors to win it 7-5. Following a break of serve in the fourth game of the third set, the Czechoslovakian duly tied up the 6-1, 9-8, 6-3 victory. Some spectators at Centre Court, though, hadn't even seen him do so; there'd been an exodus for tea before the final set commenced. As one reporter put it, 'There have been duller finals at Wimbledon, but in former years the crowd at least had the satisfaction of watching the greatest players in the world in action.'

'The ghost of Ilie Nastase haunted the men's singles final,' wrote Peter Stone. While Kodes plodded methodically and unsensationally to success, the flamboyant Romanian was only on the neighbouring No.1 Court, teaming up with Connors to win the doubles title, and the Centre Court clash, according to Stone, could have done with 'a little of the Nastase style' for 'there was no flair, imagination or excitement'. 'I felt the same way,' said Nastase later. 'All the time I was thinking I should have been on the court next door.' He'd found it hard to concentrate on his game when hearing the applause. The doubles win, he said, meant nothing to him. He couldn't even face playing the mixed doubles, so withdrew because his back was hurting again.

The *Evening Times's* Bill Brown offered an alternative view. Both Nastase and Taylor 'played like men who were suffering the tortures of the damned', he believed. 'In their heart of hearts I don't think either of them was too displeased at not gaining the title.'

In Brown's opinion, Kramer and the ATP had won a battle, and now had the whip hand. But there was still the serious prospect of full-scale war. Kramer was threatening that if there was no satisfactory change of policy among ILTF members, players might go it alone and take part in World Team Tennis, due to commence the following spring, which hoped to lure the top stars away from the ILTF circuit. Wimbledon, Rome and Paris would all be hamstrung. It was blatantly clear that you couldn't run major tournaments when the best men wouldn't play in them.

The year 1973 wasn't a vintage year at the All England Club. Whether or not the public was unhappy without the ATP stars, they still filled the courts. At 300,172, the attendance figure was the second-highest for half a dozen years. But, as one commentator described it, it was 'the ghost tournament' in which the 'absence of the biggest names in tennis took the tournament's backbone away'. It began in chaos and controversy and ran overtime, ending in anti-climax. In between, it mostly lacked sparkle, like flat champagne. There were too few upsets and there was too much bafflement at the unfamiliar names.

What zip and tingle of excitement there was had been provided by a 17-year-old. 'With everyone fearful that Wimbledon denuded of selfish stars might flop,' Peter Wilson wrote, 'a teenager with blond, shoulder-length hair became the new hero of The Championships.' To a tournament robbed of its prize jewels, Borg was a glittering presence. Playing with the calmness and conviction of a man ten years his senior, the 5ft 11in newcomer did nothing to cast discredit on his lofty ranking.

He might well have progressed further. The match with Taylor was Borg's third five-set singles encounter in a row, yet 'at 17 the bone and muscle isn't hardened enough for that' opined Wilson. The key to Borg's game was pace, but as David Gray sagely observed, he 'is not yet experienced enough to know how to slow down a player who is hammering winners all over the court'. Borg attacked but 'seemed to have no defence at all'. Trapped, 'he simply did not know how to escape'.

Fleeing the solid phalanx of idolising fans who poured over the courts to grab a piece of their sweetheart, packed the corridor outside his dressing room, or sought him out at his London headquarters was another matter. Right from the first moment he set foot on the Wimbledon court he'd become a Pied Piper. Borg, wrote David Gray, 'suddenly found himself elevated to the status of major star and pop idol'. Like a comet, he trailed a stream behind him wherever he went. Bras were proffered to him. He was flooded with letters and telegrams. The media coined a term – 'Borgasm' – to describe the rapturous response to the youngster.

Hounded by 12- and 13-year-olds, the way The Beatles had once been, tennis's first real glamour boy was actually forced to hide in his hotel room while female fans jammed the reception downstairs. He'd even had to take flight through a back window on one occasion. Borg was the first Wimbledon player to require a permanent escort – three burly policemen. 'Next time the boy comes back he'll need a bodyguard,' predicted Bill Brown.

His young air of vulnerability appealed not just to the teens but hardened Fleet Street hacks. He was a headline-writer's dream. Sobriquets often related to his nationality: Swedish Ace, Swedish Wonder, Swedish Whizz Kid. They maybe insinuated that he was some character from a comic strip, but Borg was no cartoon figure – he was very real and he was here to stay. Peter Wilson not only lauded him as 'surely the greatest player of his age' but 'a certain future champion'. 'I know my future depends on me and how hard I work,' Borg had said ahead of his first foray in the world of the Wimbledon men's singles. 'I think I can go all the way.'

No one who'd seen the teenager perform over the course of the two weeks in such an amazingly adult fashion had any doubts.

24 June – 6 July 1974

WIMBLEDON DAWNED in 1974 with its usual promise of intrigue and exciting possibilities. But the future of The Championships was the subject of some pessimistic mutterings. Professionalism might have sparked a worldwide tennis boom, with participation soaring massively, but it had also invited extensive gimmickry. What Scottish sports journalist Hugh McIlvanney termed '"Barnum and Bailey" attitudes' were progressively invading the game. World Team Tennis (WTT), a brainchild of Billie Jean King, was the latest revolutionary concept, where the first to four points won a game and matches were decided on one set only – and pleasing the fans, who were actively encouraged to hoot and holler, was almost as important as winning.

An inter-city competition in the US involving squads (of three men and three women) from 16 cities in a three-month season, WTT cut right across the European calendar. And although WTT director, George MacCall, promised a two-week break in its programme to allow its contracted players to compete at Wimbledon, stars signed up by WTT were ruled out of the French and Italian championships. European tennis administrators, especially in France, were openly scared of the threat WTT posed. Jack Kramer and the ATP board were staunch opponents. Kramer, whilst stressing that it was up to players themselves whether or not they got involved in the format, called it 'a dangerous issue', which harmed the long-range players' interest in a healthy worldwide tournament circuit. There was a genuine fear among some factions that, should the league be successful, it might spread to several months and the world's biggest talents, drawn to WTT's synthetic surfaces, would be too tired for any other competition. Including the tournament in SW19.

The *Daily Mirror*'s Colin Dunne, however, saw no cause for concern. 'For years,' Dunne wrote, 'Wimbledon has been the spiritual home of the cucumber sandwich. Middle-class, middlebrow, decent, respectable and terribly unchanging. Ladies who open bazaars leave their rose-pruning to come here to enjoy a carnival of genteel restraint in an orgy of understatement. Professionalism, commercialisation, women's lib and players' boycotts – Wimbledon has shaken them all off. Good Lord, it has even survived the Wombles.'

One Associated Press writer agreed. 'The world spins along at a maddening pace. Jets cross oceans in a matter of hours. Computers think like men. Men walk on the moon. But Wimbledon remains unchanged.' A modern breed might be 'attempting to take tennis out of 1818 stays and corsets and put it in hot pants' he wrote, but Wimbledon refused to budge. Any shift to bright pastel colours for attire had been resisted; its strict mandatory all-white clothing rule (entirely free of advertising) was still adhered to. White, not 'optic yellow', balls remained in use. As one aged Englishman remarked, 'If you want to shake up Wimbledon, you don't boycott her, you just buy up all the strawberries.'

On Monday, 24 June 1974, then, when the men's singles unwound, much was as it had always been. Yet something *was* refreshingly different. For the first time since 1971, after two years of disputes between warring factions, the field found itself with a full complement of the world's top players. With the exception of Rod Laver, who hadn't entered because he was having 'a rest from competition', all the big names were back. What was even more unusual, the star-studded line-up included not one, not two, but three players laying claim to the status of 'defending champion'.

Ahead of the 1972 Championships, the titleholder John Newcombe, barred from competing as a member of Lamar Hunt's WTT, had said, 'You can tell the guy who wins the singles this year I shall be after him in 1973.' But, prevented again from taking part by the ATP boycott, the Australian had had to wait twice as long to go after 'him'. And now there were two winners to target: Stan Smith, a narrow loser to Newcombe in 1971 before outlasting Nastase the following year, and Jan Kodes, who'd brooded since his workmanlike 1973 victory because tennis buffs, he felt, had yet to fully acknowledge his triumph.

Newcombe it was, though, who was the obvious choice for No.1 seed. The US Open champion and victor in Dallas at the recent WCT finals, the top prize of the touring pros, the player nicknamed 'Newk', was rated the world's best. Champion in 1967 (the last of the amateur era), 1970 and 1971, the Sydney-born powerhouse, an unflinching competitor, was hoping to equal his fellow countryman Laver's post-World War II record of four Wimbledon crowns and, at 7-4 on with the bookmakers, was the strong betting favourite to do so. Even some of his chief opposition, Kodes included, conceded that the athletic Australian with the distinctive drooping moustache was the man most likely to win.

Nonetheless, there were problems to overcome. With the terms of a commercial contract stipulating he had to use a wooden racket in Britain, Newcombe would have to forgo his customary steel weapon for the first time in nine months. And, as well as a two-year absence from Wimbledon itself, the player had little recent grass-court experience. A shock dismissal from the £40,000 John Player warm-up tournament in Nottingham at the hands of Roscoe Tanner hadn't helped. Newcombe's competitive talents had of late been occupied largely in what Hugh Crawford of the *Sydney Morning Herald* termed 'that curious and controversial format of World Team Tennis'. It was felt that the league with its short matches didn't build the endurance required for five-setters and seven weeks in the plastic and tinsel atmosphere of the American inter-city league may have taken the edge off Newcombe's game.

The Australian wasn't alone in being short on outdoor play. About one-third of the 128 contestants in the men's field had been playing in the US since early May, involved in WTT, activities often requiring day-to-day travelling for players and making long trips. 'I reckon all the WTT guys could be tired and in trouble,' Niki Pilic predicted. 'They've been indoors, and most haven't had a five-set match on grass for ten months.'

If the favourite faltered, others were ready, but neither Smith (No.4 seed) nor Kodes (chagrined to discover that he was seeded only sixth, the lowest seeding for a defending titleholder in Wimbledon history) were regarded as his most serious challengers. The giant Californian, Smith – Nastase called him 'Godzilla' – had found his form at Nottingham by beating old nemesis Jimmy Connors (ending a run of three defeats against the 21-year-old who, the previous year, had gained co-No.1 ranking with Smith in the US), then Tanner, before polishing off Alex Metreveli in the final. But that top prize had ended a year-long drought in which the 27-year-old had won only two WCT events.

Instead, it was Nastase, seeded No.2, and Connors (who declared himself 'highly surprised' to be seeded third) that observers rated as the top contenders. Nastase had actually done nothing that year to suggest he was ready and in the right frame of mind to win, and talked down his own chances, admitting frankly that he'd played too much, found it tough to concentrate, and was lacking in self-confidence. Psychological games? You never knew with the effervescent Romanian.

The Championships might have been dubbed the first 'real Wimbledon' in three years, but feuding and fighting still went on, with George MacCall planning a claim for $10 million damages against the ATP's Jack Kramer and Donald Dell, alleging they had a role in the barring of WTT contract players from the Italian and French championships. (The suit was later withdrawn.) Many players – members of both organisations – were caught in the crossfire, but the main victim was Jimmy Connors, part of the Baltimore Banners WTT team, whose non-appearance in Paris had denied him a tilt at the grand slam. Earlier in the season, Connors had won the Australian title.

Born into a close-knit Catholic family in East St Louis on the banks of the Mississippi in September 1952, Connors was brought up in a small town 15 miles away, Belleville, Illinois, and virtually from the age of three, when he first picked up a racket and they started throwing balls to him in the backyard, was coached by his doting mother, Gloria, herself a tennis player who'd competed in the 1942 and 1943 US championships, and his maternal grandmother, Bertha Thompson (whom he always called 'Two-Mom'). When Connors was a kid, they would overwork him at practice on the polished floor of an old local armoury that served as a community centre. 'Dances and drills made that floor mean,' he would tell journalist Frank Keating in 1981, so he learned to hit the ball early, 'pick it up and sweep at it before it could spin away'.

Raised playing in the public parks of his Midwest home, he learned quickly and developed fast. At the age of 12, Connors started to win American age-group titles. Gloria instilled in him a 'kill or be killed' attitude. By the time he was 16, the youngster had won numerous junior tournaments and established himself as a player of immense potential. But his mother, feeling she had taught him all she knew, decided it was time for Connors to take the next step in his tennis education; she opted to send him west, to Los Angeles, to come under the influence of Pancho Segura, the one-time world No.1, then an instructor at the Beverly Hills Tennis Club.

A master strategist, the unorthodox Ecuadorean, famous for his signature two-fisted forehand, worked on Connors's technique – one taught him by his mother that called for 'Jimbo' to take the ball on the rise, drive flat and deep and, at all odds, keep the ball in play – as well as the mental outlook to the game. The swank, private high school – Rexford High – that Connors attended had no qualms about releasing him at 10.30am each day to practise with the old pro. Connors's development and successes continued apace. In 1971, he made his mark in the college tennis world at UCLA, becoming the first freshman to ever win the NCAA men's singles title. After turning pro at 19, the American won his first tournament, the Jacksonville Open; the following year he took the singles crown at the US Pro Tennis Championships, his first significant title, toppling Arthur Ashe in a see-saw five-set final.

A big-hitting left-hander, noted for his potent double-fisted backhand and forehand return of serve, Connors was a fabulous talent. Lightning-quick with remarkable reflexes, his court coverage was incredible. Once his serve – well-placed but not intimidating – was in play, he was on top of the net in one bounce. His volleys and smashes were usually final. Competitive to the core, Connors was a player who had to hate his opponents. 'If I don't, I don't feel right,' he would say. If he could, he'd happily batter them into submission. Though a relatively medium-sized player at 5ft 10in and 150 pounds, he used every ounce of energy in his frame. He was a bundle of bustling aggression. 'On the court,' a journalist for the *Toledo Blade* wrote, 'Connors acts like a bull in a bull ring – fractious, always moving, almost snorting.'

But brash and brim-full of the type of self-assurance that could become confused with conceit, Connors's cockiness earned him enemies on the circuit. 'There is an arrogance about him,' the *Toledo Blade* writer went on. 'After winning a crucial point, he swaggers back into position, his shoulders stooped and his head down, all the time fingering the strings of his steel [Wilson T2000] racket. Receiving service, he spreads his legs and gets into a crouch, head out-thrust and his long hair bobbing. He acts like a man who is good at his trade and knows it.' One commentator described him as 'strutting like a little Napoleon' along the baseline.

Some of Connors's fellow pros regarded him as a smart aleck, loud-mouthed, childish. Occasionally, he indulged in mimicry intended to draw titters from the gallery – which it generally did – but his behaviour often crossed the border to the boorish and rude. When fortunes went against him, he could fly into angry tantrums, yelling malicious epithets and making gestures (typically with an upright middle finger) to spectators. Critics said he had inherited the histrionics from his doubles partner, Nastase. Stars of a maverick tour run by Bill Riordan, Connors and Nastase contaminated the air with their profanities so often they earned the nickname 'the Vulgarity Twins'.

Tennis players as a body came under attack from one American sports reporter. In a damning newspaper portrait, Will Grimsley painted most of them as arrogant prima donnas who 'swagger around in their white attire and fleecy sweaters with arms full of rackets'. 'They glower at umpires, hit balls at linesmen, bark at frightened little ball boys and at times even exchange words with spectators,' lambasted the Associated Press man. 'They are spoiled rotten.' He waded in even deeper: 'When their match is done, they shove themselves through logjams of admiring fans. They push old ladies aside and almost step on tykes with autograph pads in their desperate haste to get to the dressing room. Once there, they put themselves into an isolation booth. A press interview with any one of them is like setting up a presidential news conference.'

There were exceptions, of course. 'The Australians, as a group, are a terrific, easy-going, easily accessible mob,' Grimsley emphasised. 'John Newcombe, the best tennis player in the world, sets the pattern. He is tremendous. Arthur Ashe is another – exceptionally open, articulate, warm. Young Bjorn Borg, for all his teeny-bopper distractions is a pleasant, mature young man.'

Mature? It was still hard to believe that Borg had only just turned 18. 'Is Borg, in fact, 48?' asked *Sports Illustrated*'s Curry Kirkpatrick. 'A wizened sage of Sodertalje who went away to sleep in the mountains a long time ago and has recently awakened to discover wonder drugs, residuals, 12-channel television and the blow-dry look?' The Swede, he wrote, was 'beyond his years in poise, manner and ability'.

Since Wimbledon 1973, when he'd breathed a refreshing lungful of youthful exuberance into the moss-draped walls, Borg had been doing much the same in venues worldwide. There was never any question that he would opt for the gypsy life of the tennis pro and the following months had seen him turn professional as well as sign up to join the WCT tour – then its youngest-ever player. There was heavy money involved, but more importantly for the brightest pupil in the school of emerging young talent it was the best possible education. 'If you want to be tough, you go out and play,' Borg said. 'Bergelin [Borg's coach] says it is good for a guy to get out and burn his fingers. What that guy says is what I do.'

The answer to a promoter's prayer, Borg had fast become a tennis superstar. The Swede 'travels the worlds as a modern Magellan – and he travels with a harem and an army,' observed Will Grimsley. 'The harem – a band of giggling, autograph-hunting teenage girls – is kept at arm's length. The army that pursues him is a cordon of newsmen, radio and television crews and photographers [around 30-40] who dog his footsteps from Stockholm to Dallas, Rome to Paris, New York to London ... If Bjorn Borg sneezes, it is transcendent news to Scandinavians.' The youngster's every topspin forehand, wrote LA sports writer Joe Jares, was as big news in his homeland 'as a change in the price of herring'.

He'd been making the right sort of headlines. Notable Goliaths had been felled by the lethal forehand and his clubbed double backhands. In the second half of 1973, he was runner-up in San Francisco, Stockholm and Buenos Aires and finished the year ranked No.18. At the Stockholm Open in November, played on the indoor hard courts of the Royal Tennis Hall, both Nastase and Connors were Borg victims as the Swede reached the final before losing to American's Tom Gorman, 7-5 in the third set. Early in 1974, after competing in the Australian Open for the first time – knocked out in the third round by eventual runner-up Phil Dent – the Swede had won the Auckland Open, also played on grass, then, at London's Albert Hall, defeated Ashe and Roscoe Tanner before going on to claim his first pro tournament after withstanding six match points against British No.2 Mark Cox. In Barcelona, he crushed Rod Laver with the loss of only two games and reached the final again, this time losing to Ashe.

March saw a further meeting with Ashe (whom he beat in the final in São Paulo, Brazil), April another encounter with Laver (to whom he lost in Houston), but it was in Dallas in May that Borg really enlarged upon his growing legend at what Curry Kirkpatrick termed 'the Big Enchilada', the WCT finals, a match up of the eight top players in the world. An estimated four million people – half the Swedish population – reportedly stayed up until the early hours to listen to Tommy Engstrand of Radio Sweden doing live ball-by-ball commentary on Borg's matches. On successive nights he took Ashe apart in straight sets then prevailed over a tired Kodes in four, to reach the final against Newcombe. Following the Kodes victory, Borg had called his happy parents at 5am Swedish time. 'He's calling his parents after he wins,' said Newcombe. 'I'm calling my children!' 'I've got wine that's older than he is,' exclaimed WCT executive director Mike Davies. 'I wonder what will happen when he turns 18 and finds out the game is not supposed to be that easy.'

His stature in the game had grown considerably. So had his worldliness. Off-court affairs – meeting the press, negotiating business deals, speaking to large audiences – he handled, despite his somewhat coy nature, with precocity and charm. Borg didn't necessarily enjoy it, but willingly accepted it as 'part of the job'. On court, he now appeared totally cool, calm and collected. Composure itself. Nothing seemed to disturb his tranquillity. Never mind 'ice in the stomach', in Joe Jares's view, he had 'fjord water in his veins'. The 'BJORN IS AN ICE-BORG' headlines were already common. Arthur Ashe claimed it was easy to be so nerveless when you're 18. 'Wait for three years until Bjorn's in the top five in the world and every time he goes out there he has to prove it,' he warned. 'Then see if he feels pressure.'

Borg performed with what Curry Kirkpatrick termed an 'ingrained desire to play every point as if it were his last gasp on Earth'. Mark Cox called it the 'true spirit of idealism'. Whereas most players tended to play the significance of the point rather than the point itself, Borg went all-out offensive all the time, hitting the same way, with such savagery on every stroke, on match point as on first point. There was an almost total lack of inhibition about his game; he relied strictly on talent and inspiration.

There were still technical shortcomings, naturally. He served at times with only adolescent speed. His volley was blocked back rather than punched. The constant attacking, destructive when players fed him speed, was less effective when he was dinked around, drawn into the net. Rod Laver believed that Borg had yet to discover how to get out of a bad patch.

'The great players win even when they play badly,' he said. The Australian also recommended Borg pare down the number of tournaments he entered. 'Not so much for his health but for his mind,' Laver said. 'The poor kid will go nutty, be drained of interest.'

The 'poor kid' had no plans for any moderation just yet. Nor for temporising his boldness. He meant to grasp all he could while he could. *'Kommer alltid en Mandag'* – rough translation: 'Monday always comes' – was a Swedish expression that best summed up the youngster's whole approach. Have a nice weekend – but it doesn't last long. Nor do victories. 'I have to keep thinking this is my last tournament. Not that I'll be playing 20 years from now,' he said. 'So I must be good right away.' 'He is very dedicated,' said Borg's tutor, Bergelin. 'He works hard on his game. He spends a great deal of time practising.' Tennis was all Borg knew or, more importantly, wanted to know. Everything else was incidental. 'Maybe, of course, the naughty things are still to come. Perhaps I will break out and do foolish things,' he said. 'I hope not, because I love tennis and I really live just for that.'

His commitment was reaping dividends. In Dallas, although the Swedish prodigy, after claiming the first set, was battered by Newcombe, the favourite, he'd followed that match with 18 straight victories, a sequence that saw him capture both the Italian Open (coming from two sets to love down in the semi-final with Argentine, Guillermo Vilas, before defeating a gusty, troublesome wind and titleholder Nastase in the final later the same day) and the French Open (Borg securing the first grand slam title of his career after producing another amazing turnabout; two sets down to Manuel Orantes, he took the last three sets off the colourful Spaniard for the loss of just two games). In both Rome and Paris, Borg became the youngest-ever winner of the men's singles. Those successes had sky-rocketed the youngster to international prominence and set the tennis world talking. Experts were now showing him the utmost respect. Opponents hoped he wouldn't be lurking in their section of the draw.

Could he continue an extraordinary year by adding the Wimbledon title to his tally? No.5 in the seedings list, Borg was confident he wouldn't be affected by the intense atmosphere at an event of such magnitude any more than in other big European tournaments; his declaration that he feared no one had caused consternation among some veteran Wimbledon observers. Despite his great run, the 18-year-old faced a formidable job. The younger generation might have been, as Noel Coward once wrote, 'knock knock knocking at the door' but Newcombe for one wasn't too worried about the audacious new brigade coming through. (Along with Borg, there were other exciting prospects like the rising Indian champion, Vijay Amritraj, the big-serving Tanner from the US, and Britain's Buster Mottram.) 'You can't take much notice of their wins over some of the older players. Wimbledon is a test of tactics and experience,' he insisted, warning that it would take more than youthful strength to take the trophy. 'Matches on Centre Court at Wimbledon are won and lost up here,' the 30-year-old Australian said, touching his head. 'Ability and power are not enough.'

As well as the old guard at full strength aiming to keep out the youngster, the almost uninterrupted schedule had left Borg physically and mentally jaded. His winning streak had come to a crunching halt the previous week when, beginning his Wimbledon warm-up, the Swede was hustled out of the first round of the John Player Tournament in a 105-minute marathon by self-exiled Czech, Milan Holecek, 5-7, 6-3, 12-10. Coming just 48 hours after the final at Roland Garros, it was perhaps unsurprising. 'I desperately need a rest,' Borg admitted following his defeat. The loss at least allowed him a few days to recharge his batteries, though he would be uncomfortably short of match play on grass before he reacquainted himself with Wimbledon's lush turf. Until the Nottingham event, he hadn't played on the surface since Forest Hills the previous September when he'd come unstuck in the fourth round of the US Open against Niki Pilic.

Whether or not Borg would set the tournament alight with his tennis, the Swede was bound to once more be a magnet for the gangs of infatuated teenage and sub-teenage girls who, as Will Grimsley put it, 'pursue him like a pack of hungry hounds'. With the Swede's impressive string of victories under his belt, the ranks of swooning Borg-maniacs were only going to have even more new recruits. 'They'll probably have to erect crash-barriers to hold the girls back,' predicted Hugh Crawford, while Grimsley warned that 'if he doesn't go all the way, Wimbledon's ivy-covered brick walls may be torn down'.

Tournament officials were taking no chances. They'd ordered extra stewards to guard any court where Borg was playing, and keep at bay the hordes that sought his autograph, the clothes off his back or, better still, a lock of his Prince Valiant-length mane. Mobile barriers had indeed been installed to protect the player from the anticipated rush of gasping adolescents. All England Club secretary, Major David Mills, had even written to the headmistresses of 300 British schools asking them to warn their girls of the dangers of Borg-chasing. 'Wimbledon, they should remember, is no pop concert,' Mills informed them.

In spite of the adulation, the quiet, unassuming youngster had thus far taken it all in his stride. 'I am conscious all the time that it would be easy to get big-headed,' Borg said. 'I watch myself carefully and remind myself that my job is to play the best tennis I can and not to play at film stars.' There was 'a problem of privacy', of course, and, he confessed, the autograph hunters did make him 'a little nervous', but Borg was adamant that his young fans' presence at matches wasn't too off-putting. 'It's good. I like it when they cheer for me,' he said. 'You always like the support.'

Nevertheless, security arrangements were said to be the tightest ever for the start of a Wimbledon fortnight. On the morning of the opening day, Centre Court and its surrounds were combed by staff before spectators were allowed in. Police and plainclothes detectives mingled with the early arrivals. They would soon have their first real test. After an uncomfortable-looking Kodes opened his defence with a laboured triumph in a staccato match with 28th-ranked American Sherwood Stewart, the Centre Court's green carpet played host to Borg's clash with Briton, Graham Stilwell. And in contrast with the Czech, Borg looked completely at home on it. For the most part, anyway.

In the 1969 Davis Cup, Stilwell had enjoyed a superb run, helping Britain to the brink of the challenge round before losing to Romania (despite Stilwell bettering Nastase in one of the singles rubbers). He was ranked tenth in the world at the time. But the Essex player's career had languished since then. Still only 29 – though, as *The Guardian*'s David Gray pointed out, with his short, stocky build and hirsute top lip, he 'might have stepped out of any Victorian print' – Stilwell was now considered well past his peak and at the veteran stage.

Against Borg, on an afternoon of almost tropical heat, he seemed slow in reaction to begin with. Borg, on the other hand, electrified the gallery with the zest and variety of his play. With his topspin forehand carving out winners, the crowd favourite almost effortlessly cruised through the first set. In the second set, though, the young Swede's play went from slick to slack. Stilwell, more used to the surface now, began to find openings on Borg's forehand side, playing the delicate angled shots he did so well given time. Stilwell held his service to love for 5-4, then went to 30-love with two passing shots on Borg's serve, before forcing a mistake for the set.

Borg's play was still inconsistent in the third set and though he had five points for a 5-1 lead, he failed to convert, before letting his concentration slip again. Stilwell came surging back to 4-4. But Borg responded forcefully; he broke then served to love to take a 2-1 lead in sets, and after that there were no lapses. Serving effectively, with aces coming thick and fast, Borg turned on the power, accelerating away. Stilwell, wasting too many simple shots and never really working hard enough, was unable to contain him. After breaking to lead 2-0, the Swede gave Stilwell no chance to level and, with the loss of only one more game, sealed a 6-1, 4-6, 6-4, 6-1 victory.

It was a tough opener. One in which Borg, in one journalist's assessment, had given a 'typically casual performance'. Whether that was a compliment or a criticism wasn't clear, but the 18-year-old did commit too many errors for his own liking. He blamed it on fatigue. 'I had one week off in February and that's all,' Borg said post-match. 'I think probably after the Davis Cup (he was due on duty for Sweden versus Italy) I'll take two and a half or three weeks off. I'm going to find a sunny beach and just lie there.'

When Borg dropped a set to Stilwell one pundit had wisecracked, 'If Bjorn loses, the airport telephones will be flooded; there will be a mass exodus and a lot of open seats around Wimbledon.' However, despite some anxious moments, he was never in danger of relinquishing the match. Nor, to his relief, any of his garments or locks of his hair. Smuggled into the ground by a secret entrance, Borg apologised afterwards for having to dodge his schoolgirl followers – 'I don't like disappointing the girls,' he said – but was grateful for avoiding 'all the ballyhoo'.

The *Daily Mirror*'s Colin Dunne thought it would actually all be a lot rowdier. Expecting to see 'the T-shirted commandos from the world of the top twenty storm the citadel', instead he witnessed a gathering of small girls who 'didn't seem like Slade ravers. They seemed mostly to be called Katie and had ponies called Twinkle and their T-shirts only temporarily replaced the public-school blazers.' At Centre Court, they'd all been decent, well-mannered and respectable. 'The few pale teenaged squeaks of ecstasy were drowned beneath the polite patter of applause from pink manicured hands,' Dunne wrote. 'For all it mattered, he [Borg] might just as well have been bjall bjoy.'

Perhaps he missed what Robert Musel, reputedly the man who coined the nickname 'Elvis the Pelvis' for Presley, was witness to. 'The stampede towards the players' dining room where the 18-year-old Swede had taken refuge caught the stewards by surprise,' Musel reported. 'One of them gasped, while pushing back the throng: "Imagine what it would be like if he could also sing."' (After his first Wimbledon, offers of recording contracts had actually come Borg's way.) Borg's worshippers certainly had good voices on them. 'The chants of "We want Borg" – unprecedented in the prestigious birthplace of competitive tennis – brought a storm of shushing from the older generation, but to no avail,' Musel wrote.

While Roger Taylor, unseeded and unfancied this year, made an early exit to beanpole Australian Dick Crealy, all the favourites enjoyed first-round victories, though Nastase, typically moody and wayward sometimes, was given a fright when he lost a set to Jiri Hrebec, the Czech who had a Davis Cup win over Newcombe to his credit. For the *Evening Times*'s Bill Brown, though, 'the excitement of watching the further progress of the best thing to happen to men's tennis in a long while' was the biggest hook. 'He may just have turned 18,' Brown wrote of Borg, 'but to see his tall, broad-shouldered form lumbering back to the baseline for all the world looking like John Wayne plodding along the streets of some cowpoke town is to watch complete maturity.' That maturity, however, went briefly AWOL in Borg's next match.

On a wet Wednesday, as temperatures plummeted, the heavens opened – 'a godsend for the gardeners of London who have been waiting for rain for weeks, but a real dampener for tennis enthusiasts,' commented Brown – and didn't close for the best part of the day. When play began at 5.30pm, Borg became locked in a late-afternoon duel with Australian Ross Case on No.2 Court – and nearly forfeited the match in a fit of pique.

After 22-year-old Case, one of his country's most promising players, who'd beaten both Tony Roche and Newcombe to reach the semi-finals of the Australian championships earlier in the year, had taken the first set 6-3, Borg fought back to win the next two, 6-1, 8-6 (Case missing a point for the third set at 5-4), but early in the fourth, as the skies grew gloomier, so did Borg's mood. Complaining it was too poor to see, the Swede wanted the match called off for the night. Having already appealed about the fading light at 1-1, Borg, after losing the next game to love, put on a sweater and was about to leave the court when the umpire ordered him to carry on. When he promptly dropped his service, Borg returned to the court side, got into his orange tracksuit trousers, picked up his rackets, and motioned with his head and hands that he was stopping. 'I don't care what you say. I am not going to play,' he told the official. 'If you want to scratch me, scratch me if you like.'

It took Bergelin to tame his wilfulness. 'It is idiotic to be disqualified for something like this,' Bergelin told his young charge. After an argument with the assistant referee, Fred Hoyles, who came on to the court, Borg was given the choice of either continuing or forfeiting the match. 'It's not too dark for Newcombe,' one spectator yelled. As the crowd began to slow handclap, Borg grudgingly returned and again took up his position. But after losing two points tamely, he angrily and quite deliberately slashed two shots high and far, way over the stands towards the players' tearoom before smashing his racket to the ground. At the end of the game, with Case 4-1 up, play was finally halted for the night on that very uneasy note, despite the Australian protesting that the light was still good enough to continue. Borg, hustled away by Bergelin, stalked off to the dressing rooms.

The Swede's behaviour irked the tournament referee. A 'very disappointed' Captain Mike Gibson said he'd be having words with the player – 'He only hurt his cause by such silly actions' – and his coach, though there was no question of disciplining him. (Borg received a private lecture from Gibson, but was perhaps fortunate not to be punished further.

By attempting to leave the court before play was suspended the youngster was, in fact, forfeiting. Gibson might well have disqualified him and there were suggestions that, had it been any other player, he would have done so.)

Bergelin pleaded the 18-year-old's case. He described Borg as looking 'pale and nervy', promising 'as soon as he is out of the men's singles, I am sending him home for a complete rest'. A decision was made to withdraw from the mixed doubles – much to the disappointment of Borg's American partner, Pam Teeguarden.

The overnight break was clearly a tonic. The following day, on another rain-blighted afternoon, a much sunnier Borg started off brightly, resuming with an ace, and played well on the damp surface, continually catching the Australian slow to react with drop shots. But after breaking Case in the seventh game to 30, and with the rain beginning to fall, Borg again dropped his service to fall 5-3 behind and on the verge of possible calamity, before a downpour sent the players and spectators scurrying for shelter.

Two hours later, when play resumed for a third time, Case, at 5-4, had a set point, but Borg saved it, won the game and the next two as well, serving out the 12th game to love to settle the match 3-6, 6-1, 8-6, 7-5, and leave Case completely demoralised. Borg's haste was timely; soon after, the heavens started to pour once more to play havoc with another day's schedule.

Afterwards, Borg showed remorse for making a fuss the previous evening. He hadn't done himself any favours; throwing a game in irritation had only required him to work harder to make up the leeway when play began on Thursday. Harder work was the last thing he needed. The Swede reiterated how fatigue was hindering him. 'I'm not playing as well as I usually do. When you're a little tired it's difficult to concentrate,' he told reporters. 'I'm fine for one set, but then I have to work.'

Being forced to make short but vulnerable progress past a mass of hysterical youngsters before and after matches didn't help. On the

Thursday against Case, because of the rain, Borg endured four hazardous journeys, two out and two back. Every time 'the 18-year-old Adonis', as Will Grimsley called him, took to the court or returned to the dressing rooms, exposed to a walk across the main concourse, he was shuffled along in the centre of a moving cordon shadowed by a security force of three uniformed policemen (assigned to a special 'Borg patrol') and two stewards.

But even then it was a battle. After Borg had beaten Case, his protective escort immediately surrounded him but were jostled and pushed as they struggled through what Bill Brown described as 'the swirling, panting mob'. In the stampede, other spectators were charged aside, a policeman's helmet came off, and one elderly steward was even knocked down.

Before the match, making a foolish attempt to answer the question, 'What's it like to be an idol of the girls?' – 'I slipped behind a posse of lovelorn weeny-boppers, who were hunting for that sweet potato, the Golden Wonder from Sweden' – Brown had found himself 'practically grounded purée in the rush' when Borg appeared. 'His effect on the girls of St Trinian's is quite remarkable,' Brown wrote. 'They go into a frenzy of squeaks and grunts, roll their shrewd eyes at one another, hum silly tunes, and cackle with delight. "Have you touched him?" "Ooh! I nearly got a piece of his shirt." "These horrid policemen won't let us get near him. Ooh, they're not fair."'

Brown had already noted Borg's passing resemblance to John Wayne on court. Now, as an enveloped Borg trudged slowly to the dressing rooms following his win, the youngster appeared more like the actor in one of his Western films 'being taken to the sheriff's office before facing the noose'. (Ironically, as well as whodunits, the Swede's favourite TV *was* American Westerns. Borg rarely watched TV replays of Wimbledon matches – not even his own.) 'I'm glad I'm not Borg,' Brown concluded. Ross Case echoed that sentiment. 'I would not like to be him, having all the girls running after him and never being able to go anywhere without being bothered,' said the Australian. 'I feel sorry for him. I'm certain he would prefer to be just like the other tennis players, to go where he wants without problems.' Even after he'd left the stadium, Borg's pursuers, their screams audible throughout the grounds, the *Glasgow Herald* correspondent observed, 'stayed and searched for any young man with long, blond, and curly hair'.

It seemed inevitable now that the All England Club would have to restrict Borg's appearances to the Centre Court and No.1 Court – the easiest to police. However, while it might be safer to play all Borg's games there, the public without tickets for those courts had as much right to see the Swede as those who had tickets. It was a situation no player other than Borg had ever created at Wimbledon. Drobny had his admirers, as did beret-wearing Frenchman Jean Borotra, one of the famous 'Four Musketeers' from his country who dominated tennis in the late 1920s and early 1930s, and whose supporters sported white gloves and large hats and carried umbrellas. But, said the *Herald* man, 'those followers were dignified and more likely to recourse to smelling salts'.

Of the more than 50 matches scheduled on Wednesday and Thursday, only half a dozen were completed, three of those seeing Newcombe, Nastase (wearing 'the smile of Lewis Carroll's Cheshire Cat' apparently) and Smith squeeze in victories to make the third round. Kodes was also safely through. On Friday, the sun shone for the first time in three days, though waited until mid-afternoon to do so and there were yet more interruptions for rain.

The hide-and-seek showers had meant frequent delays – Captain Mike Gibson said they were the worst since 1968 – and all but thrown the tournament off course. Never had so many people paid so much to see so little tennis and at Wimbledon you paid your money, you took your chances with the unpredictable British weather: there were no refunds for spectators. The breaks were so ludicrous, one match, between the Australians Tony Roche, the 1968 runner-up, and John Alexander took 74 hours to complete.

So, on Saturday, 29 June, in an effort to have all the titles decided by the following Saturday, the most long-established tennis tournament of them all broke with another tradition. In days gone by, the afternoon start gave bowler-hatted bankers and stockbrokers the chance to put in a hard morning's work and motor to suburban Wimbledon in time for a chicken and champagne lunch before the tennis started. Now, any modern-day moneymen would have to get a bit of a shift on. For the next three days at least, the starting time for the day's play was moved to midday.

The Wimbledon committee did consider having matches on the Sunday, but paying to see professional sport on Sunday was still forbidden by law in England and the prospect of opening the grounds free to the thousands of noisy schoolgirls certain to be attracted by Borg (and other handsome youngsters) was too daunting.

The compressed programme, though, meant that, with some players involved in singles, doubles and mixed doubles as well, they might be on court once, sometimes twice a day every day as the finals neared. The tournament, ever more gruelling, was certainly no place for the weak. 'In the end, it's physical fitness that wins Wimbledon,' said Arthur Ashe. 'Mental toughness, too, but you can't be mentally fit without being physically fit.'

The American was one player who wouldn't be winning the men's singles in 1974. The Championships went into its second week with all the seeds intact in both the men's and women's singles – a post-war record that owed more to the rain than the rankings – but that was soon to change. On the second Monday, the tournament, after a predictable first week, plunged into drama. The rain gave way to a gusty wind that swirled around the grounds and made playing conditions difficult, particularly on the two show courts. Paper cups were blown about. The balls behaved in peculiar ways. And there were two major upsets.

The dismissal of eighth seed Ashe was the first. Twice a semi-finalist, in 1968 and 1969, losing each time to Rod Laver at his peak, Ashe was beaten in four sets by the explosive, high-bouncing serve of his doubles partner, 22-year-old Roscoe Tanner. Once touted as tennis's next superstar even before he turned pro – in 1968, while still an amateur, he'd won the very first US Open – Ashe had never quite reached the pinnacle many predicted for him. Now 30, he had 'remained a player in the front row of the chorus and no more', in the opinion of a *Glasgow Herald* correspondent. 'He does not seem to have a champion's urgency.'

The other seed blown out of Wimbledon in the blustery weather was Borg.

In his delayed third-round match, Borg faced Egyptian Ismail El Shafei on No.1 Court. A muscular, well-built 26-year-old from Cairo, where he'd graduated from university in economics and political science and was still a resident, El Shafei, after a long first-round five-setter versus Onny Parun, had come through his next match with Jurgen Fassbender in more routine fashion. A left-hander, El Shafei, who'd given Rod Laver problems in the past, was the man largely responsible for putting Britain out of the Davis Cup that year. The career of Egypt's top player, who'd emulated his father by becoming his country's national champion, had been dotted with breaks from tennis, including one for military service in the Arab-Israeli war. On this day, he barely had to do battle.

After leaping from a window to avoid the legions of schoolgirls besieging his Swiss Cottage hotel before the match, then being hidden in the women's dressing rooms to avoid even more groupies once he reached the All England Club, Borg came on to court out of an unexpected entrance. But once there, he was left cruelly exposed by his opponent. Just 59 minutes after the start of the match he was making a shock exit.

Visibly exhibiting the effects of an arduous year's campaign, Borg appeared off-colour from the outset. Instead of his normally accurate serves and first volleys, his play was sloppy and slipshod. The young Swede displayed neither spark nor enthusiasm and looked, in David Gray's description, 'like the blighted hero of some bleak Scandinavian play unable to find any cause for pleasure or optimism in his situation'.

El Shafei, conversely, was fully fired up. He was quick at the net, volleying sharply. Though not with any great power, he moved the ball about the court, his best shot – a two-fisted backhand down the line – forcing his opponent into numerous errors. Rather than go for big serves, he sliced them as wide as he could, knowing Borg would struggle to return. After a point for a break early on, his only one of the match, the Swede never remotely looked like tackling that awkward, swinging delivery. In El Shafei's 12 service games, the long-haired youngster won only ten points. Three of those were from double faults. The unranked Egyptian also lobbed well ('it's difficult to volley or smash in the wind,' he said later). And, acting on the pre-match advice of Ross Case and Arthur Ashe, he tried not to give Borg any pace. The game plan worked perfectly.

El Shafei who, like Borg, had won Wimbledon as a junior (in 1964), raced into a 4-1 lead before taking the first set two games later. And midway through the second set, the match was ostensibly all over. The fifth seed, overcome by what the *Daily Mirror*'s Peter Wilson termed 'a kind of unutterable weariness', seemed resigned to his fate. After making each sub-standard shot, Borg merely shook his head and moved to the other corner of the court. A net cord helped El Shafei to a service break to go 5-3 up. He took the next game and a two-set lead. Though Borg won the opening game of the third set, it was his last success. After both players had a chance of taking the third game, the Egyptian claimed another crucial break. And Borg virtually gave up altogether, making little or no attempt to return balls – purposely hitting the ball into the net sometimes – and serving double faults, one reporter even observing that 'At the finish, Borg laughed and threw away points, as if telling the fans he was surrendering without further fight.' It was either through sympathy or shock that the crowd didn't boo him.

Completely outclassed and on the end of a comprehensive 6-2, 6-3, 6-1 drubbing, the 'Swedish angel', as one paper named him, hadn't so much crashed down to Earth as fallen with hardly a flap of his wings. For El Shafei, lightly regarded going into The Championships, and who'd never before advanced beyond the second round, it was the biggest win of his career. For the 'golden boy, who had played so many bold shots and endured so much in Paris and Rome,' as *The Guardian*'s David Gray put it, it was an uncharacteristically quiet submission. 'He did not look very interested,' Bergelin admitted afterwards, 'and it's not often I see him like that.'

Even his rival was surprised how meekly the Swede had capitulated. 'He [Borg] either gave up or felt too tired to fight back,' El Shafei surmised. Borg made no excuses, but baulked at insinuations that he'd thrown in the towel. 'I am not happy about my form at Wimbledon. I did not have the power I usually have, but any impression I may have given that I gave up in the third set was false,' he said. 'I could not bring myself to concentrate and am happy to go home to rest.' He planned to have a holiday at his parents' summer home, mostly swimming and fishing.

Borg's elimination had, in one reporter's view, thrown 'a pall over this aged complex'. David Gray called the death of the Swede's Wimbledon dream 'depressing and disastrous'. The lack of mass schoolgirl hysteria was a sure indicator. 'The gymslip army didn't cheer. The matrons from Surbiton were silent,' Gray reported. 'No one even dreamt of running on to the court at the end.'

With the 18-year-old gone, the tournament became largely about a player at the other end of the age scale. The following day, another long one starting at noon, more seeds exited. Nastase was also a goner, beaten by American Dick Stockton. His attitude to the whole affair casual, the Romanian clowned around now and then – on one change of ends in the fourth set he borrowed a spectator's umbrella and stood ready to receive service – but the 23-year-old 6ft 2in native New Yorker Stockton, handed a bye into the last 16 when Buster Mottram withdrew with a severe throat infection, was the only one laughing by the end, securing a first success against Nastase in three meetings and a stunning four-set upset. Seventh seed, Dutchman Tom Okker, bettered by Metreveli, and (after conquering Tony Roche) 12th seed and 1972 semi-finalist Orantes, another victim of an El Shafei giant-killing act, joined Nastase in the limbo.

Following his victory over Ashe, however, Roscoe Tanner – his service so scorching early on his opponent was 'threatened with being burned alive,' reported the *Glasgow Herald* – fell to Ken Rosewall, the ninth seed ultimately teaching the American a lesson in a dynamic victory. And it was the nostalgic progress of the 39-year-old Australian, lovingly known as 'the Little Master' by his fans, 'Muscles' (because you didn't notice them) by his mates, which really became the story of the tournament.

Except for the years when the door was closed to professionals, Rosewall had been coming to Wimbledon since 1952, though this was actually only his tenth time competing. A flawless technique and unbending concentration had been the basis of an extraordinary career. King of the pros in the late 1950s and early 1960s, Rosewall was a worthy world No.1 for many years, but Wimbledon was the one major honour he had never won. Twenty years earlier, aged just 19 years and nine months, Rosewall had faced Jaroslav Drobny, then considered a veteran at 33, in the 1954 final. The spectators figured Rosewall still had plenty of time to win at Wimbledon and they made Drobny their favourite. Drobny won in four sets.

But despite one of the greatest backhands, and appearances in two other singles finals at the All England Club, Rosewall had never claimed the men's singles crown – one of two players, Pancho Gonzales was the other, whom the BBC's long-time voice of Wimbledon, Bill Threlfall, felt should have done so. 'He has fought three great finals, losing each time to an opponent who pulled out the game of his life,' Threlfall said. 'Drobny in 1954, Lew Hoad in 1956, and Newcombe in 1970.' The match with Newcombe was the first five-set final since 1949.

Still carrying only 142 pounds on his 5ft 7in frame, his hair as coal-black as the day he started touring the world as a 17-year-old, the pint-sized shotmaker from Sydney was, in Will Grimsley's words, 'just a watch fob of a man' but one who possessed 'a tennis game that is pure poetry and a backhand as deadly as a rattler's tongue'. The *Glasgow Herald* noted his glorious volleys 'which he picks off as if plucking cherries from a tree'. Due to turn 40 in November, age may have been against Rosewall, but the desire to be a champion plainly still burned. 'You've got to have some goal or aim to keep you going,' he said. 'From the time I first held a tennis racket I've thought of Wimbledon. Even in this day and age of big-money tournaments, Wimbledon maintains this magnetism.'

After looking positively surgical in removing compatriot Barry Phillips-Moore in straight sets, Rosewall then survived a splendid second-round four-set match with Vijay – a Hindu name meaning 'Victory' – Amritraj, 20 years his junior, whom he'd also beaten at the US Open at Forest Hills the previous autumn. The greatly talented Amritraj was reckoned to be second only to Borg as the world's most gifted younger player and probably the most dangerous unseeded player in the tournament. He and Rosewall were, the *Glasgow Herald* reported, like 'a pair of fine art dealers when it comes to playing the game in the classic manner' (compared with some of tennis's furniture removers). But in an absorbing encounter of pinpoint accuracy and flashing skill, hailed by the crowd on No.1 Court, it was 'age, wielding a rapier', wrote Robert Musel, '[that] disarmed youth armed with a cutlass'.

Rosewall followed that with a win against Swiss maintenance mechanic Petr Kanderal, then his hugely popular conquest of Tanner, and had now emerged as the sentimental selection to take the title that had always eluded him. In the quarter-finals, again backed by the gallery, the ageless warhorse gave an exhibition in beating John Newcombe that left 14,000 on Centre Court gasping for breath between cheers. 'Newk', one of the biggest favourites for years, had opened Wimbledon impressively against Frenchman Georges Govern, then beaten fellow Australian Geoff Masters and Niki Pilic (in a repeat of their 1967 semi-final) before running out an easy winner against American Erik van Dillen. When he faced Rosewall, he had yet to concede a set. But Rosewall, defying both his advancing years and the breezy, bitterly cold conditions, and although meekly surrendering the second set, was at his magical best, recording an astonishing 6-1, 1-6, 6-0, 7-5 victory.

When he completed a comeback against the redoubtable Stan Smith in the semi-final, Rosewall had the Centre Court crowd rising to its feet in wild appreciation. Smith, who'd concluded the rag-to-riches story of El Shafei, outplaying the Egyptian in a close-fought last-eight match, had been two sets to love up, before the gritty Australian, stroking the ball impeccably, took a giant step towards adding the Wimbledon trophy to his cabinet. It seemed that age, rather than decaying Rosewall's game, had improved it.

Now the only barrier standing in his way was Jimmy Connors. For most of the tournament, tabloid interest had centred as much on Connors's off-court romance as on his tennis. He and the 19-year-old Chris Evert, seeded second behind Billie Jean King in the women's singles, were a couple who were due to be wed in Fort Lauderdale, Evert's home town, in November that year. The young duo, in addition to reaching their respective singles finals, had also been highly touted to play winning roles in the men's and women's doubles (both were ultimately ousted in the semi-finals), but withdrew from the mixed doubles because of what an understanding Captain Mike Gibson called 'an impossible schedule'.

Connors's manager Bill Riordan wasn't worried however many games the American had to play. 'I've never known an athlete in any sport who handles pressure as well as this kid,' he said. 'He thrives on pressure.' His journey through the fortnight hadn't always been a smooth one. Sporting a sweater on a cloudy, chilly day, Connors had first beaten big Ove Bengtson, Borg's compatriot, in four sets but then had a very narrow escape en route to victory over Phil Dent. A burly, dark-haired 200-pounder, Dent, the son of a Sydney taxi driver, was a typical, chance-loving, beer-drinking Aussie off court, a gambler on it who went for broke nearly every shot. It almost paid off. In an epic five-setter started 24 hours earlier and three times interrupted by rain, Connors slugged it out on Centre Court with the 24-year-old, runner-up to the American in the Australian Open earlier in the year, just squeezing home 10-8 in the final set. He had been 5-6 and 0-30 down before running off four straight points to avoid disaster.

After that near-fatal collision, Connors followed up with a straight-sets win over Italy's Adriano Panatta and then, volleying sharply, his baseline shots sizzling, beat Jaime Fillol of Chile for the loss of an early set. In the quarter-finals, a scrappy, scrambling Jan Kodes was eventually wiped out in a three-hour five-set cliffhanger, Connors ending the Czech's bid to retain his crown by taking the final set 6-3.

The semi-final, played on No.1 Court, pitted Connors against compatriot Dick Stockton who, serving powerfully, his return of service deadly, had trounced tenth-seeded Metreveli. With Smith facing Rosewall, it was the first year since 1947 that three Americans had been in the last four. Stockton had the chance to become the first unseeded player to reach the final since Kurt Nielsen of Denmark in 1953. He knew Connors well. The two men had competed against each other since they were tykes. But on the day, it was 21-year-old Connors who gained the upper hand over his slightly older opponent, overcoming a poor first set to defeat the New Yorker in four sets, afterwards saying that the organisers of the French Open had probably done him a favour by refusing him entry. Connors was able to get in a couple more weeks' practice on grass at Manchester and Nottingham instead.

After Chris Evert, on the Friday, became the youngest winner of the women's title in 22 years, eliminating Olga Morozova, the first Russian to reach a women's final, 6-0, 6-4, the No.3 seed now had the chance to make it a unique double for the American sweethearts. It was a scenario similar to 1954. This time, it was Connors who was favourite, with spectators expected to be cheering loudly for the middle-aged Rosewall in the hope he could finally end his Centre Court jinx in finals and land the big one that had always evaded his brilliant reach.

Talking about his opponent before the final, Connors called Rosewall 'a legend' – and asked, 'How do you beat a legend?' The answer was: quite comfortably.

After 12 days, on eight of which the schedule was either wrecked or shuffled out of order by rain, The Championships ended in a blaze of sunshine – and a disappointing spectacle. In their only previous meeting, two years earlier, on a hard court in LA, Rosewall had won easily. But the conditions were far different now, and Connors was a much tougher competitor. As Bill Riordan noted, 'That was before Jimmy got good.' In a match that lasted only 90 minutes, Connors showed just how good he'd gotten.

Keen and hungry, the American, playing what he termed afterwards 'unbelievable tennis', started like a whirlwind, pressuring Rosewall from the opening point, never once letting him find his normal touch. His serves like hammer blows, his returns pummelled, Connors's heavier range of weapons destroyed his opponent. The perfect blend of finesse and fury, the energetic youngster was in irrepressible mode.

In a deliberate change of tactics, instead of rushing to the net at the first opportunity, Connors held back, engaging Rosewall in a duel of groundstrokes, hitting the lines with blistering pace before moving in. His volleys, firm, deep, and sliding away, were dispatched accurately and convincingly. Rosewall simply lacked the tools to cope with such a fired-up adversary. In a brutally one-sided final, the overwhelmed Australian never had a chance. Connors defeated him 6–1, 6–1, 6–4.

In the afternoon sun, as Connors waved aloft the giant golden Challenge Cup, presented to him by the Duke of Kent, the Queen's cousin, his fiancée watched in the stands. The media would label their triumphs in the singles events 'The Lovebird Double'. The younger generation were no longer just knocking at the door, but had barged through and slammed it behind them.

Holding Miss Evert's hand in the post-match press conference, Connors said he had never played a better match. 'Winning is like a dream come true,' the new champion enthused. 'When I was six I dreamed of it happening.' Only the fifth left-hander, after Norman Brookes, Drobny, Neale Fraser and Laver, to win Wimbledon, he became the youngest champion since Lew Hoad, two months younger at the time, beat Rosewall in 1956. A one-time boy wonder, like Borg, Connors had proved he could produce his best on the biggest occasion. And at the Mecca of tennis too.

Pancho Segura was certain that his protégé was now the No.1 in the world. 'He's another Laver,' Segura raved. 'He's a killer.'

Laver, like Connors, first won Wimbledon as an eager youngster of 21, then went on to dominate the courts around the globe for over a decade. Might Connors do the same? He was already being spoken of as one of the all-time greats. Rosewall thought so. 'Jimmy has got his whole future in front of him,' he said. 'He could do anything.'

But what of Borg? After the highs of winning in Italy and France, a comedown was perhaps inevitable. From the start it 'always seemed a doom-laden Wimbledon for him', summarised David Gray. 'He never looked as if he believed he could win – and yet at 18 it must be hard to consider the possibility of defeat.' A fairly dismal campaign had brought into doubt the youngster's ability to stand up to the strain of a major, two-week-long tournament coming so soon after another one. Worn out by his exertions on the continent, he'd had little will to see Wimbledon through. Borg suggested that the following year's preparations would include Rome or Paris, but not both. 'His problem is that he wants to play singles, doubles and mixed,' Bergelin said. 'Obviously you can't do that all the time.' Borg's coach acknowledged that, in general, 'He must take it much easier.'

Whining about weariness heading into Wimbledon, Borg certainly looked half asleep against El Shafei. Gray believed that the excuse, as reasonable as it was, had weighed heavily upon the Swede. '"Fatigue" ought it be a banned word for tennis players,' he wrote. 'If they are fit enough to enter a tournament, they ought not to complain publicly of tiredness – mental or physical – afterwards. It is a little unfair to those who beat them.'

El Shafei's slaying of the young Viking warrior was unimaginably easy, and while it came on No.1 Court, one of the fastest, which suited the Egyptian more, Borg's conqueror questioned whether the Swede, worn out or otherwise, had the game to be successful on such pacy surfaces. 'He's at his best on clay, because he has a lot of time to play his shots,' the Egyptian had said after his surprise win. 'I don't think he's at ease on grass.'

'It seems absurd to classify Bjorn Borg as a boy when he is so very much a man,' Bill Brown had put forward in the *Evening Times* earlier in the tournament. Even so, his failings had exposed a certain frailty and shown that the player was still a callow youth with much to learn and many answers to find. If Borg was to prove the naysayers wrong and get to the top of the Wimbledon class, ahead of him there was evidently a great deal of lengthy and laborious work.

23 June – 5 July 1975

JIMMY CONNORS had spent most of the day in bed, dosing himself with antihistamine drugs to suppress symptoms of what he described as 'the worst hay fever I've had'. Connors and pollen were natural enemies. It was Sunday, 22 June 1975, the eve of the 89th staging of the Wimbledon Championships, and he'd suffered a chronic attack. The 22-year-old's confidence, however, was in its usual rude health. 'I may be the only junkie to win Wimbledon,' he joked to reporters. 'And I will win,' he said. 'Not even hay fever could put me off.'

The man from the banks of the Mississippi had every reason to feel so self-possessed. In 1974, with a 99-4 win record, Connors was easily the most dominant player on the circuit and, at the end of the calendar year, had a firm, double-handed grip on the ATP No.1 ranking. Of the 21 tournaments he'd entered, he won 15, including three of the four grand slam singles titles. In September, a first US Open crown had been added, when Connors thrashed Ken Rosewall again in straight sets in the final at Forest Hills, losing only two games all match. Nine further tournaments had already been won since the start of the 1975 season. And although he'd lost his Australian crown to Newcombe, four months later a victory against the same player in a one-off, winner-takes-all, $500,000 challenge match in Las Vegas had all but confirmed him as the finest player on the planet.

The relationship with Chris Evert, however, had failed to last the distance. On the Saturday evening of his victory in 1974, Connors and his fiancée had danced the first dance at the traditional Wimbledon ball – the tune, 'Girl of My Dreams' – and the pair left for the US the next day with a promise that they'd return the following year to try to become the first married couple to win the men's and women's singles titles. But wilting under the pressure of their respective quests to be number one, Connors and Evert had subsequently split up. A few weeks before the planned wedding, it was postponed and finally cancelled.

Seeded No.1, Connors craved a second consecutive Wimbledon men's singles title so badly he'd passed up both the Italian and French Opens to play in two grass-court tournaments in Britain instead. Contrary to a widely held opinion about him, personal pride and satisfaction were stronger motives than money. It was the prospect of entering the record books rather than the prize on offer that Connors rated most highly. Cynics, of course, implied that, already a millionaire, Connors could afford to have ideals.

At 5-4 on to become the first American since 1945 to retain his crown, Connors would begin his defence as the hottest favourite since the days of Laver in his pomp. The left-hander looked a good bet. And this year, for the first time, Wimbledon customers who fancied a punt could do so inside the grounds; bowing to popular demand, the All England Club was allowing one of the biggest firms of bookmakers, William Hill, to set up a tent – right next to the champagne bar – to take wagers on the tennis. Players, however, were warned they faced expulsion should they themselves be tempted to gamble.

Beaten twice in two weeks in those pre-Wimbledon warm-ups – first by Bernie Mitton at Chichester then by Roscoe Tanner at Nottingham

– Connors emerged in typically pugnacious mood. 'Don't worry about a thing,' he reassured any doubters. 'Everything will be all right by Monday.' It wasn't only tennis court battles that were concerning him. On the Saturday, as the American started his final practice session at the Queen's Club, Bill Riordan revealed that the player, already involved in several lawsuits – filing actions against Commercial Union, the insurance company that sponsored the Grand Prix, plus various executive members of the ATP (for restraint of trade), and being countersued along with Riordan for alleged libel and slander by Jack Kramer – was now embroiled in yet one more legal squabble, this time with Arthur Ashe.

Ashe, the first African-American selected for the US Davis Cup team, found Connors's attitude towards representing his country in the competition an irritation; when it came to the annual international event that dated back to 1900, Connors, Ashe felt, didn't have a sufficient sense of patriotism. In March 1972, Connors had travelled with the team for a match against Jamaica. He was supposed to play in the fifth rubber – the US had already won the tie – but, while he was in the West Indies, Connors's beloved grandmother died following a heart attack so he flew home for the funeral. He hadn't played for his nation since.

Connors claimed that he had been libelled in a letter penned by Ashe to a group of 16 American players in which the president of the ATP (since June the previous year after Cliff Drysdale stepped down) allegedly said that Connors was not the right man to judge who should captain the US team in forthcoming competition. He was suing Ashe for $3 million damages. It was an allegation at which Ashe professed astonishment.

Ashe, like Connors, had foregone the chance of the title and money in Paris, spending two weeks preparing for Wimbledon by playing in comparatively minor events on English grass. After capturing the Kent Championships title, beating Roscoe Tanner 7-5, 6-4 in the final, again like Connors he'd exited in the quarter-finals at Nottingham. But, after a strong record in Lamar Hunt's WCT tournaments leading up to the season-ending finals, Ashe's victory in Dallas in May had been his fifth title of the year and the 31-year-old, despite his sixth seeding, was heavily backed to do well in SW19.

Nevertheless, with the names that in the past were always in contention either missing – Laver, Newcombe (who was injured), Orantes – or had lost form with age – Smith, Roche, Kodes – it was the fresh-faced stars of the new youth movement who were earmarked as the likeliest contenders for Connors's crown. 'If 1974 was a watershed in world tennis with youth supplanting the established names,' predicted the *Sydney Morning Herald*, 'then Wimbledon 1975 is the beginning of a new era.'

It was Bjorn Borg, of course, who was leading the field of would-be title bidders. At No.3, he'd received his highest seeding thus far. In Dallas, Borg had taken the first set in the final against Ashe, but a five-set semi-final rollercoaster with Rod Laver – Borg afterwards describing the victory as his 'finest win' – had left the Swede drained and unable to continue the fight against Ashe as he all but conceded the final games. But after surrendering his Italian title later that month (beaten in the quarter-finals by the graceful Mexican and eventual champion Raul Ramirez), Borg was in superb form at the French Open, dropping just one set all tournament before defeating Guillermo Vilas, 6-2, 6-3, 6-4, in the final, to become champion again. Only in 1970 and 1973 had the final in Paris been briefer.

On the slow clay surfaces of the Stade Roland Garros, Borg played some devastating tennis but, as he admitted, adjusting himself to the more rapid pace and shallower bounce of grass at Wimbledon would again be problematic – possibly even trickier than usual, as the courts were reported in questionable condition following a cold, wet spring. Borg had skipped Nottingham too. Curry Kirkpatrick compared the Swede's task to 'what a dangerous stroll down the lane following a romp in the bramblebush was for B'rer Rabbit'.

The 22-year-old Vilas was seeded No.4. A comparative unknown before, in one year the supremely fit Argentinean, a muscular left-hander, who, like Borg, relied heavily on topspin for his successes and had a weakness as a volleyer, had emerged from the tennis netherworld, topping the Grand Prix points table for 1974 before giving a wonderful grass-court display against defending champion Nastase to claim the year-end Masters title in Melbourne in December. The southpaw who began the year as an obscure pro had pulled off the upset of the decade, also beating Newcombe, Parun, Borg and Ramirez en route to the final, and many experts tipped Vilas to confirm the sensational form he'd shown in Australia at Wimbledon. A stomach complaint had subsequently kept the Latin American out of competition for three months, however. He'd yet to fully recover his confidence or timing. Borg had beaten him soundly in Paris.

The one real surprise in the seedings was Ken Rosewall. Now 40, the wily veteran, though severely limiting his tournaments in the past year, had played superbly whenever he had appeared. All the same, he declared himself astonished at his second-placed seeding behind Connors. Neil Ross of the *Sydney Morning Herald* was sceptical too: 'Life, they say, begins at 40, but surely they did not mean for a professional sportsman, especially an exponent of a punishing game like tennis where youth is an all-important factor?'

If Connors was determined to justify his own place at the head of the table, initially he was allowed only 27 minutes in which to do so. After two weeks of heatwave conditions, which had seen record crowds revelling in the fare on offer at cricket's first World Cup, Wimbledon's run of bad weather over the previous few years continued; right on cue, a steady curtain of drizzle descended, umbrellas sprouted like mushrooms and up went the Centre Court rain tent to blot out everything for the next three and a half hours. When play in all of the men's first-round matches ceased (around 2.33pm), the American was leading 4-2 in his clash with the young British Davis Cup player John Lloyd.

On a damp evening, when it eventually resumed, Connors completed the prolonged traditional opener, polishing off his 20-year-old adversary 6-2, 6-3, 6-1, but the scoreline somewhat flattered the defending champion; in the first two sets, 13 of the 17 games went to deuce. Connors often had to struggle to establish his authority. Ranked only fourth in Britain, Lloyd, whose professed pre-match ambition was 'to be spared humiliation', was as unreliable as the weather but battled bravely and stretched the American without ever posing a genuine threat.

Afterwards, the Briton's unstinted support from the home crowd drew envious noises from Connors. 'I wish the crowds in America would be to me like the English are to their own players,' he said. Virginia Wade, the leading British female player, reckoned a homegrown crowd hungry for victory was more a hindrance than a help. 'You can't concentrate for worrying that they are expecting too much from you,' she countered. Wade believed that if Connors were British the murmurs of dismay or clatter of applause that attended every point to deafening decibels would be as much a mental hazard to him as they were to the native players.

For Borg, deafening decibels were pretty much the norm at Wimbledon. On No.2 Court, the Swede, drawing his customary flock of schoolgirl followers, chiselled out a 6-2, 6-4, 6-4 win over Venezuela's No.2 Jorge Andrew, but it was a subdued performance, giving little cause for hysteria from his teenage army, the victory earned, according to *The Guardian*'s David Gray 'against a background of muted screams from the gallery'.

After trouble adapting to the grass, Borg soon got his topspin forehands going and moved along well enough to lead by a set and 3-1 before the break for rain. When they resumed after the interruption, the court seemed damper and more slippery than the others. Borg, especially, was careful where he placed his feet. Andrew, with less to lose, took a few more chances. Twice Borg went over when the Venezuelan lobbed him. Such was Borg's restraint that each of the last two sets was decided on a single service break. Unable to dart about with his usual briskness, Borg seldom raised his play to his own acceptable standards. Only in the last two games of the match, when he put the pressure on Andrew, did he look anything approaching world-class. Borg's match-winning point, a delicate stop volley, was perfection.

Borg was besieged by mobbing fans as he made his way to and from the court – he had to run the gauntlet four times because of rain stoppages – but the scenes were not as wild as the previous years. The 19-year-old, wearing a white headband around his long blond locks for the first time at The Championships, was also sporting a newly sprouted wispy beard around his jawline, the *Daily Mirror*'s John Jackson suggesting that it'd put off some of the Swede's fan club. 'It seems they prefer Bjorn shorn,' he punned. 'Maybe they don't like me anymore,' Borg commented. 'Maybe it is not the year for blonds.'

He might have been right. Two fair-haired players were the first seeds dispatched to the sidelines. Young New Yorker Vitas Gerulaitis, a finalist in the US Pro Indoor at Philadelphia in February, and one of the most mobile players in the game, was the first to bow out, the No.14 seed beaten in five sets by seasoned Australian globetrotter Ray Ruffels. Stan Smith soon followed, the genial American humbled on No.3 Court by 22-year-old South African Byron Bertram in 64 minutes, winning just four games in a shattering defeat. Bertram, a winner at the Wimbledon junior event in 1969 and 1970, had since failed to fulfil his promise mainly because of national service and a succession of injuries, and had only returned to tennis in May after eight months out following arm surgery.

Those early casualties came on the Tuesday. After a first day of rain and bad light, when more than half the 64 men's singles matches weren't even started, blazing sunshine thankfully became the norm and fans bombarded the All England Club in vast numbers. On a scorching Wednesday that drew a biggest-ever crowd of 37,081 – at 4.30pm officials ordering the gates closed, as a safety precaution, for the first time since 1949 – Connors, after announcing to the Centre Court 'it's such a lovely day', survived both another bout of hay fever and a rigorous examination from Vijay Amritraj.

In the steaming heat, the rangy Indian, who'd outlasted Borg on grass in the second round of the US Open the previous autumn, forced the American into a first-set tiebreak but was, in the end, tamed in straight sets. Connors was still concerned with his allergy, mostly because it was affecting his ears. 'Sometimes I think it is more important to hear the ball than to see it,' he commented.

Following Connors on to Centre Court was Borg, who faced Milan Holecek, the experienced Czech, now based in West Berlin and awaiting US citizenship. The high-pitched squeals of his young girl fans were the only thing likely to stop Borg hearing the ball, but in the first set any thrilled shrills were in short supply as their hero strained to find his rhythm. Playing much the better tennis, the 31-year-old right-hander Holecek won it after a single break of service. But if thoughts of repeating his conquest at Nottingham the year before went through the Czech's head, Borg quickly dismissed them. The Swede, steadying his game, turned the match in his favour with a solid display, eventually earning a 3-6, 6-3, 6-4, 9-8 win.

At 6.30pm there were still thousands of potential onlookers stranded outside the courts demanding entry as the early leavers departed. They must have sensed what they were missing; it was a day when the men's second round sizzled with emotion, upset and, in Ilie Nastase's case, fury. And, as Australian writer Peter McFarline put it, 'the seeds fell out of the Wimbledon fruit bowl'.

No.12 Kodes (ousted by Queenslander, Geoff Masters, despite winning the first two sets) and tenth seed John Alexander (beaten by another Queenslander, the unknown 20-year-old Paul Kronk, an Australian junior champion three years earlier) both bit the dust. But the chief shock was the defeat of Nastase.

Disqualified by the referee Captain Mike Gibson for his vicious displays of temperament during the Coca-Cola Hard Court Championships at Bournemouth in May, Nastase had initially stated he would not play Wimbledon because Gibson was also the referee there. The Romanian was quoted as saying of Gibson, 'He is the worst referee in the world. He thinks he is God, or a little higher.' He'd had a change of mind, however, and, seeded fifth, was back to playing the perfect gent when disposing of Teimuraz Kakulia of the Soviet Union in three sets on No.2 Court in his first-round match. He'd even found time to flirt roguishly with a lineswoman – 66-year-old Doris Bartlett – who'd reversed a decision (she'd first called 'out') after Nastase had gone down on his knees to her at the net. He then continued his charm offensive at the end of the first set, insisting on carrying the same official's chair to the opposite end of the court when she wanted to shift position, taking her arm for a courtside stroll before kissing her hand.

The merry mood of tennis's clown prince didn't last for long, though. Against 29-year-old Sherwood Stewart, a lanky, bearded Texan (whom one journalist likened to a 'pine tree' and Reginald Brace of the *Glasgow Herald* said had 'the touch and physique of a lumberjack'), the Balkan maestro lost an electrifying five-set encounter on No.1 Court, the match turning in the closing stages of the final set on a cruel call that, for once, Nastase seemed correct in disputing. With Nastase serving at 40-30, within a point of making it 4-4, Sherwood steered a curling backhand down the line and it looked suspiciously wide. However, the linesman, despite Nastase's appeals – he smashed his racket to the turf, cracking the shaft, argued with the officials and conducted the crowd in a hysterical chant of 'out, out' – insisted the ball was in. Umpire John Palmer called 'deuce' and a dejected Nastase, in Brace's words 'like a schoolboy who had just lost his weekly allowance', played on, but had clearly had the wind taken out of his sails. He lost that game and the next two as well to go tumbling out of the tournament.

On Thursday, after three days of upsets, the seeds had a calm passage but Borg's wasn't without its disquieting moments. 'There is no question of Borg being moved to Centre or No.1 Court,' Captain Mike Gibson had said earlier in the day. 'It's not our problem that he is being mobbed by girls.' So, as planned, for his third-round match with Jaime Fillol the Swede found himself on No.3 Court – and it almost proved very costly.

With another gigantic crowd – 38,844 – filing through the gates, the lanes between the outer courts were so jammed the players had difficulty getting to their matches. Borg inevitably was among them. The Swede might have received his usual heavy police protection from his adoring fans to reach the court but once there he was again at the mercy of their shrieking. And their chatter too. Against the Chilean, in temperatures that soared to 80°F, he lost the first set in just 15 minutes without registering a single game. Fillol, who'd seen off Roger Taylor convincingly in the first round, was Chile's leading player. Quick over the ground, his chief weapon was a strong serve, which Borg routinely failed to deal with. The youngster had even greater trouble, though, coping with his own supporters.

Throughout the set, sitting at the edges of a congested court, 'the large, scarcely clad army of "Bjorn's birds,"' as Peter McFarline described them, tried talking to him as he stood waiting to receive service. They called to him all the time, they yelled and they cheered. The 19-year-old's name was repeatedly cried out. Disturbed by the din, the Swede became so angry he smashed balls aggressively into the net and out of bounds. 'With all that screaming and chattering, I just could not concentrate,' he said afterwards, 'and I got really mad.'

At a signal from the player, Lennart Bergelin asked a steward to appeal for silence. To add to Borg's distraction, the steward kept giving stentorian orders to the crush at a decibel level that caused Bergelin to ask *him* to keep quiet. Borg looked in trouble and confessed later he thought he'd struggle to get back into the match. His focus returned, however, and with it his form. Finally taming Fillol's service, Borg improved greatly to outclass the Chilean as the computer ratings said he should, coming through 0-6, 6-4, 6-4, 6-3. But it was hard going.

An unhappy Borg told reporters post-match that playing under such circumstances was 'impossible'. His coach protested that the attentions of the squealing schoolgirls were killing Borg's tennis. 'He has lost all his concentration and is under enormous pressure,' a fatherly Bergelin said. 'Right now, he's a very confused boy again.'

The predicament of where to put Borg's matches without exciting a hysterical reaction surfaced once more. 'That means the Centre Court or No.1 will obviously have to bear this cross,' reckoned Reginald Brace, 'until he reaches the later rounds or becomes an old man of 20.' The following day, for the match with American old-stager, Marty Riessen, he was back on Centre Court. Captain Mike Gibson denied that the golden boy was being given preferential treatment, however. It was 'the best [match] of the day,' the tournament referee explained. 'After that, he [Borg] could be back to the outside courts again.'

The match with the 33-year-old Riessen, a Wimbledon quarter-finalist in 1965, was also the first clash of the seeds. After days of great heat, the courts were getting patchy and worn, the ball skidding awkwardly. But on the dry, dusty Centre Court, Borg made an encouraging start. Racing around like a frisky foal, he hit killing volleys and some magnificent forehand passing shots, taking the first set 6-2 in only 21 minutes, after breaking in the sixth game helped by a double fault from Riessen on game point then clinching the set in the eighth when the American again double-faulted on Borg's first set point.

Borg had beaten the Illinois-born Riessen earlier that month in Rome but the 13th seed, who'd dumped out the gifted Charlie Pasarell to make the fourth round, was more at home on grass and made the Swede fight tooth and nail for every point. Twice he broke Borg's service to take the lead in the second set when the 19-year-old's concentration seemed to waver and he began netting simple volleys. But the contest brought out Borg's grittier qualities. Each time, he came back, Riessen's poor approach shots allowing Borg to pass him on either side as he rushed the net. At 7-6, Borg made the decisive break, three unforced errors by Riessen and a fine volley by Borg earning him a two-set lead.

The American contributed much to an entertaining match – he took the third set 6-4 – but never really showed the form that had won him the US Pro Indoor title earlier in the year, and, under the pressure of Borg's ferocious forehands, faltered on the most vital points. If ever Borg got into trouble, he simply hit the ball harder than ever. In an unequal last set, the youngster ran away with it, 6-1.

Borg wasn't the only one deluged by female fans wherever he went. A rival in the heart-throb stakes had emerged in the shape of Guillermo Vilas. Not dissimilar to Borg in appearance, with his unkempt mane of brown hair kept in check by a tight headband, Vilas had intense, Byronic looks. He was a robust athlete with bulging forearms and tree-trunk thighs. Rex Bellamy described him as 'a poet built like a wrestler'. Away from the courts, the man from Mar del Plata, who spoke near-perfect English, was quiet and polite, renowned for his artistic nature – Vilas wrote both verse and music. He and Borg had become close associates on the tour. They'd formed a doubles partnership (though at Wimbledon, after winning their opening match, would withdraw from the competition, handing a walkover to their opponents, Austin and Owens).

In the singles he'd advanced well, winning his first three matches without dropping a set then bettering Sandy Mayer who'd earlier knocked out 15th seed Onny Parun. Along the way, Vilas, with his forceful play, had become a big crowd favourite, taking the girls by storm. Amidst those encircling him begging for autographs after each of his matches, some had even brought him presents, which he gratefully accepted. However, in the quarter-finals, Roscoe Tanner brought him only grief. With a virtuoso display of big serving – the blond American paceman registered 23 aces – the No.11 seed toppled Vilas in a testing five-setter, his heavy artillery ultimately proving too much for the Argentinean.

Borg's quarter-final was against Arthur Ashe. After finding his talent for tennis as a skinny seven-year-old on the outdoor courts of Virginia, Ashe had had to fight racial prejudice for it to flower, as he grew up in a segregated environment in the south in the 1950s, the son of a policeman from Richmond. Denied entry to clubs and competitions because of the colour of his skin, Ashe refused to be deterred. The scrawny youngster eventually broke the barriers of a stuffy, white man's sport and became accepted in the swankiest country clubs the world over.

After winning his native title in 1968, Ashe became more active in Civil Rights work, a significant voice in the war against discrimination. Apartheid-ruled South Africa's repeated refusal to grant Ashe a visa to play in their championships was the direct cause of that nation losing status in international tennis (Ashe wasn't allowed to compete in the South African

Open until 1973, where he lost in the final to Jimmy Connors). Ashe was a gentle and intellectual man with a good temperament. Tall – 6ft 1in – and lean, his slightly frail appearance belied the fierceness of his serve and backhand. When in full flow he was a wonderful mover, a free hitter of amazing winners with an excellent serve-and-volley game.

A Wimbledon semi-finalist in 1968, losing a tough match to Rod Laver, Ashe again lost to Laver at the same stage the following year but only after the American took the first set easily with what he said was 'the best tennis I ever played'. He was the No.1 star of the US Davis Cup team and won his second grand slam singles title by taking the Australian Open in January 1970, albeit versus a shallow field. But the chief criticism levelled at him was that he struggled to keep the pressure on permanently at the top level when necessary. Ashe had become known as a 'choker' – a player who came up short at the really big events. In September 1972, after reaching the US Open final for a second time, he'd led Nastase two sets to one with a break point to take a 4–1 lead in the fourth set, but blew it and the match. 'Among the traditional sights in sport,' wrote Joe Jares of *Sports Illustrated*, 'is Ashe putting an easy volley into the net on a crucial point.'

Wimbledon glory had been a lifelong dream. Many believed that time had run out on Ashe achieving it, but the player himself, now Miami-based, wasn't among them. And this year he was making a spirited bid. Having negotiated a tricky opener versus Sydney-born South African Bob Hewitt, when his play had often been inconsistent and he'd hardly looked the potential champion, Ashe was far more comfortable in sweeping past Japan Davis Cup player Jun Kamiwazumi, before showing no compassion in demolishing compatriot Brian Gottfried in just over an hour.

That authoritative display was followed by a less impressive triumph in four sets over Graham Stilwell, the Briton now ranked just 15th in his own country, whom Ashe, in 1969, had also beaten at The Championships.

Stilwell had had to win three qualifying singles to even get into the tournament and was in Wimbledon's fourth round for the first time. But the American, despite a crop of volleying errors that cost him the second set, finished strongly to reach the last eight for the first time in six years.

In scientific tests, Borg had been, as Joe Jares indelicately put it, 'proved to have the pulse rate of a corpse'. It was measured at only 35 beats per minute, half the norm. Helena Anliot, despite Borg stating their relationship wasn't 'serious', was reportedly still the girl who could set his heart really racing. And when photos of the couple, taken while they walked hand in hand, were published, Borg's hackles were raised too. Already annoyed by the more unflattering attentions of the press in his native country – he'd been upset by a headline in one Swedish newspaper, after a defeat by a lesser-known countryman, which read: 'IS THIS THE END OF BJORN BORG?' – Borg went into the meeting with Ashe angry with certain sections of the British media after the pictures of him and his girlfriend had gone to print.

He also faced Ashe with an injury. On the morning of the match, the Swede was practising with Vilas at the Queen's Club when he sustained a pulled muscle high in his right thigh. He'd slipped on grass wet from the sprinklers. In spite of that, when play on Centre Court got underway in the early evening of another day of bright sunshine and dry heat, Borg began like a bomb. In a blistering attack, the youngster – 'giving his imitation of Thor' wrote David Gray – unleashed a stream of thunderous forehands and explosive backhands that flashed past the American and left him merely groping. Aces were slammed down. Ashe, looking unusually unsure at the net, won only three points as Borg raced into a 4-0 lead. When he took the first set 6-2, Borg appeared to totally have Ashe's measure.

There were few signs of discomfiture. But the 19-year-old, as he revealed later, had felt the pull again – 'it was a bad pain' – as early as the fifth game, and soon found himself considerably hampered, unable to move swiftly forward to the net or to his right without it hurting. Borg did his best, but, after dropping service to fall behind 1-3 in the second set, his pain became more apparent; he flexed his leg and made a gesture of resignation to Bergelin sitting in the stands. Although he pulled back to 3-3 and continued to serve well, after blowing a point for 5-4 on Ashe's service, Borg finally lost the set following an erratic game in which he hit two aces, served a double fault and, after Ashe executed a cross-court backhand from the baseline that ripped past Borg for advantage, finally mistimed an easy forehand volley. Now, 'under heavy scrutiny from all the amateur physiotherapists in the press', reported David Gray, he looked tired and dispirited.

Though first to break service, for 2-1, in the third set, the Swede was immediately overhauled and again sent Bergelin a signal of distress, appealing that he could not keep going. The coach signalled back for him to soldier on, which he did, wrote Geoffrey Green in *The Times*, 'like a good king who is the slave of his people'. But the more Borg toiled, the greater Ashe's confidence grew. The American's backhands kept pulling in points. His volleying was stronger, his serve more powerful. Borg, resting between games with his head in his hands, was put under ever-increasing pressure.

In the 14th game, 6-7 down, having saved one set point, Borg served on a second and, when his service was hammered back at him, he lost his grasp on his racket and it fell to the court. The French Open champion – 'out of his depth like an abandoned ship' wrote Green – was now a disconsolate figure. He spread his arms in despair. Borg's juvenile supporters, who'd queued all night and through the day, many playing truant from school, cheered him on, but their loyalty was in vain. The handicapped Swede hadn't much hope against an opponent who was now playing very well.

In the fourth set, he could offer only token resistance. The odd spectacular shot was made when the ball came right to him but, although he won the second game, Borg amassed only nine points in all of the set. He took just four points in the last five games. Once, when Ashe won a game with a service that looked dubious, the crowd protested and the umpire ordered the point to be played again. But Borg declined. He just sat down, towelled himself and prepared for the next game. He finished the match a virtual cripple and on the end of a 2-6, 6-4, 8-6, 6-1 defeat. 'I had no chance once it went,' Borg acknowledged after his elimination. He'd been in too much agony to even bend his knees. 'It was just bad luck,' he reasoned.

Ill fortune or not, it meant a third successive year without getting beyond the last eight, and was tough to take. 'I am very disappointed,' Borg said. 'It's hard to get things like this at Wimbledon, which is such a big tournament and terribly important to me.' Ashe, unsurprisingly, had seen Borg's injury and taken advantage of it, albeit, according to Geoffrey Green, 'in a well-mannered, kindly way'.

Now, in a battle of the veterans, the American faced Tony Roche, at 30, a year Ashe's junior. The Australian, a winner in Paris in 1966 at the age of 21, and beaten by Laver in Wimbledon's first Open final, was once tipped as the heir apparent to 'Rocket Rod' before a nagging elbow injury – a pain Roche likened to someone jabbing an ice pick into his funny bone every time he struck the ball – threatened to put him in permanent tennis limbo. But with his days as a top-rank player looking numbered, Roche had taken an unusual route to recovery; up in the mountains of Manila, a Filipino faith healer named Placido, so Roche's story went, opened the player's ailing left arm with his bare fingers and extracted three blood clots. After a brief two-week recuperation, Roche resumed playing and had suffered no further elbow problems since.

Roche hadn't played a singles tournament all year while he healed following an Achilles tendon operation, but on his way to the semi-finals had outmuscled Ken Rosewall – afterwards, Rosewall, saying that the yearly pilgrimage was too great an effort for him, prophesised he would not come back to Wimbledon, and he never did – then emerged victorious from a heart-stopping, five-set thriller against Tom Okker, the whippet-quick Dutchman who'd beaten him in the Nottingham final.

The clash with Ashe, the only right-hander in the semi-finals, proved to be a rather dour five-set tug of war. In an evenly balanced but gruelling serve-and-volley duel, Ashe, who had been beaten easily by the brawny Australian at Nottingham, always looked the better player, his finer stroke play more appealing on the eye than the rugged determination and muscular effort of Roche. It ultimately tipped the scales, but it took nearly three hours and 61 games before the New South Wales man was at last subdued and Ashe emerged victorious to ensure a final spot for the first time. His opponent on 5 July: Jimmy Connors.

Playing with what one commentator termed 'the precision of a finely-oiled machine', the No.1 seed had practically eased through the first four rounds. After dispatching Lloyd and Amritraj, Connors produced superlative tennis in beating Mark Cox, brushing aside Britain's top-rated player with a merciless destruction. Against big-serving Phil Dent, a man he feared after the Australian almost eliminated him in 1974, the now even-money favourite was just as masterly when smashing his way to a 6-1, 6-2, 6-2 win. Connors quelled Dent's all-or-nothing game so efficiently, he even impressed himself. 'I played really good, didn't I?' he said afterwards.

Connors, in Rex Bellamy's words, 'flung his racket at the ball as if intent on testing the manufacturer's products to the limit'. It was said of him that he hit every ball as if he despised it. 'That's not quite right,' Connors responded. 'I hate balls. I never autograph balls. Me and tennis balls never get along very well. I try to hit them so that they don't come back and when they do, they really hurt me.'

Mexico's Raul Ramirez (who'd edged out Adriano Panatta) was the next to feel the full force of Connors's high-powered, super-positive tennis, the Omar Sharif lookalike battling desperately in the heat, looking dangerous for two sets, but in due course having no answer to the grass-blasting forehand drives of the American. Although seeming more vulnerable at times against the eighth seed, Connors played what he called 'really tough tennis' when he needed to, and took just two hours to blaze his way to another straight-sets success.

In the semi-final, Connors came up against fellow left-hander Roscoe Tanner. The tall Tennessean, who'd knocked out another hard-hitter, Mike Estep of Dallas (victor against his boyhood friend Sherwood Stewart), was one-one on grass with Connors, having beaten him in straight sets in Nottingham. But that was just a Wimbledon warm-up and, on this day, the champion was at his very sharpest. In 80 breathtaking minutes, bouncing about the wearing turf with jaunty confidence, hitting dazzling groundstrokes that awed the capacity Centre Court crowd, Connors delivered a five-star performance that he later eulogised as being among 'the best-ever'. Tanner was tamed 6-4, 6-1, 6-4. So exhilarating was Connors that pressmen were stunned to silence; veterans were comparing his display with the golden days of Hoad and Laver. At Wimbledon, there was no higher praise.

The 22-year-old had reached the final without dropping a single set, only the third man in post-war years to do so. (Tony Trabert in 1955 and Chuck McKinley in 1963 were the others. Both went on to win the title in straight sets too.) A prime factor behind that, he said, was Ilie Nastase. After his loss to Stewart, the Romanian might no longer have been competing in the singles but he'd still had a big part to play. Daily practice with his close ally and doubles partner had been one of Connors's secret weapons. 'Every day he [Nastase] plays different,' Connors explained. It had sharpened his game against any sort of tactics. Or so he believed. For he wasn't prepared for what Arthur Ashe was soon to offer him.

Ashe, who would turn 32 five days after the match, called reaching his first final in 12 years of trying 'a prophecy fulfilled'. He'd set himself two targets for the year. Winning the WCT title, he'd already achieved. Now, the man who'd had much difficulty with his contact lenses against Roche had his sights firmly fixed on the next. 'The first part is over and because I have sacrificed so much for this goal, I can only hope the second part goes well,' he said.

The first black player to compete in a Wimbledon men's singles final, Ashe stressed that he wasn't thinking of himself as a hero in the eyes of black Americans. Talk of his colour was passé, no longer a novelty, he said. ('Nobody talks about Evonne [Goolagong Cawley] being aborigine or El Shafei being Egyptian.') Though it did add a little pressure, he admitted, especially when West Indians and other blacks in Britain had sent him notes saying, 'You've got to do it for us.' The bookies, however, could see only one winner. Connors, seeking to become the first American to win two straight men's titles since Don Budge in 1937 and 1938, was the most prohibitive favourite in Wimbledon history, at odds of 3-20.

Due to meet in a law court as well as on a tennis court, the two men weren't exactly on each other's Christmas card lists. They had very little in common, said hello but that's as far as it went. Even so, both insisted that there would be no special animosity on the day; the multi-million-dollar lawsuits in litigation between them wouldn't add any venom to the contest or affect their play. The final, the first all-American one since 1947, when Jack Kramer smothered Tom Brown with the loss of only six games, would be 'just another day at the office,' Connors said.

Billed by Reginald Brace as a 'Mr Confidence against Mr Cool' confrontation, it was also their first meeting on grass. The pair had squared up three times before, on clay and concrete courts, and Connors had won them all, losing just two of 11 sets to Ashe in their matches to date. But Ashe, sitting in the stands, had watched how Tanner was pasted by Connors. He spent hours thinking how he would play. On the Friday night prior to the match, at a Hawaiian-themed restaurant, Trader Vic's, part of the Hilton chain, Ashe dined with Donald Dell, Charlie Pasarell and Fred McNair, a 24-year-old American in his first WCT season, and hatched a battle plan. Convinced that the way to destroy his seemingly invincible nemesis was to feed Connors 'junk', Ashe decided to ditch much of his usual slash-and-burn power game in favour of denying Connors pace, frequently chipping his groundstrokes low and short, lobbing often, as well as swinging his serve out wide to Connors's backhand in the deuce court. The strategy worked to perfection.

After Connors won the first game on serve, the 7-1 underdog, with clever, calculated changes of speed, length and direction, took the final by the throat and rarely let go. Hitting the ball with immense control, playing soft, quiet shots here, harder ones there, Ashe moved Connors about, never letting his younger opponent settle into any groove, only going for an outright winner when a clear opportunity arose and repeatedly making it. Time and again Connors's service returns were, wrote Brace, 'reduced to the level of peas fired at a tank', as Ashe served with depth and penetration before advancing quickly to the net and confidently knocking off volleys.

For the first two sets, Ashe played almost immaculate tennis. While Connors raced around the court at breakneck speed, hitting everything as hard as possible, often into the net, Ashe's far subtler approach worked a treat. He took the opening set 6-1 in 20 minutes; the second by the same margin in 23 minutes. With Connors down 3-0 in that second set, a voice called out from the crowd, 'Come on, Jimmy, try.' 'I am trying, for Chrissakes!' a frustrated Connors screamed back. Yet despite the urgings of Bill Riordan and Nastase from the crowd, plus an inspirational note received from his mother several years earlier, which was stuffed inside his sock and he read during breaks, Connors remained thrown off his stride, the usual rapier-sharpness of his Wilson T2000 racket all but blunted.

Only in the third set did he find some momentum. After taking it 7-5 then going 3-0 ahead in the fourth set, a comeback looked on. Ashe appeared to be fading a little. But Connors missed a point for a 4-1 lead and that was that. His resistance collapsed and Ashe, now reverting to his normal array of topspin backhands and well-placed forehands, allowed his arch-rival only one more game. At 5-4 up, Ashe meditated at the umpire's chair and, in the next game, proceeded to hammer his way into tennis history. When Connors, 40-15 down, dived for a kicking service and ballooned a two-handed return back to him, Ashe put away a forehand from the net and the ambition of a lifetime was achieved. In two hours and four minutes, wrote Peter McFarline, 'the racket and cool brain of Ashe performed what most people thought could only be done by a miracle or a machine-gun'.

At the end, reported Reginald Brace, 'there was a great roar of applause as the Centre Court hailed King Arthur', and Ashe turned to the players' viewing area with a clenched right fist, aimed it seemed at Riordan and Nastase. While the capacity throng delighted at Ashe's victory, a sombre Connors quickly shook his opponent's hand at the net but the two men did not speak. Connors, Ashe claimed to reporters after the awards ceremonies, had 'choked' in the match, a comment that wasn't well received when relayed later to Connors. 'I do not choke, my friend,' he snapped. 'I came here with my head high, and I can go out of here with my head still high.'

Head high perhaps but no longer sporting the crown. Ashe's triumph was one for brain over brawn as much as anything. He played what one commentator later described as 'one of the most intelligent tennis matches ever seen in the 98-year history of Wimbledon'. If he was watching the final at home in Sweden, where he'd returned to have his groin problem attended to by a doctor, the young man that Ashe defeated in the quarter-finals can only have looked on in total admiration. And maybe, just maybe, the odd thought or two ran through his head about how very different, but for an unfortunate injury, things could well have been.

21 June – 3 July 1976

IN 1976, Wimbledon – 'That nerve-tingling compound of dreams and drama,' as *The Guardian*'s Rex Bellamy billed it – might still have been 'the game's supreme festival' but in a sport making ever faster strides forward, and moving nearer the showbiz category, The Championships was increasingly viewed in certain quarters as being out of step. In an age of ultra-professionalism, it still had the trappings of a bygone era. The prize money on offer for the men's singles winner, for example, although a record £12,500 was to be had this year, was chicken feed compared with what could be earned elsewhere, sometimes by one player for a single match.

One critic described the fortnight as 'almost like a walk back through the 19th century'. Another accused the All England Club of being 'a quaint old club outside London steeped in history but stuck there'. Above all, its detractors felt that, while the Americans, in response to the public demand for tennis slower than the serve-and-volley game that had kept Australia at the top of the international tree through the golden era of the 1950s and 60s, had plumped largely for synthetic, all-purpose, all-year surfaces, and most of the major European titles were played on clay, Wimbledon had stubbornly clung to its grass roots – remaining loyal to courts that were now regarded by opponents as anachronisms.

In 1974, the rain that disrupted the tournament had raised the possibility of changes in the format of future Wimbledons. Bad weather meant that rescheduled matches had to be crammed in close together and players had even less breathing space in between matches than usual. Wimbledon was becoming 'more a test of stamina than skill,' one journalist observed. Matches weren't delayed or postponed every year but inclement conditions were an underlying problem. A problem that, some modernists believed, could be solved if the All England Club was to lose its lawns.

In SW19 and at Forest Hills, Rudyard Kipling's words, 'If you can meet with Triumph and Disaster/And treat those two impostors just the same …', hung above the players' entrance to the world's two most famous centre courts. But even at the West Side Tennis Club in the States, where the Tudor-style clubhouse was as much a part of tennis lore as Centre Court, those triumphs and disasters were now being met on clay, the grass surface having been replaced after years of complaints about its impact on the ball's bounce. Aside from the Australian Open, Wimbledon now seemed like a last green oasis in an artificial world.

Though a 'Dig Up Wimbledon' campaign had yet to materialise, pressure for change was growing. Many players made no secret of their dislike for the grass-court game, reiterating the remark made in the early 1960s by a former player, Jan Lundquist of Sweden: 'Grass is only for cows – not tennis players.' They hoped for some kind of perfectly predictable surface to be laid instead. The quick and sometimes slippery surfaces required not just a different technique but a fresh mentality. Adriano Panatta, after his conquests at the recent French and Italian championships on clay, claimed it was almost impossible to win those two tournaments then Wimbledon as well.

The peculiar international calendar didn't help. The programmers complicated the lives of the touring pros by scheduling Wimbledon only a week after the French Open ended. The players ideally would have liked three weeks to tune up and shake the clay-court habits from their systems. Arthur Ashe called it 'ridiculous'; the ATP, he said, was going to press the question with the national associations.

Seeded fifth for Wimbledon, the tall, dark, handsome Italian, Panatta, was riding the crest of a wave. A stylish player with a big backhand, the baby-faced 24-year-old was a threat to any player; though, as he'd recently proved, he was most at home on clay and confessed that he felt his seeding was too high. In Paris, Borg was one of the dashing Roman's victims, surrendering his crown in a four-set quarter-final. It was the second time Panatta had defeated Borg at Roland Garros.

Though his early elimination upset him deeply, the Swede consoled himself with the thought that his preparation for Wimbledon would be more thorough than usual. *The Guardian*'s previewer suggested that at least the youngster wouldn't 'arrive in Wimbledon looking quite so wan'. Bergelin told him that the setback in France could actually prove to be 'very good'. Borg's coach had long been concerned that the player needed to slow down, play less. 'All [the] time I am seeing him,' he'd said earlier in the year, 'he look[s] more or less half-dead.'

He wasn't the only one worried. 'A lot of people are beginning to wonder if Borg is being burned out and sabotaged by his own schedule-makers,' wrote Curry Kirkpatrick. The Swede's business affairs were handled by Cleveland attorney and entertainment entrepreneur Mark McCormack, head of the International Management Group (IMG), who'd started with golfer Arnold Palmer and built an empire around scores of the world's premier sports figures. According to Kirkpatrick, McCormack's people 'seem to be under the impression that a day off will turn their prince into a frog'. Borg was still only 20, but, wondered Anne Simpson in the *Glasgow Herald*, 'it could be that his triumphs are a bitter-sweet experience. Is Borg too much of a genius too soon?' There was no doubt, Simpson wrote, 'the pressures of international tennis are far more ferocious than in the early, gentlemanly days. Aggro seems to suit the pace of tennis now.'

During 1975, Borg had played almost ten full months, enjoying 12 singles tournament victories. His diary in 1976 was just as full: Atlanta, Toronto, Palm Springs, São Paulo, Monte Carlo and Stockholm just a few of the places Borg had wielded his racket in top-level competition in the early part of the year. Half dead or not, in the six months leading up to Wimbledon, Borg had achieved two major ambitions. The previous December, he'd set a record winning streak of 19 singles matches as he helped Sweden, almost single-handedly, to their first-ever Davis Cup success, beating Czechoslovakia 3–2 in the final in Stockholm. It was an ecstatic moment for him. Then, in May, in the sixth annual WCT finals in Dallas, Borg came through the eight-man shoot out to become champion for the first time, defeating Vilas in the deciding match, 1-6, 6-1, 7-5, 6-1.

Now, just over two weeks after departing the teenage ranks, Borg was entering his fourth Wimbledon still unsure whether he could ever play well enough consistently to succeed there. Others had their doubts too. Fellow players still saw him as a clay-court specialist, someone whose stroke technique wasn't best suited to shots that tended to keep low and shoot. His serve was still suspect, his volleying mediocre. Although Rex Bellamy suggested that Borg, seeded No.4, had 'growing cause to feel that his empire need not be restricted to slow courts', Borg realised that, to meet the special demands that grass made on a player, being, as Bellamy called him 'a superb competitor with ice in his veins' wasn't enough; he needed to alter his style. In particular, as *The Observer*'s Hugh McIlvanney put it, to 'increase the violence of his service'.

Since the start of the year, he'd been working on it a lot. But with Wimbledon looming, his efforts had intensified. For two weeks on the lawns of the Cumberland Club, a small, exclusive, 1,000-member professional men's club in West Hampstead just over three miles from the Park Lane hotel where he was staying, Borg had been toiling ever more diligently. Guillermo Vilas had brought him to the club. There, the Argentine and Panatta sparred with Borg. But it was developing his service that was the Swede's prime focus. Hours were spent on the practice courts until he had just what he wanted.

Under Bergelin's instruction, Borg shifted the position of his left foot, so that it became a little straighter, from almost parallel to almost perpendicular to the baseline and pointing to the net. Instead of tossing up the ball more to the right side, Borg threw it up in front of him. Now when he served, hitting through the ball with his body moving forwards, he gained rhythm, consistency and power. There were far fewer mishits. He had much greater accuracy. The change would prove vitally important.

Bergelin also convinced Borg that he needed to be more aggressive; not playing an out-and-out serve-and-volley game but venturing to the net more, so that opponents never knew exactly what he was going to do. By working on that, too, the Swede revamped his volley, improving it noticeably. Now he was coming to the tournament not with any hang-ups about the surface but with a hungry expectation.

A player with whom Borg was yet to get to grips with was Jimmy Connors. After a single early victory over the American, Borg had been unable to beat him in a major tournament. The previous September, 'the Brash Basher of Belleville' (as eminent tennis journalist Bud Collins nicknamed Connors) had bettered the Swede on the new surface at Forest Hills, knocking out Borg at the semi-finals stage of the US Open, with Borg playing through the two and a half hours with his racket hand raw from blisters. Connors had suffered a surprise straight-sets defeat to the Spaniard Manuel Orantes in the final, but he'd then beaten Borg in the final of the US Pro Indoor in Philadelphia in February 1976, when the Swede had all but quit in the third set, losing it to love. A record crowd of 14,000 at the Spectrum courts took special notice of Connors's self-proclaimed new image: he was changing his style, he said, and trying to be 'nice'.

Anyone who'd backed Connors in 1975 had got their fingers burned, but only a brave man would bet against him wresting back the Wimbledon crown in 1976. The authority, arrogance and obstinacy of the left-hander was still the most potent mix in the game. Now weighing in around 160 pounds, 20 pounds lighter since the 1975 Championships, the newly trimmed-down slim Jim was desperate to prove that his defeat to Ashe was, as Rex Bellamy put it, 'a comma rather than a full stop'. Expert opinion had it that the Ashe-Connors rivalry would be renewed but, despite Ashe's top seeding, it was the No.2 seed Connors that most people's crystal balls showed ramming home the last point of the tournament.

He wasn't lacking in match play on grass – a dozen games in two weeks – and, although he'd lost to Roscoe Tanner in the final of the Kent Championships at Beckenham then been forced to share the John Player title in Nottingham when rain reduced his final with Nastase to a watery farce, the 23-year-old was in fine fettle. Returning from the wilderness of failed careers as a singer and an actor – among other attempts to break into the entertainment field, Connors had recorded and performed on ABC TV's *Saturday Night Live with Howard Cosell* a song called 'Girl, You Turn Me On' penned especially for him by 'My Way' composer, singer Paul Anka, but it was never released – he wasn't short of his usual swagger, either. 'They will all know that Jimmy Connors is back at Wimbledon,' the American vowed. 'I'm leaving singing and acting to those who can do it. I'm just a tennis player – but I'm a hell of a good one.' The lawsuits were dropped; the quests for notoriety, he promised, were behind him.

Ashe suggested a levelling up in men's tennis; the talent of the 128 players who would begin fighting for the title was so evenly divided, he believed, any player could beat any other at any time. His own objective was simply to still be in the draw come week two. 'If you can get to the second week of Wimbledon,' he said, quoting Lew Hoad, 'it's anybody's ball game.'

After the brilliant run that had seen him win 61 of 69 matches during a two-year span, including five tournaments at the start of the year, Ashe had been in indifferent form in recent tournaments. Were the momentum and motivation that helped him spring his surprise successes the year before still there? Friends said he did not seem the hungry, eager, new Ashe who had shown up in Dallas in May 1975. A first-round defeat in Nottingham was hardly ideal preparation for the 32-year-old titleholder.

And, indeed, as the big tennis festival began in scorching sunshine with swarming shirt-sleeved crowds, the American still appeared a tad uncertain, commencing his defence with a ragged performance, serving ten double faults and taking nearly three hours to defeat Ferdi Taygan, ranked only 57th in the US. The defending champion came within a point of losing the first set to the 19-year-old amateur but eventually wriggled through. 'He did not look,' noted the *Glasgow Herald*'s reporter, 'the man most likely to cause a riot in the betting shops.'

On the opening Monday, the 24,500 fans who sauntered into the All England Club saw no big upsets. All 14 seeds – two of them, the short, speedy American known as 'Fast Eddie' Dibbs and Jan Kodes, had withdrawn due to injury before the tournament started – made it safely over their first-round hurdles. Borg did so in style. The night before, so high were the temperatures, David Lloyd, the 28-year-old brother of

John, slept on a mattress in the garden of his London home in Kingston Hill. It was on the recommendation of Lloyd, who'd first seen Borg as a 14-year-old playing in the Scandinavian Open, that Slazenger signed the Swede to use their rackets when he first joined the professional circuit. In Borg, Lloyd had sensed someone special 'wrapped in a charisma you couldn't put a finger on'. On No.2 Court, Lloyd got to witness just how appealing the Swede could be; the No.4 seed eased to a 6-3, 6-3, 6-1 win, totally outclassing the British Davis Cup player. Borg's serve, both first and second, was particularly formidable.

That serve was equally as destructive in his next match. For a second successive Wimbledon, Borg faced up to Marty Riessen on Centre Court and, for a second year running, dismissed the challenge of the American, this time racing to a 6-2, 6-2, 6-4 victory in yet more sweltering heat. Riessen, playing at slams since the late fifties and at Wimbledon since 1961, had 15 years on Borg but experience counted for nothing as the Swede crashed 14 aces by his opponent's outstretched racket and, on a day of no upsets but a lot of close calls – Newcombe (tenth seed), Gottfried (14) and Fillol (13) all squeezing out of difficult situations before prevailing – was as impressive as anyone. Anyone other than Connors, perhaps.

Connors, watched by his new constant off-court companion, the former Miss World Marjie Wallace, sitting with Connors's mother, was at his awesome best in his opening match, thrashing Antonio Zugarelli, though the lack of respect he showed the Italian – Connors indulged in some on-court horseplay – earned the wrath of the Centre Court crowd. The wildest ovation came when Zugarelli finally broke the American's serve.

He then disposed of 22-year-old Stephen Warboys with the nonchalance of a spectator dispatching their strawberries and cream. The 6ft 4in Englishman, a runner-up at the Wimbledon junior event in 1971, had once been the youngest-ever member of Britain's Davis Cup squad and seemed on the threshold of an outstanding career but had never quite reached the top. Warboys was led a merry dance as Connors waltzed into the last 32, treating his opponent almost with contempt.

As the seeded players continued to charge through the draw in the searing heat, some spectators didn't fare so well. On the Thursday, the temperatures hovered around 35°C and in the unseasonal conditions scores fainted in and around the baking Centre Court; fans, standing shoulder to shoulder after lining up for hours outside the club, went down like tenpins. More than 500 had to have first-aid treatment.

With the courts becoming glassy and treacherous, fast services became lethal weapons. In his third-round match, Borg faced one of the game's top speed-merchants, Australian Colin Dibley, whose serve had been measured the previous year at 148mph. The 31-year-old right-hander had been part of arguably the greatest Davis Cup team in Australia's history, one that recorded a famous 5-0 victory over the United States in Cleveland in December 1973. He first met Borg soon after, in the early part of 1974, when he was asked if he'd play doubles with the Swede in a tournament in Dibley's native Sydney. Bergelin had told Dibley that 'He's not going to know too much about what to do.' They won the competition.

In April of that year, Borg, pairing up with Ove Bengtson, was on the opposite side of the net to the Australian in a doubles clash as they defeated Dibley and Laver in the quarter-finals of the $50,000 Kawasaki classic in Tokyo. And at Wimbledon the 20-year-old once again got the better of the one-time world No.26. Dibley, a quarter-finalist in both 1971 and 1972, served well, but Borg served better, scoring another commanding win, 6-4, 6-4, 6-4. 'I don't think I'd ever lost to anyone who stayed back on grass before that match,' Dibley would recall years later.

Now, on grass as perilous as an ice rink, the seeds started to topple. The 32-year-old Dutchman Tom Okker (9) became the first, eliminated in a dull three-set encounter by Phil Dent. For the 26-year-old, who'd earlier come through a five-setter with John Lloyd, it was the first time he'd beaten Okker in a tournament. Fellow Australian John Newcombe, though, fighting all week against stiffness in his serving arm, found the going too tough against unseeded Bernie Mitton. After struggling through a five-set losing doubles with long-time partner Tony Roche against Gottfried and Ramirez, and then surviving 42 aces from John Feaver in another five-setter, the old lion simply did not have enough left for the bushy-bearded South African. Jaime Fillol, vanquished by big-serving Onny Parun, was another distinguished victim.

The biggest third-round casualty was the highly regarded Panatta. Against the unseeded 32-year-old Charlie Pasarell, Panatta, the great escape artist – he'd saved 11 match points in his first-round match with Kim Warwick before winning the Italian title and another before claiming the French over Vilas – failed to survive Wimbledon, letting slip a two-set lead. At 3-3 in the final set, Panatta stopped to care for a wounded sparrow, which he carefully deposited in the cupped hands of a spectator, and perhaps became distracted – he lost the next three points and ultimately the match.

Borg had his own injury to tend to. On the Saturday, he was due to face Brian Gottfried, the American who'd never previously progressed beyond the third round. But the Swede's participation in the match and the rest of the tournament was thrown into doubt when, on the Friday night, partnering Vilas in a doubles victory over Australians Richard Crealy and Kim Warwick, Borg aggravated a muscle in his stomach. Rumours circulating initially indicated it was another groin problem.

The pain was so severe, Bergelin asked Fred Hoyles (now tournament referee after Captain Mike Gibson's retirement) to hold back the singles match until Monday. But Hoyles, a Lincolnshire farmer, insisted the order of play remain, leaving Bergelin seriously mulling over pulling Borg out of

The Championships. It looked like Wimbledon might be losing the No.4 seed without a shot being hit in anger. 'He [Borg] had a similar injury three years ago and then it took a month to clear up,' Bergelin said. 'It seems it always happens in a match on grass in England.'

Forced to withdraw from the doubles – the title, ironically, eventually won by Gottfried in tandem with Raul Ramirez – Borg also had little choice about his fourth-round match: he would only be able to play with the aid of a pain-killing cortisone injection. He decided to go ahead. And the jab did the trick. Gottfried, the No.14 seed, went up against the Swede having faced three fellow Americans in the previous rounds, taken to four sets by Tim Gullikson, before surviving two successive five-setters against John Andrews then Bob Lutz, a quarter-finalist in 1969. A hard-working, if unadventurous, player with an ultra-reliable forehand volley, he was meeting Borg for the very first time. But like others before him, the man from Fort Lauderdale found Borg's savage strokes, hit so high and with so much spin, nigh-on impossible to attack. He was no match for the 20-year-old. Borg, despite discomfort, moved smoothly about the court, returning well and serving superbly. The American was demolished 6-2, 6-2, 7-5.

It was yet another day of testing weather – conditions that helped bring about the downfall of the defending champion. Out of form, Arthur Ashe, after his first-day scramble, for the second day running had muddled through in uncertain fashion against an opponent who wouldn't normally be expected to extend him – this time taken to four sets on No.3 Court by the unheralded Australian Allan Stone, a player ranked only ninth in his native country. 'CHAMP NEARLY A CHUMP' headlined one newspaper post-match.

A more convincing victory followed, a sharper Ashe dismissing Australian champion, 6ft 2in Mark Edmondson, in three sets in the sweatbox of No.1 Court (which, 'banked more than any other at Wimbledon', was 'paradise' for a wide service on either side, Ashe said afterwards). But then, troubled by poor serving, woeful forehand volleying and erratic net play, Ashe surrendered his crown, blasted out of The Championships on the end of a stunning upset by the unranked 21-year-old Vitas Gerulaitis, who'd lost to the reigning champion in all three of their previous meetings.

After winning the first two sets against the scraggy-haired New Yorker, Ashe, weakening under the burning midsummer sun as Gerulaitis clawed his way back, lost the next three sets in a near three-hour epic. One journalist observed that in the final two sets Ashe looked so wearied he was 'holding his racket as if it were stone'. The player offered no excuses except to say he felt flat after establishing his lead and was 'just dead' by the end.

One of the fastest rising stars on the American scene, Gerulaitis had started 1975 ranked 21st in the US but, after scoring a series of wins over such names as Okker, Ramirez and Alexander and leading the Pittsburgh Triangles to the WTT championship, had risen to No.4. A dynamic figure in the Borg style, Gerulaitis, unseeded this year, had earlier seen off Britain's Mark Cox, and said after beating Ashe that he had been prepared to treat Wimbledon as just another tournament but was inspired by a letter from a former Australian Davis Cup captain. 'Harry Hopman wrote to me and said that only great champions win Wimbledon,' Gerulaitis told reporters, 'and it changed my thinking completely.'

Asked who he now fancied as his successor, Ashe said: 'I'd put my money on Nastase or Connors, but Charlie Pasarell could be the dark horse if he plays on Centre Court during next week.' Pasarell, with whom he had founded the National Junior Tennis League, was Ashe's best friend, and the game of the engaging, intelligent Puerto Rican, Ashe felt, improved 50 per cent in Wimbledon's main arena – 'but anywhere else he's [just] Charlie'.

He wasn't a dark horse for long. After staging a stirring mid-match reversal to progress from a five-set thriller with Dent, Pasarell, famous for a nerve-shattering five-hours-12 minute slog in 1969 with 41-year-old Pancho Gonzales that stretched over two days and went some way to prompting the introduction of the tiebreak, faced Nastase in the quarter-finals. While Connors had enjoyed the company of Miss Wallace, Nastase had a somewhat less glamorous consort; concerned that his notorious temperament might get the better of him once again, the Romanian had retained Fred Perry to guide him through the tournament. Perry had mentored Nastase to victory at the US Open in 1972. Striving for a low profile, Nastase had consistently refused to meet newsmen in case he said anything out of line, and had leaned heavily on Perry's advice. 'He's made up his mind to be a loner this time,' Perry had said at the start of the fortnight.

It was evidently proving beneficial. After dealing comfortably with Nikola Spear, and then another Yugoslav, Zeljko Franulovic, an old hard-court adversary, the Romanian advanced in 101-degree heat with a straight-sets win over Australia's Kim Warwick, a player with an explosive disposition the equal of Nastase, and there was a sneaking feeling in the Wimbledon air that this could be his year. Something in the atmosphere that had always seemed to constrict Nastase was gone. He was full of decorum and good humour, and had yet to put a foot wrong. Some of his play against Franulovic remarked the *Glasgow Herald*, 'had the mark of magic'.

Despite a brief flare-up with the umpire en route to a victory over Parun, the newfound maturity of the man, according to the *Herald*, 'involved in more scenes and disputes in world tennis than his rivals have served double faults', was in evidence once more when a beautifully stroked defeat of Pasarell confirmed Nastase's position as the new title favourite. Calm and disciplined, his concentration unflickering, Nastase scarcely made an unforced error in a display of all-court mastery. The highest remaining seed, he was yet to drop a set.

Neither had Connors – up until the quarter-finals. With Ashe out of the running, the path to another title looked clear for Connors. He was playing as if in a hurry to get there – and out of the frying sun – as soon as possible. After the slaying of Zugarelli and Warboys, the American blitzed his way to another clinical destruction, this time against El Shafei, before, in more business-like fashion, calmly accounting for old rival, the 16th-seeded Stan Smith, on a Centre Court where it was so hot it set off a fire extinguisher.

In the last eight, Connors met Roscoe Tanner, there after a fourth-round straight-sets victory against Niki Pilic. He'd dropped only 29 games, the lowest by any player left in the tournament. Yet Tanner, one of only two men to have downed Connors in 1976, was not the slightest bit awed by his opponent. 'I've beaten him before, so why not again?' he snapped at reporters barraging him with questions beforehand about his supposedly slender chances. Why not, indeed.

Tanner, with his supersonic service, had been racking up aces in each match. Against Brazil's Carlos Kirmayr he'd hit 28. For Connors, though, he served harder than he ever had.

Uncorking his usual quota of winners – 19 aces in total – his cannonball blasts kicked up dust and skidded away at such a speed they were hard to follow. When one thunderous delivery thumped a linesman at the back of the court, the official let out a loud 'ouch'. Even one of tennis's best returners couldn't cope. All a punch-drunk Connors could offer was a limp racket and a few four-letter words. Overwhelmed by his fellow left-hander's uncomplicated but deadly game, the firm favourite was scuttled out 6-4, 6-2, 8-6.

A dejected Connors, wrote the *Glasgow Herald* correspondent, 'departed like a man suffering from shell shock after taking an unprecedented battering', afterwards giving no interviews and driving off in a blue

Mercedes with Miss Wallace, instructing reporters to 'Go away and leave us alone.' According to Connors's ex-manager Bill Riordan (suing the player for £80,000 over his dismissal the previous year), the presence of the player's girlfriend and mother at the tournament was too big 'a distraction' for Connors – 'When you are playing tennis at this level, you cannot afford to be rushing around after your girls all the time,' Riordan said – and had cost him the title (as well as Riordan an £8,000 bet he had on Connors to win).

Hailing from Lookout Mountain, Tennessee, Tanner, a professional since 1972, practised firing his high-velocity torpedoes by aiming at tin cans piled up at the other side of the net. They were often left in a dented, battered heap. He now had Borg in his sights. Instead of partnering Vilas in the doubles, Borg had met his friend in the quarter-finals on a No.1 Court in a poor, parched state, the No.6 seed having chipped away at the granite-like Tony Roche, wiping out a two sets to one deficit against the 12th-seeded Australian left-hander before coming through. Borg and the twin hair-banded top spinner had a rivalry dating back to 1973, a friendship even longer. Whenever they played, Borg, by his own admission, had to pretend that Vilas, three years his senior, was somebody else, just 'another guy over the net'. It evidently worked. Borg's victory over Vilas in the WCT final made it six wins in a row in the Swede's favour at big events, a fifth success in six matches in the past year.

Though beaten in Paris in the last eight by eventual runner-up, America's Harold Solomon, the swashbuckling Argentinean had a game wonderfully suited to clay and hard courts but seemingly lacked the confidence to reproduce it on grass. He was meeting Borg on the surface for the first time. Borg was only able to make it after more pain-numbing jabs. Aware of the dangers of taking the injections, he'd decided the risk was worth it. And once play began, fans would never have guessed there was anything amiss. 'The last man Borg's supposed stomach strain seems to be troubling is Borg himself,' observed the *Glasgow Herald* afterwards.

Against Vilas, on a court regarded as possibly the fastest in the world, Borg bounded about with haste and certainty, hitting multiple winners with his vicious forehands and almost completely subduing his rival by sheer power. He 'ran like a deer, leapt about as if on springs and served and smashed like a low-flying bomber' wrote Rex Bellamy. A Swedish reporter at the tournament believed that Borg cleverly used their doubles matches and practices to assess the Argentinean's deficiencies. 'Bjorn has made him [Vilas] his patsy ... He's got him taped,' he stated. It certainly looked that way.

Though continually applying a freezing ice-spray to his mid riff at each break, Borg seldom seemed troubled by his injury or his opponent. Vilas tried to play Borg from the baseline and it was no contest, though the strong, barrel-chested left-hander didn't help himself by serving ten double faults. For the bewildered Argentine, Rex Bellamy remarked, it was 'more like playing two hostile Steve Austins than one supposedly ailing friend'. He was on the end of a crushing 6-3, 6-0, 6-2 defeat, and the Swede had reached the semis for the first time. It was, *The Guardian*'s David Gray reported, 'a devastating performance for an invalid'. Gray proposed, 'Perhaps Vilas, the real sufferer, should have been injected instead.'

Although acknowledging he was scared he might do further damage to his muscles by playing, Borg was defiant. 'I'm prepared to put up with anything because I want this title so badly,' he stressed. Combating an injured stomach muscle was one thing; facing 'a one-man firing squad', as the *Glasgow Herald* labelled Tanner, was another. The grass on Centre Court, browned by the sun and scuffed by ten days of hard play, had put an even greater premium on big, blistering deliveries. It was tailor-made for the Tennessean. 'If he serves well, then what can I do?' a philosophical Borg asked pre-match.

Thankfully for Borg, Tanner was never able to match the electric pace or precision he'd had against Connors. As the American lost some of his control in a stiff cross-breeze, many of his first serves were off target. If anything, his second service, often with a wicked high kick off the dusty, sun-scorched surface, reaped a richer harvest. As expected, it was a duel of hard-hit shots and heavy topspin – a 'sledgehammer affair' *The Times's* Geoffrey Green named it – in which the two players bludgeoned each other throughout. But in an encounter described by David Gray as 'full of brief rallies and sudden blows', it was Borg who struck the most decisive ones.

In the whole match there were just two breaks of service, and only six games went to deuce. Each time the break went to Borg. In the seventh game of the opening set, after paving the way with a winning backhand service return, then following it with an angled backhand drive that left Tanner unprepared, he hit two incredible forehands in one rapid rally to break at 4-3. And, when Tanner was unable to take advantage of three double faults in the tenth game, Borg then settled the set 6-4 with an ace. He registered eight in all.

In a long second set that, in Green's words, 'continued to throb with power', both players served at peak form throughout, but at 5-4 up, with Borg serving, Tanner held a set point only to lob out and, when games eventually went to eight-all, he came to rue his missed opportunity. After losing the first point to a blazing Tanner ace – the fifth of his ten in the match – the Swede claimed six points in a row, eventually taking a tense tiebreak 7-2, the American putting another nail in his own coffin at set point against him by taking his eye off a Borg topspin lob, which, as he scrambled helplessly back to his baseline, bounced off his ankle.

The third set threatened to go the same way. Tanner spurned further chances in the seventh game when he had Borg 15-40 and in the ninth when he led 30-0 on the Swede's serve but that was the nearest the 23-year-old got to a break. Borg, reported Green, 'unsheathed his claws with more beautifully-judged passing shots as the defeat slowly but surely closed in on the sturdy American like a cloak'. When Tanner served to save the match at 4-5, he got only one first service in. Twice he made his second serve kick shoulder-high, and each time Borg ran around the ball and smote a topspin forehand down the line. The final winning shot was a backhand pass.

In an accomplished, if not artistic, victory, Borg always touched greater heights than the inconsistent American. After again going against medical advice, Borg played with ruthlessness as cold as the aerosol spray he administered to his middle, letting nothing – neither his double fault at set point in the first set nor his pain – worry him. Despite his injury, the whip-like Swede, according to the *Glasgow Herald*, 'looked the fittest man in Wimbledon'. Tanner was another foe surprised by the vast improvement in Borg's service. It was 'very much better than I expected', the seventh seed admitted after.

Aged 20 years and 27 days on the Saturday of the final, Borg was the youngest finalist since Rosewall in 1954. The man he would confront in the cauldron of Centre Court was Nastase. In his semi-final, the rumbustious Romanian had met Raul Ramirez, the first-ever Mexican to reach that stage of the competition and, like Nastase, one of the world's top shot-makers. Seeded eight, the tall, elegant Ramirez, who'd lost his Italian title when he was beaten in the first round but was a semi-finalist in Paris, had made the last four by halting Vitas Gerulaitis's chase for the coveted crown, his all-round superiority too much for the young American. Gerulaitis, a car fanatic who drove a white Rolls Royce – he used to have a Lamborghini 'but it gave me too much trouble so I traded it in' – had promised himself a $20,000 Dino Ferrari if he won the tournament. It would have to wait.

Overcoming a swirling wind, Nastase and Ramirez manufactured a match regarded as the best seen at a rather flat tournament – 'the equivalent

of an oasis of sand in a desert of grass' Rex Bellamy called it – one full
of artistry, graceful stroke play, rallying and retrieving, all played at a
breakneck speed. There was little to choose between the two but it was
Nastase who, in Peter Wilson's words, 'used his racket like the philosopher's
stone to turn what has often been so leaden at Wimbledon into gold'. He
carved out a 6-2, 9-7, 6-3 victory to reach his second final.

Given that the courts were faster than ever, there was a certain irony
that two players brought up on clay should be contesting the final. With
the vivid contrasts in personality and playing style – the dark, volatile
Nastase, capable of any shot or quirk of behaviour versus Borg, fair, strong
and stern – the ingredients were there for a close and thrilling one. Only
three times before had Europeans collided at the last stage. In both 1935
and 1936, Fred Perry had beaten the German, Gottfried von Cramm, while
1973 had seen the Kodes-Metreveli clash. But unlike three years earlier,
this promised to be a classic between two of the game's idols.

Despite suggestions that Nastase, at 29, had a more urgent incentive
to win, Borg was desperate to seize his opportunity. 'It is my dream to
win Wimbledon,' he affirmed, 'and I want to win *this* time.' It was the
Romanian, though, who'd had the edge in their previous meetings;
he'd come out on top in seven of their ten matches. And while it was
hardly surprising, as Nastase was almost ten years older than Borg, more
significantly, maybe, he'd beaten the Swede on two recent big occasions
– in the final of the Commercial Union Assurance Masters at Stockholm
(annihilating the hometown hero, 6–2, 6–2, 6–1) the previous December,
and in the semi-finals of the Avis Challenge Cup in Hawaii in May (before
defeating Ashe in the final).

But the uncertainty remained whether the brittle genius could handle
his moods as well as he could handle a tennis racket. Borg had said that it
was common knowledge among players that if you could get Nastase to lose

his cool there was a good chance of beating him. Some players admitted that they deliberately tried to unsettle Nastase during matches, knowing full well that if his hot-headedness boiled over his game fell apart.

'This time I have come to play tennis and that's all,' Nastase had promised earlier in the tournament and, for the most part, he'd been true to his word. He and Connors had raised the ire of officials when arriving on court for a second-round doubles match wearing bowler hats and rugby jumpers – a stunt similar to one they pulled the previous year in a Dewar Cup final when clowning their way through the match drinking champagne while again sporting bowlers on their heads. But umpire Eric Saville wasn't laughing; he made them remove the jerseys – Nastase, a red one with No.13, Connors, a green one with No.12 on the back – that contravened Wimbledon's predominantly white clothing rule, and the joke turned sour for the vaudeville act who exited to Syd Ball and Pilic in five sets. That aside, Nastase had kept his displays of tomfoolery to a minimum.

His semi-final, however, had seen his hair-trigger temperament get the better of him. In an outburst of irritation at dropping a service game, he argued with photographers, upset by their flashlights and machine-like clicking, issuing threats and two-fingered V-signs, and even took a swipe at one happy snapper sitting in the Centre Court front row, hitting him with a big green towel the player had been rubbing himself down with. At the end of the match, he'd walked off backwards as a final gesture against the cameramen. Ramirez readily confessed afterwards he'd hoped Nastase would really lose his rag. He hadn't. But, in Peter Wilson's opinion, the Romanian had 'the recurring attitude of a disgruntled, mongrel dog'. It was too easy to set him barking.

Should Nastase's interest wander, Borg was just the man to step in and take every advantage. Throughout the course of the fortnight, all calculated self-discipline, Borg had displayed unwavering focus. Nothing had penetrated the steely carapace; his attention span was unbroken. A perceived change in how he was now followed (or, rather, not followed) hadn't done him any harm. 'With the maturing of his play,' one reporter noted the day after he beat Vilas, 'has come the mellowing of his audience … even last year a young lady gave Centre Court added colour by dancing her pleasure at his every point while waving aloft her bra. Yesterday, apart from a brief outburst of Scandinavian "hurrahs" instantly silenced by Borg's finger across his lips, the elimination of Vilas was completed with no more decibels than came from the decorous clapping of the mums.'

Perhaps it was the more stringent security, possibly the shaggy beard fringing his once boyish face and making him look, in Geoffrey Green's view, 'like a pirate', but the days of eager young females chasing him across the manicured lawns appeared to be over. Maybe it was just Borg's crossing the threshold from his teens into his 20s that was sufficient to banish the boppers. In a 1973 *TV Times* feature about the rise of sporting pin-ups, Jimmy Hill had written, 'The one sure thing is that teenage adoration is transitory and a heart-throb seldom lasts for more than three or four years before the next dynamic 19-year-old captures the young fan's imagination.' Whatever the reason, the lack of attention had obviously profited Borg.

Nevertheless, it was Nastase who was heavily favoured to win. And when the final began on one of the hottest and most humid days of the year – the Duke of Kent arising to remove his jacket then sit in his shirt sleeves; an example that was followed by various other dignitaries including the Lord Mayor of London – the third seed looked very much like fulfilling the bookies' confidence. Borg won the toss and elected to receive. If it was an attempt to psych out the Romanian, hoping to break Nastase before he warmed up – a ploy many players used – it failed. On the patchy Centre Court grass, it was Nastase who began the slicker.

With a succession of volleys, half-volleys and passing shots, Nastase took the first three games, saving a break point in the opening game to bring it home after a service winner then drawing first blood, breaking Borg to 15 in the second game after a fine backhand fell on the baseline. Nastase had to stave off another break point in game three, hitting a volleyed winner to get out of jail before closing the game with a forehand, but at 3-0 up he looked well in charge. 'Come on, Borg,' came a frustrated yell in a Swedish accent from the back of the stand.

It was very nearly 4-0; in the next game Nastase had three break points but was repelled on each occasion, Borg then banging in a backhand volley before forcing his opponent to net and put his name on the scoreboard for the first time. Two games later, the youngster was level at 3-3. After Nastase served the first of his three double faults and a scorching Borg forehand winner blazed by him in game five to pull the break back, Borg, serving deep and fast, then held to 30 and the match was all square. Nastase won the seventh game, to love, but after that initial advantage it was his only success.

The Romanian's touch began to desert him and mistakes crept into his game. At 4-4, he revealed the first real cracks, missing with two volleys, one into the net and one yards out of court, as Borg scored a crucial break of serve. 'I saw he was getting nervous,' the Swede said afterwards. 'I know him very well and I can tell the signs.' Minutes later, he was looking even edgier; Nastase saved one set point with a backhand pass but Borg, with two crashing service winners, took the spoils and a one-set lead.

He raced through the second set in just 21 minutes. Love-one and 15-40 down, Borg slammed two aces, saved a third break point with another service winner, then reached advantage playing cat-and-mouse around the net before punching home a forehand after a long baseline rally for one-all. Nastase was broken in the following game after a sloppy forehand flew well out and for the remainder of the set, despite some marvellous retrieving shots, couldn't hold the rampant Swede.

While Borg, all fearless aggression, clubbed every ball as if he meant to split it in two, Nastase looked for the most part inhibited, cautious and often negative. His play was lethargic and slow, his magic wand turned into a piece of lead. Too frequently drop shots and lobs were turned against their perpetrator. No matter how deftly the Romanian would slide the ball into little pockets across the court, Borg, wrote Rex Bellamy, was 'nimble enough to reach most shots with a second or so to spare, so that he could organise limbs and racket for the best possible riposte'. Borg, with his familiar gait, ambled from court to court on the changeovers but, once the ball was in play, showed the blinding pace of an Olympic sprinter.

If Nastase's fans hoped for the blood to start coursing through his veins they were disappointed. 'We waited for the recovery or the explosion,' wrote veteran tennis writer Laurie Pignon. 'Neither came in the second set.' There was only a brief attempt at unsettling his adversary. As one of Borg's thunderbolts hurtled past him in game four, Nastase clutched his stomach in a mocking impersonation of a man suffering great pain around the ribs, as if asking the 'invalid' how he possibly could be hitting the ball so fiercely. Far from being upset by his opponent's implied doubts about the genuineness of his physical problems, Borg – who later revealed that, two hours before taking to the court, he'd taken three cortisone injections – took it as a positive. It was then that 'I knew he was gone,' Borg said post-match.

Even a note of encouragement passed to him by fast friend Connors, sitting courtside – 'It was just a love letter,' Nastase joked when asked about it later – failed to do the trick for the man from Bucharest. After Borg had broken again to lead 5-2, in the next game when a service from Borg was called out, Nastase politely insisted on counting it as an ace and the ruling was changed in the Swede's favour. Nastase's sportsmanship was heartily applauded but there was surely no clearer indication that he wasn't really himself. Borg, firing four winners, won the game to love and went two sets up.

In the third set he began like a world-beater. After breaking in the opening game with the aid of a blinding volley, Borg eased through his first two services games winning both to love, and was racing towards victory. From the seventh game of the second set to the fifth game of the third, Nastase won only eight points. With the baked turf giving the ball a higher, truer bounce, Borg capitalised. At 3-2 up, the No.4 seed flashed two topspin forehands past a floundering Nastase as he went adventurously to the net, his rifle-sharp shots so accurately placed he might have been looking along a gun barrel.

As Borg's dominance increased, the capacity crowd swung behind Nastase trying to urge him to greater effort. Nastase tried to respond but several times easy points slipped away as simple volleys found the net or his usually expertly controlled backhand was too long. In the rallies, the Swede nearly always got to the net first to smash away winners.

The Romanian wasn't quite done. Trailing 3-4, Nastase, after killing a backhand at the net and then wrong-footing Borg with a forehand cross-court, had two break points – but he muffed them both. A Borg volley and a rather frail service return undid Nastase's good work and, when the No.3 seed put a tame forehand into the net after a baseline duel, Borg took the game and a 5-3 lead. Nastase, 'who started like a thoroughbred racehorse', one American journalist noted, was ending 'like a tired and dispirited carthorse'. But with the Swede serving for the title at 5-4, his rival geared himself for one last desperate push.

Egged on by the crowd roaring their approval, the cut-and-thrust missing since the early exchanges returned. A spirited rally at the net had Nastase volleying away a winner to lead 0-15 and then he held two break points at 15-40. This last-ditch effort seemed of no avail, though, as Borg got to deuce with a service that Nastase could only net and then outlasted his opponent in a rare long rally. When Borg met Nastase's attempted pass with a forehand volley at the net, he was presented with a first Championship point. But after Nastase's venomous volley again made it deuce, he followed it with a smash before sending over a backhand from midcourt that Borg netted and then stroked a perfect backhand down the line, and it was level at 5-5. It brought the loudest cheer of the afternoon.

The charge was short-lived, however. Seeking a way back into the final, the Romanian found Borg refusing to allow him entry. After the next four games went with service, at 7-7 Borg upped his game again. As Nastase repeatedly failed to get in his first service, Borg hit two magnificent passes, one that gave him a 40-30 lead, and when another powerful two-fisted backhand had Nastase groping and failing with a relatively straightforward volley, Borg gained a critical 8-7 advantage.

This time, there was no slip. The young Swede, his blond locks flying beneath his headband, streaked across court to pick up a Nastase stop volley and whipped it a couple of millimetres over the net just out of the Romanian's reach. Then Nastase produced another out-of-character error, netting a volley he should have put away. Borg then volleyed a winner to earn himself a second match point. When a kicking serve to Nastase's backhand corner was returned into the net, the title was his. He hurled his racket and a ball exultantly heavenwards, let out a tearful whoop, pushed back his headband then buried his sweating face in his hands; Nastase, after hurdling the net, planted a congratulatory kiss on his conqueror, then embraced him as the two men walked off court. Moments later, handed the trophy by a now-jacketed Duke, the new king of Wimbledon held it aloft and took the acclaim of the capacity crowd.

In a near-flawless exhibition, Borg committed only four unforced errors all match. His win – secured in only one hour 49 minutes – 'represented one of the most classic examples of swift, inexorable destruction The Championships have seen' wrote Hugh McIlvanney. In *The Observer* man's opinion, 'Some of the Swede's shots were struck with the kind of uninhibited violence that Arnold Palmer once put into his golf shots.' Both his service and his return were 'superhuman', marvelled Peter Wilson. Borg's raw, brute strength he likened to that of the heavyweight boxer Rocky Marciano.

The world's most gifted touch player had been, Ronald Atkin reported in *The Observer*, reduced 'to sweaty misery'. Borg, according to David Gray, had left Nastase 'in retreat, struggling to survive in the face of some of the most devastating attacking tennis that Centre Court has known'. Gray described the Swede's display as 'cold-blooded and efficient'.

Rather than Nastase, it was the 20-year-old, in the eyes of Frank Keating of *The Guardian*, who played like 'the calm, wizened old campaigner'. Aged only 19 years and five months, an Englishman, Wilfred Baddeley, had triumphed in 1891 before Wimbledon truly was international, while America's Sidney Wood was 19 and eight months when, in 1931, Frank Shields, another American, was forced to default because of an ankle injury. But the Scandinavian phenomenon became the youngest champion of the modern era (as well as the first male player to have won both the Wimbledon junior and adult titles), and, as Peter Wilson put it, 'neither of these [other two] performances can be compared with Borg's'.

His victory was achieved, opined McIlvanney, 'with a blend of cool thoughtfulness and ferocious animal power, with a mature and deadly resolution that was almost impossible to reconcile with the fact that only two men in history have taken the title at an earlier age'. At the same age, Laver had yet to gain a major title, and even the prodigious Rosewall had only two significant wins to his name. The legend that said that Borg's feet of clay, so to speak, was his grass game – and any nagging doubts of his own – had surely been laid to rest. His talent would brook no such confinement in the future.

The first-ever Swede to have succeeded to tennis's most sought-after title, Borg was also the first champion to charge through an entire Wimbledon without losing a set since Chuck McKinley of the US in 1963. The final had seen, David Gray wrote, 'a brisk determined newcomer … rising to the occasion at exactly the right moment'. 'I have certainly never played better on a fast court than I played today,' Borg told reporters. 'Grass is now my favourite surface,' he said. To any of his opponents listening, it must have sounded like a truly ominous note.

20 June – 2 July 1977

AT 1.00PM on a cold and gloomy Monday, 20 June 1977, shortly before he launched his bid for a second successive Wimbledon men's singles title, Bjorn Borg was striding out on to Centre Court. Not donned in his already iconic vertically striped Fila top and shorts, the red, white and blue headband, and Tretorn plimsolls, with a Donnay tennis racket in hand, dressed for battle on the groomed green grass, but wearing a smart two-piece suit and walking along a crimson carpet.

Along with the reigning women's titleholder, Chris Evert, the Swede was one of a cavalcade of 41 former and current champions paraded before a packed crowd as the band of the Welsh Guards played Verdi's triumphal 'Grand March' from his opera, *Aida*, and each presented with a silver commemorative medal from the Duke of Kent, President of the All England Club since 1969.

The 'Parade of Champions', a nostalgia-drenched, awe-inspiring ceremony marking the centenary of The Championships, revived vivid memories of the dramas and disappointments seen during Wimbledon's first 100 years, the men and women who had left indelible impressions. A span of 64 years separated the 21-year-old Swede from 85-year-old

American Elizabeth 'Bunny' Ryan, winner of a record 19 doubles titles from 1914 to 1934, who'd hobbled slowly across the court on crutches to receive her medal. Britain's Kitty McKane Godfree, now 81, was also present. France's famous 'Four Musketeers', including 82-year-old Jacques 'Toto' Brugnon, with ages totalling 306, were there too.

However, one past champion was missing. As the celebrations went on, ending with players linking arms for 'Auld Lang Syne' and blowing kisses to spectators, Jimmy Connors was nowhere to be seen. The American, seeded No.1 and 9-4 favourite to recapture the crown he'd won in 1974, had entered the pre-Wimbledon Queen's Club tournament hoping to get his first outing on grass in a year, but was forced to withdraw because of what was thought to be a bruised right thumb, injured while practising with John Newcombe, now the ATP president. It actually proved to be a cracked bone. Granted a request for a day's grace, his Monday match rescheduled for the following day while an orthopaedic splint was fitted, Connors had been invited to join the procession as well as attend a special champions' luncheon in the members' enclosure.

But not only did he fail to reply to the invitation and then not appear but, according to club officials later, he also sent no explanation nor an apology. When asked by reporters about his absence, an evasive Connors only compounded the controversy by saying first that he didn't know about the event, then that he 'was busy' and finally that 'Maybe I was seeing my doctor.'

The latter would have been the most legitimate excuse, but it transpired that the American had been hitting balls 200 yards away on Court 13 at the back of the grounds with his old buddy Ilie Nastase. 'When I arrived in the dressing room the champions were going out on court,' Connors explained. 'It was Rod Laver's turn to go next. I looked at him and ...' Connors stopped and shook his head. He'd tried his best to make it to

Centre Court, only to be shut out at the gate at the last second. Instead, he kept an appointment with his doctor who wanted to check on his fracture.

Unsurprisingly, the left-hander was in trouble before he'd even stroked his first two-fisted backhand. The man the press loved to hate had supplied his detractors with yet more ammunition. A chilly, overcast opening day was nothing to the frosty reception the player now judged as 'the Rude American' was given by the press. Fleet Street's criticism was blasted from almost every newspaper. 'Champion in disgrace' the *Daily Express* headlined with the following day. 'Connors snubs Royals', was on the front page of *The Sun*. 'If a charming 85-year-old lady on crutches feels proud to take part in the centenary celebrations,' wrote Laurie Pignon in the *Daily Mail*, 'it is inconceivable that a young man cannot bother to walk a few hundred yards with a bad thumb.'

To add to that thumb, Connors received a severe rap on the knuckles, Major David Mills, the All England Club secretary, considering the American's behaviour as 'an extreme discourtesy', and informing the press that a 'very upset' Wimbledon committee, while sending a medal to each of the 11 other champions who'd forwarded apologies, would not be issuing Connors with one, only a stern reprimand.

Connors's failure to show overshadowed what was an emotional start to the tournament. His attitude towards the birthday festivities might have been questionable, but few could argue with Connors's top seeding. The boy from Belleville had once again been belting opponents left, right and centre, a dominant force on the exclusive but demanding WCT circuit for the remainder of 1976 after his Wimbledon disappointment and the first half of 1977. Only four players – Borg, Dick Stockton, Nastase and Panatta – had beaten him since the start of the year.

On all four occasions he'd met Borg in 1976, Connors had won. Crucially, in the September, with 'the best tennis I've ever played', he'd defeated the Swede 6-4, 3-6, 7-6, 6-4 at Forest Hills to claim a second US Open title in three years. In May 1977, he'd also taken the $200,000 first prize in the WCT final in Dallas, overcoming Stockton, exacting revenge for a defeat in five sets by the same player at the US Pro Indoor in Philadelphia in January.

No top seed had won Wimbledon since Stan Smith in 1972, but Connors was determined to end that record and, as the *Sydney Morning Herald*'s Brian Mossop phrased it, 'snatch back the candy from the 21-year-old Swede'. Connors was regarded as the toughest and most successful competitor in the draw, though it was still perhaps a little surprising that he was twice as strongly favoured by the bookmakers as Borg. The race for No.1 in the world was hardly settled. Borg had taken more than his share of the spoils over the season.

At Forest Hills, he'd actually edged Connors in points, 123 to 121, and Connors knew that the youngster was pushing harder all the time. 'I can't count him out anymore. It was five seconds after the last point that I realised the match was over,' Connors had said after the final. When he was asked where Borg had improved, 'Everywhere,' came the reply.

Curry Kirkpatrick called them 'magnificently matched adversaries' destined to rule the roost for years to come. 'By the time Jimmy Connors and Bjorn Borg finish up their series of Great Debates ... both should be old enough to require wheelchairs and wise enough to give the game of tennis back to somebody else.'

In January 1977, Borg earned a victory over the American in a Pepsi Grand Slam match played on the outdoor green clay courts at the Mission Hills Country Club in Boca Raton, Florida, and Kirkpatrick saw it as a significant result. In their seven previous matches, Borg had won only once – in the very first meeting, in the semi-final of the 1973 Stockholm Open, when the emerging Swedish star triumphed 7-6 in the deciding third set

– but, combining well-chosen lobs and a clever little low backhand chip shot with his characteristic looping topspin forehand, he upset Connors 6-4, 5-7, 6-3 and, in the *Sports Illustrated* writer's view, had proved 'that if you punish a child enough he'll learn to do things right'. The win at the invitation event, which brought together four of the world's top players, had not only avenged Borg's US Open loss, but more importantly had thrown 'the monkey of self-doubt off his back'. Borg now had faith in his ability to get the better of the American.

Borg's first Wimbledon title had brought him fresh confidence. It also increased his already huge wealth. A lucrative pattern was set long before his success in SW19, not least because he'd joined up with IMG, the sports management company who'd realised and exploited his income potential from the off. Along with his winnings from matches, various endorsements – for Saab cars, SAS airlines and Kellogg's cereals, for example (as well as getting paid simply for sporting the right headband, wristband, shoes and racket) – had already earned Borg a small fortune. His deal with the Italian clothing firm of Fila, alone, was believed to be worth about $400,000 a year, including royalties. But the money continued to flood in. In early February 1977, the Swedish star signed a three-year contract estimated at $1.5m to play World Team Tennis for the Cleveland-Pittsburgh Nets. From May, with the exception of Wimbledon, the US Open and Swedish Davis Cup competition, he would devote the rest of his 1977 efforts exclusively to WTT, his acquisition seen as a major breakthrough for the league.

Borg, feeling that 'Europe really holds no challenge for me. I did everything there,' thought 'why not?' The faster courts on the WTT circuit, requiring hustle and aggressiveness, would also help him prepare for Wimbledon. The pot was sweetened even further for the Swede when his Romanian girlfriend, Mariana Simionescu, was added to the Nets' roster, joining Borg in a 'sweetheart team'. Mariana, winner of the 1974 French Open junior girls' event and a Wimbledon junior finalist the same year, had met Borg at the French Open in 1976. After Borg asked her to go out with him and his coach for a meal on 10 June, Lennart Bergelin's birthday, the pair began dating. By November they'd announced their engagement. They'd become inseparable, Mariana following Borg all over the world, cheerfully accepting the routine of jet-hopping and living out of a suitcase that came with his life. Alongside Bergelin, she was now a regular fixture at her partner's matches.

As part of the recognition of its past, Wimbledon inaugurated its Lawn Tennis Museum, with exhibits and artefacts – rackets, fashions, the first grass-court tennis balls, and tennis 'sets' in the shape of cardboard boxes containing the equipment needed for 'the new game of lawn tennis' – dating back to 1555 and telling the story of a game once played for fun, weather permitting, on English weekends. The museum ostensibly doubled as a hall of fame. Whether Bjorn Borg would ever find himself a place in it, time would tell.

Despite cutting a swathe through the field in 1976 he was, to a degree, still an unknown quantity on grass. 'Any man can win Wimbledon once,' Rod Laver had said. 'Only a real champion can win it twice in a row.' There remained many, his fellow players included, who questioned whether the youngster, with his style far more readily tailored to clay, could pull off a repeat performance. Borg hadn't competed on grass since the Nastase final. Nor had he played any tournament tennis since April when he won Nice, Monte Carlo and Denver in successive weeks before turning to WTT.

It didn't take the defending champion long to dispel a few of the doubts. Playing the time-honoured Centre Court first match as titleholder, Borg began his campaign by making light work of the powerful but erratic Italian Antonio Zugarelli. Hitting five aces in his first two service games, before breaking in the fifth to lead 3-2, then winning the first four games of the second set, Borg dashed through the first two sets 6-4, 6-2. And though a more determined Zugarelli emerged in the third set – the Italian changing his tactics, coming to the net at every opportunity, and causing Borg some bother – the Swede was never really extended.

Zugarelli won the first game of the set to love and games then went with service until the 15th, when the Italian committed four errors to drop his service to love. Borg then served for the set and match and won to love. If anything, the court, soft underfoot after two weeks of rain, caused Borg more alarm than his opponent. During the ninth game of the third set, the Swede slipped on the moist grass and fell heavily, though his game remained unaffected.

On that opening day, low temperatures and a chilling north wind kept the number of spectators down to less than the organisers had hoped but those there waved their patriotic flags and witnessed a major shock. Against John Lloyd, despite taking the first set, Roscoe Tanner was the man who suffered it. The fourth seed, winner of the Australian Open earlier in the year after wiping out Vilas in the final, was undone by his own misfiring first serve and an inconsistent backhand.

After it looking early on like the Briton was on court only in the role of sacrificial lamb, Lloyd punished the American's weak second service, picking him off time and again, and with Tanner surprisingly unable to match his opponent's serve-and-volley game, Britain's 22-year-old Davis Cup player registered a 3-6, 6-4, 6-4, 8-6 triumph and arguably the biggest first-day upset in a decade. 'I think all the seeds have a tendency to get nervous in the first round,' Lloyd said modestly. 'That's the time to beat them.' The 16th-seeded American Harold Solomon, eliminated by Steve Docherty of Australia, was another saying an early goodbye as The Championships got off to a form-shaking start.

One seed who rarely exhibited anxiety whatever the round was Connors. The American was bound to pay for his no-show, though. The Wimbledon committee had already made their feelings known. Now it was the turn of the spectators. On the Tuesday, as he walked out for his match against Briton Richard Lewis, a rangy left-hander ranked ninth in the country, Connors ran a gauntlet of unprecedented hostility from Wimbledon's normally sedate fans, a large percentage of the 14,000 around Centre Court eschewing their usual politeness to show their anger at his Monday boycott. There were boos, cat-calls and hisses as he entered. Sir Brian Burnett, Herman David's successor as All England Club chairman, even walked out. It seemed more like a pantomime stage than the stately, Elizabethan-style arena; these were sounds long-time observers couldn't ever remember hearing before, let alone for a former champion.

As Connors went to his baseline to start hitting up, the noise was cranked up in volume. The villain, nonetheless, remained unperturbed. Soon settling down in the old, familiar surroundings, the 24-year-old, sporting a steel splint on his injured thumb, displayed an even steelier nerve, never letting his resolve falter as he charged, albeit seldom at more than half throttle, to a 6-3, 6-2, 6-4 victory, thoroughly outclassing the big, loose-limbed Lewis. 'It [the crowd's reception] just made me play better,' he commented afterwards. The mood of the fans did actually melt a little as the match progressed and Connors's finest shots were applauded. At the end, although he received only a mild ovation, conciliation was in the air.

After virtually no grass practice leading up to Wimbledon, Borg conceded that his preparations had not been adequate. He got plenty of time on court in his next match, however. On Court 14, Borg faced Mark Edmondson in a singles match for the first time on any surface – they'd met once at doubles though Edmondson said he could recall little about it – the burly Australian having struggled to advance in a fluctuating five-setter over unranked American Mark Wayman in the first round. And on a sunny day that saw 37,393 – a new one-day record attendance – packed into the grounds, Borg at one stage looked poised to make a hasty exit from the tournament.

'Obviously it's a tough one, but I'll be doing the best I can,' Edmondson stated pre-match, but no one foresaw that the former Australian Open champion's best would see him on the brink of pulling off a sensational result. Edmondson, with a stocky build, long and wild hair, and a handlebar moustache – 'a large man, broody and menacing', in Rex Bellamy's description – looked more like an Aussie Rules footballer than a tennis pro. On court he was all raw power. Arthur Ashe, who'd beaten Edmondson the previous year, had said of him: '[He] walks around like a man possessed – caning everything.'

Against Borg, for the first two sets, his cavalier play completely threw the No.2 seed out of his stride. Showing no sign of nerves or the ankle injury that had hampered his build-up, the 22-year-old took them both, the second from 2-5 down. Borg recovered his composure, claimed the third set easily and gradually played himself into touch. But at 4-4 and 30-30 in the fourth set (Borg serving) he was living on a knife edge. 'Borg, like most Swedes, tends to be gloomy, inviting nightmares but eventually responding to the summons of the alarm bell,' Bellamy wrote in his match report. The 21-year-old did precisely that; he rallied again, won the set and went on to record a 3-6, 7-9, 6-2, 6-4, 6-1 success.

He was lucky to win, he said afterwards, though added that 'If you can play a hard five sets on grass, it is good.' He did himself a disservice; it was more through pluck than luck. Facing possible extinction, an instinct for survival kicked firmly in; Borg's indomitable will, seemingly impervious to blows, married with his tremendous court skills saw him through.

Edmondson, who lost 7lb in the course of the match, readily admitted that he 'just couldn't keep going'.

Borg wasn't the only one struggling. While Connors – made to look like a novice when losing a second-set tiebreak 7-1 – took four tiring sets to overcome his heavily moustached fellow American Marty Riessen, other seeds fared far more miserably. Arguably the most improved player in the world, No.5 Brian Gottfried, who'd reached eight finals earlier in the year and won four of them, came up against and went down to the notoriously erratic Byron Bertram, while his doubles partner, the seventh-seeded Raul Ramirez, after boosting his confidence when winning at the Queen's Club (defeating Mark Cox), was another casualty.

The Mexican, a semi-finalist in Paris, had opened with a win against Peter Fleming but in a tightrope match lasting ten minutes short of four hours was beaten by Tim Gullikson, the right-hander of the tennis-playing Wisconsin twins prevailing despite suffering cramp in the latter stages. Adriano Panatta (No.10), proving once again that he was better on clay and a good attacking player with little defence, was another to go out, downed by Sandy Mayer.

There were yet more turn-ups to come. In the third round, Wimbledon dipped into its bag of surprises again and left Guillermo Vilas the victim. Now coached full-time by Ion Tiriac, the South American, who'd dropped only three games in thrashing Gottfried in a drizzly French Open final, was gunned down by unheralded Californian, Billy 'The Kid' Martin. The boyish, blond-haired youngster, who'd been American tennis's 'Rookie of the Year' for the previous four or five years, was being helped by, among others, Borg's coach. Lessons from Bergelin (plus practice sessions with Rod Laver) had prepared Martin for the match. The 20-year-old was also not shaving during the tournament in the hope it might bring him the same luck as Borg.

It all worked. Martin – the 'Santa Baby' born on Christmas Day 1956 – produced a sparkling performance to back up the promise he had shown in landing the Wimbledon junior title in 1973 and 1974. Third-seeded Vilas, looking tired, his play mistake-littered, was humbled in straight sets. 'It was not a contest,' reported the *Glasgow Herald*, 'it was a stroll in the sunshine.' Elsewhere, another American, the experienced Bob Lutz, also went out, the No.15 seed losing in five sets to Kim Warwick, the Australian vanquisher of David Lloyd in the previous round.

The temperatures were rising and the grass was becoming faster. With record numbers cramming the grounds, the crowds flowed like lava from court to court, some players taking ten minutes to squeeze their way through the throng along narrow paths to the outer courts. Borg had no such trouble – either with congestion on the promenades or his next opponent. On Centre Court, he beat Niki Pilic in relatively untroubled fashion. The Yugoslav veteran, who'd earlier destroyed Vijay Amritraj, made Borg fight all the way, but, after two tight sets, was finally ground down, the Swede finishing at a canter to win 9-7, 7-5, 6-3 and go serenely on.

With Connors also making the last 16, defeating Cliff Drysdale, the way to a date in the final for the two top seeds was becoming ever more clear-cut. Against the Texas-based South African, Connors, after the heavy criticism he'd come under, turned on the charm in an attempt to win back the crowd's respect. Drysdale, 36 and well past his mid-60s peak that had seen him twice reach the semi-finals, took advantage of some lackadaisical play from the 24-year-old to give Connors a good workout but the American was never under great pressure; he even allowed himself the luxury of playing the fool – heading the ball on one occasion and clowning with spectators – before emerging an emphatic winner.

By the end of the week, the inaugural boos for Connors had turned to more appreciative noises. On No.1 Court, after a four-hour, blood-and-guts battle with Stan Smith that could have gone either way, Connors, grunting 'like a shot putter' according to the *Sunday Times*'s Brian Glanville, progressed to the quarter-finals. But it took five sets and some breathtaking brinkmanship before he overcame the 11th seed.

Smith, who'd seen many lean years since his Wimbledon triumph, found a fair measure of his old flair and in the final set the 1972 champion had Connors at his mercy and a packed crowd right behind him – the spectators applauding each winning shot by Smith, wrote Glanville, 'as though it were a blow against the powers of darkness' – only to spurn a heaven-sent opportunity. A squandered point that would have given him a service break and a 4-2 lead cost Smith the match, Connors producing a devastating burst that finally clinched victory. 'It was one of the best matches I've ever played,' Connors said after coming off court, before snapping, when someone asked if he felt at all sorry for Smith, 'No. It's war out there, man.'

Borg's passage into the last eight was a little less fraught. In the fourth round, he met Wojciech Fibak. In the previous round, having already survived one five-setter (versus Jaime Fillol), the 24-year-old Pole had accounted for Britain's Buster Mottram in another, battling to victory on a packed Centre Court heavily behind their homegrown hope. Fibak, with only two years' experience on the circuit, had enjoyed a rapid rise to prominence and was unlucky to finish runner-up to Manuel Orantes in a five-set Masters final in Houston in December 1976 after leading 2-1 in sets and 4-1 in the fourth.

A victor over Borg in Monte Carlo the previous year, the man from Poznan was expected to really test the Swede's mettle. A few know-alls felt he might even prove the surprise packet at the tournament. But on the same day that his Romanian girlfriend was putting Britain's Virginia Wade through an ordeal before losing 9-7, 6-3, Borg barely made a false move. On No.1 Court he removed the right-hander with by far his most convincing performance of the week.

With Fibak proving a resilient and worthy opponent, pushing Borg back with finely angled shots, plenty of variety, and the occasional drop shot at the net, matters were reasonably even for the first ten games. Borg, though, always seemed to have the edge, suggesting that at a critical moment he would steal ahead. He did. After games swayed to and fro with service, a backhand gave Borg the break in the 11th. He then served out the first set with Fibak netting a forehand at set point.

The multi-lingual Fibak, who'd studied law at Adam Mickiewicz University (though dropped out with a dream of becoming a film director), was also a man of great tennis intelligence. He played a clever, adventurous game. But he struggled to cope with the Swede's tremendous athleticism. Borg 'leaped around the court like a great bronze cat', wrote the *Evening Times*'s Bill Brown, and serving strongly and volleying acrobatically outplayed the Pole at both the baseline and the net. A break ahead, Borg, with a fourth ace of the match to reach set point, took the tenth game of the second set to love, and from then on there was really no way back for his moustachioed opponent.

If the weather was a bit dreary, Borg's tennis wasn't. The longer the afternoon went on, the more in charge he was. His serving, thunderous at times, became ever heavier, his returns sharper. Whenever he wanted to, he appeared able to pull aces out from his sleeves. On the big points, he just slipped into a faster gear. Towards the end, Fibak was reduced to a sheer survivor. When a service winner pumped down the middle sealed the third set 6-2, and victory, the capable Pole was finally overcome by a man who had just too much for him.

Next up was Nastase. The 31-year-old had been his predictably unpredictable self. After putting out Tom Gullikson, the older of the two brothers by five minutes, he'd come from behind to win in five sets in the second round against Andrew Pattison, kept his court antics to a minimum as he defeated 18-year-old Californian Eliot Teltscher, before recovering brilliantly from a tentative start to top old enemy Tom Okker in a two-hour duel overflowing with rich talent.

The sixth seed's clash with Pattison, though, had been tainted. Forced to fight back from a two-set deficit, Nastase, ill-tempered throughout, had edged the tall, blond Rhodesian but only with the aid of his old tricks and childish tantrums. When Pattison was leading with a service break in the fourth set, Nastase started acting up, becoming abusive and insulting to a linesman and the umpire and causing a ten-minute delay when forcing referee Fred Hoyles to come on to No.2 Court, at one point ducking behind the green canvas surrounding the court.

The Romanian's stalling tactics worked. Distracted and upset, his concentration in tatters, poor Pattison folded, and was so incensed at the end he refused to shake his opponent's proffered hand, while Nastase was then given a police escort back to the locker rooms as an angry crowd shouted at him. Pattison later accused Nastase of 'behaving abominably' and 'breaking the rules of the game that play must be continuous'. Had Wimbledon officials not been so cowed, Nastase may well have been ejected from The Championships.

Against Borg, it took only ten seconds for another bout of petulance. The first eruption came over a linesman's delayed call, when a drive by Nastase cleared the baseline by inches. Although late, the call was correct, but Nastase being Nastase was prepared to claim it was in, only to be told firmly by umpire Jeremy Shales to play on. An even more heated argument was raised over the third point, Nastase arguing that his service had touched the top of the net on the way over. Again, Shales ruled against the Romanian and, to add insult to injury, Borg won the game with a shot off a net cord. Nastase had a word with all three officials who had offended him, and promptly lost the second game as well without scoring a point. At the end of it, as he crossed over, he tossed a ball between Mr Shales's legs.

In the third game, as he dropped his service for the second successive time, it was the courtside photographers with whom Nastase saw fit to disagree. It looked like turning into a farce rather than a tennis match. Nastase's shenanigans, of course, cut no ice with Borg. Staying composed throughout the incidents, he simply concentrated on the task in hand: knocking out his opponent in the quickest time possible. Borg won the first eight points in a row. It was only in the middle of the fourth game that he made his first unforced error.

Walloping the ball with tremendous force and unfaltering accuracy, Borg's groundstrokes were shattering. Nastase, looking 'as lonely as a lighthouse' to Rex Bellamy, was passed almost at will, his tennis 'like some pretty but fragile craft smashed into sadly anonymous wreckage by a storm that had crossed the sea from Scandinavia'. Under considerable pressure from Borg's service, and finding his own serves thumped back at him, Nastase was made to look downright mediocre.

The champion sped around like quicksilver. 'Everywhere Nastase looked, there was a Borg – all of them playing marvellous tennis. The Swede seemed to flutter about the court like a moth,' Bellamy observed. 'Even when he [Nastase] played what he thought was a winning card – a drop shot, a cross-court volley or a lob – the tall Swede was there to trump it,' reported *The Guardian*'s David Irvine. After 16 minutes of unremitting attack, Borg thundered down an ace to go one set up. He'd taken it to love with the loss of just seven points. Two of those the Romanian was fortunate to win. Borg, playing 'like a mad man' according to Bill Brown, simply blew his opponent right off court. Bellamy described him as 'inhumanly good'.

A contest threatened to break out in the second set. In the fourth game, Borg, after a double fault – one of three in the match – was broken for the only time. But with a point for a 5-2 lead, Nastase struck a couple of weak forehands to let Borg back in and thereafter the Swede never looked likely to lose his grip. In the 13th game, flashing two superb passing shots that kicked up chalk on the sidelines and following it with a drive so fierce that Nastase could only put it wide, Borg made the break to lead 7-6. Nastase had a point for a break back, but hit a poor return, and again, with an ace, Borg rounded off the set.

After that, Nastase seemed more intent on winning a personality clash with umpire Shales than fighting back. Shales, a 34-year-old Bank of England official, won it game, set and match. At 1-0 up in the third set after holding service, Nastase appeared to deliberately aim a forehand drive at Borg advancing to the forecourt, and when the Swede stared back at him and asked angrily, 'What you do?' Nastase swore at him, his bad language earning him a caution from the umpire.

Then, after more delaying tactics and some quite deliberate provocation following confusion over a replayed point, Nastase was officially reported to the referee, Shales ringing Fred Hoyles on the telephone on his chair, but leaving his microphone on for the entire Centre Court to hear. This was all in the second game.

Nastase – 'like a little boy who had been given a public spanking' wrote Peter Wilson – did play on, but Borg, patrolling the baseline totally unperturbed, whipped in three more serves to win the game and then raced to victory. After breaking the Romanian in the fifth game with the aid of a Nastase double fault, Borg again remained unflustered in the next game as Nastase tried yet more time-wasting ploys – complaining, jokingly this time, about a bird's feather that had floated down and landed on the court just in front of him – winning it to go 4-2 ahead.

There was little else for Nastase to laugh about. Against the splendid virtuosity of Borg's all-round game, Nastase simply fell apart and the Swede wrapped up the set, 6-3, and his victory. It was a clinical 98-minute elimination that had observers calling it the best tennis of the tournament thus far. In David Irvine's view, the champion had given 'another murderously cold and unanswerable performance'.

For Nastase, though, it was, wrote Australian journalist Peter McFarline, 'another chapter in the story of the Romanian's inability to mask his shocking temperament with his God-given skill'. Shales confessed afterwards he couldn't 'understand the man's mentality'. Inevitably, Nastase saw himself as the victim. Even long after the match, racing to catch a Paris-bound plane, he was still fuming as he went through Heathrow airport. 'I did not have any argument with the umpire,' Nastase insisted. 'He picked one with me. He wanted something to happen. He was totally biased. The umpire knew of my reputation and deliberately tried to start something.' And what about the near-decapitation of Borg when the entire court was open? 'I wanted to smash the ball very hard and unfortunately it hit Bjorn. It was not because I was angry. It was an accident.'

Regardless, Borg was still in one piece, and the semi-final pitted him against Vitas Gerulaitis. The 22-year-old New Yorker, his slim legs, broad shoulders and mane of blond uncombed curls giving him the appearance of Borg without a beard, was a fine, feisty athlete with a superb physique, extremely nimble around the court. His service return was one of the best in the game. Six weeks before, after reaching the semis at the WCT finals, he'd collected his first major title when becoming the Italian champion – the first American since Barry MacKay in 1960 to do so – though Gerulaitis was threatened with a $16,000 fine for skipping WTT to go to Rome.

In SW19, seeded eight, he was looking in good nick, having too much speed and all-court skill for fellow American Tom Gorman before disposing of Gene Mayer (Sandy's brother) and Jonathan Smith of Britain. Despite dropping a set for the first time, Gerulaitis, adapting better to the bumpy grass, then saw off ninth-seeded Dick Stockton and, in the quarter-final, faced Billy Martin.

To reach the last eight, the stocky, athletic Martin, playing his third left-hander in a row, had recovered from 2-5 down in the fifth set to defeat Britain's last hope, the 14th-seeded Mark Cox, with another strong serve-and-volley game. But the 20-year-old Californian had also spent five hours on court the previous day playing doubles and, against Gerulaitis's superior experience and stamina, those efforts proved too much of a drain. After the first two sets had been shared, the New Yorker, his groundstrokes more severe, his volleying keener, took the next two, both 6-2, to come out on top.

A self-confessed ladies' man with a love of discos (the Big Apple's notorious Studio 54 nightclub was a regular haunt, though Gerulaitis himself hated his 'playboy' tag – 'I don't drink and I don't smoke, so why playboy?' he would say forcibly), the Brooklyn-born son of a Lithuanian immigrant had nevertheless buckled down to take advantage of his tennis talent. Under the guidance of 38-year-old Aussie, Fred Stolle, himself a former Wimbledon favourite (a runner-up three years running, beaten in 1963 by Chuck McKinley and by compatriot Roy Emerson in both 1964 and 1965, though rated as a much better doubles player than a singles star), Gerulaitis had improved enormously – especially his service.

He and Borg, the extrovert and the introvert, had become close – Borg's friendship with Vilas having waned somewhat after the Swede's relationship with Mariana began. Having played for hours together on practice courts around the world and frequently engaged in exhibition matches, they knew each other's games intimately, almost telepathically. In the week before Wimbledon, they'd knocked up together for over 30 hours.

Although already an established threat to the older generation of men's stars, after winning in Rome, Gerulaitis realised that he'd been settling on the fringe of the world top ten and that, he said, 'made me play all the harder' at Wimbledon. He was a fighter, perhaps with no one great shot, but sheer persistence alone hadn't carried him to the semis. He'd played a lot of excellent tennis.

Far from being overawed at the thought of meeting Borg – 'The fact that he is champion, although a very good one, will mean nothing to me' – Gerulaitis was optimistic about his prospects. 'I feel I have a great chance,' he said. 'I just can't start making careless errors.' Their back-and-forth duel, fought at a sizzling pace for just over three hours, was among the most gripping seen on Centre Court for years.

In the first two sets there were just two breaks of service. Borg, with two immaculate lobs, gained an edge in the very first game, on to which he held tightly to take the opening set; Gerulaitis's chance came in the sixth game of the second set and when he buried a backhand volley – 'as decisive as a guillotine' wrote Peter Wilson – he claimed the crucial breakthrough before levelling at one set all.

The two young gladiators fought a mesmerising battle, 'a contest', described David Irvine, 'full of subtle turns and twists, brilliant manoeuvring and fierce hitting, light and colour and a hundred different changes of pace'. Rallies were long and pulsating. Balls were landing plumb on the lines. For Peter Wilson it took him back to the classroom 'for since my schooldays I've never seen so much chalk flying'.

In the third set, Gerulaitis initially broke away but was immediately caught, saved five break points in the fourth game and held on until the eighth before an outstanding forehand pass gave Borg the advantage and eventually the set. In that eighth game, Gerulaitis had served his ninth – and final – double fault. He had to go for broke with his second service, according to Wilson, because 'Borg was lashing the ball so hard that it was likely to go down Gerulaitis's throat and give him a second Adam's apple.'

Gerulaitis, though, was anything but done. Bounding eagerly to the net, and flashing along it like forked lightning, he was, Rex Bellamy said, 'gambler and acrobat in one', his agile play and finely judged volleys equalling whatever Borg could offer. In the fourth game of the fourth set, a Borg double fault – he served only two – gave the American a break at 3-1 and, playing with supreme verve and enthusiasm, Gerulaitis proceeded to even things up once more at two sets apiece.

In the final set, the player affectionately known as 'the Lithuanian Lion' continued to roar. Gerulaitis appeared to be assuming control. At 2-2, Borg's composure slipped ever so slightly for the first time; after questioning a linesman's call – 'I saw him frown at an official' Gerulaitis joked later – he still seemed bothered when play resumed. Gerulaitis, with a succession of textbook volleys and two backhand returns that Borg barely waved a racket at as he was passed, played his finest game of the match to break the Swede's service to love, and it boded ill for Borg.

But, typically, he showed his true champion quality. At 40-30 down in the sixth game, he found fresh reserves. After staying back on his second service, when he eventually charged the net, Gerulaitis was off the mark with a forehand volley from Borg's attempted backhand pass and the score was deuce. 'I made a mistake,' Gerulaitis rued afterwards. 'I missed with my first service and when I spun my second service, I should have gone in.' It was a costly decision. Two points later, a running forehand down the line then a vicious backhand return that shot away off Gerulaitis's racket, saw the Swede level once more.

The large crowd was held spellbound. At times, it was almost exhausting to watch as the two rivals hared around chasing lobs, retrieving from their baselines and scrambling to the net. At 5-5, with Borg serving, the excitement edged towards the breath-stopping. The game went to deuce three times. Watching on intently in the stands, Bergelin sweated marbles, an anxious Mariana chewed on her gum. But Borg, 'teetering on the brink of a plunge to oblivion', as Bellamy put it, never once flinched. He held his serve and, after raising his game at 6-6 to hold again, this time to love – 'a circumstance as rare as a rose on Christmas Day' wrote Peter Wilson – then came the crunch.

Gerulaitis, serving to save the match, gave way against Borg's savage returns and failed with first a volley then an overhead backhand smash. That made it 15-30. The American attacked at the net on the next point, and Borg lobbed him. Gerulaitis scrambled backwards, swinging his racket above his head, but missed the ball. The Swede had two match points. He only needed one. From Borg's service return, Gerulaitis hit a weak low shot that dropped wide and the match finally slipped from the American's grasp.

At 8pm, in the twilight, it was all over. As the sun lowered in the sky, the entire Centre Court crowd rose to give both men one of The Championships' most rapturous ovations. The pair had scaled unprecedented heights. Dan Maskell, commentating for BBC television, called it 'the finest match for sustained brilliance over five sets I've ever seen at Wimbledon'. Others lauded it as one of the great encounters of all time. 'Beauty should be enjoyed, not measured,' Rex Bellamy eulogised. 'But how to describe this sample, save in terms of three dazzling hours of summer lightning?'

The victor himself said it was the best match he had played in two years, since beating Rod Laver in the 1975 WCT finals in Dallas. Borg had endured – 'he always had more versatility and soundness in his groundstrokes and, eventually, the composure to recoil from adversity to triumph,' in Bellamy's opinion – but he'd been stretched, in Wilson's words, 'until you could almost hear the sinews creaking'.

It had taken the centenary Championships at Wimbledon to produce the four youngest men ever to reach the semi-finals. One of those was a most unfamiliar name: John McEnroe, or J.P. McEnroe as he was listed at the tournament. Ranked 270 in the world, though second in the US junior list behind Larry Gottfried, McEnroe, 18 years and four months old, had only left high school in May before embarking upon his first trip to Europe, and had come to London scheduled to contest the junior title.

But after negotiating his way through three qualifying rounds at Roehampton he'd earned a place in the 128-man draw for the men's singles and, once there, his wickedly hit shots, accurate serving and all-round aggression had effectively disposed of four older, more experienced players to reach the last eight: Ismail El Shafei, the London-born Colin Dowdeswell (then representing Switzerland), Karl Meiler (who'd put out John Lloyd in the second round) and Sandy Mayer. After Connors's shunning of what Bud Collins called the 'Golden Oldies party', McEnroe had become the hottest story of the tournament. He'd made a bigger impact on Wimbledon in one week than many players made in a lifetime.

Born in Wiesbaden, West Germany, where his father, John Snr – now a successful corporation lawyer in a prosperous Wall Street firm – had been a personnel officer in the US Air Force, McEnroe had grown up in a comfortable middle-class family in suburban-like Douglaston in the New York City borough of Queens, a 15-minute ride from Forest Hills. Gifted with an inbuilt affinity for sports, he could hit a thrown ball with a bat when he was just two. After receiving his first racket at the age of eight, almost all he wanted to do was walk to the one tennis club in the community, where his mother and father were members at the time, and keep whacking balls. He was really rather adept at it. Boys five or six years older were soon suffering defeats at his tender hands. Like the young Borg, McEnroe had a fierce longing to be the absolute best. Even injury couldn't discourage him. Once, as a child, he fell whilst on a bicycle and broke his left wrist, but didn't tell anybody. He kept playing tennis until one day a bump came up on his arm and X-rays then revealed a fracture.

McEnroe was the product of the Port Washington Tennis Academy on Long Island, coached by the world-acclaimed Australian Harry Hopman. One of America's leading tennis factories, it was an extremely competitive environment, but the kid survived it. He was tough. His rise through the junior ranks had little to do with the luck of the Irish; the left-hander showed an extraordinary talent. Coming to Europe unchaperoned, he'd won the junior title at the French Open as well as the mixed doubles crown, partnering Mary Carillo, his best friend from the old neighbourhood. The 20-year-old Carillo had no doubt that her doubles cohort was destined to go far. 'He is one of those people you just know are going to make it big, no matter what they do,' she said. 'Some people are just naturally winners. John McEnroe is like that.'

At Wimbledon, after sweeping into the quarter-finals, the startling assault on the title by the unheralded unknown continued when, after displaying poise, precision and power, McEnroe emerged from a lengthy five-set match with Phil Dent to reach the last four. No player had ever advanced to the semi-final after surviving the lottery of the qualifying competition. He was also the youngest men's semi-finalist in 100 years. It was one of the most remarkable debuts in the tournament's history.

'The manner of his progress suggests a glowing and prosperous future,' the *Montreal Gazette* stated. But it wasn't just the teenager's tennis that had stood out. The feisty Irish-American's journey hadn't been an inconspicuous one. As Ted Green (in the *Toledo Blade*) punned, McEnroe had 'made a name for himself, not only for the way he swings a racket, but for the racket he makes while swinging it'. His court manners had already drawn one rebuke from Fred Hoyles. 'I told him to be careful and warned him that if he persists with his bad language he will be fined,' Hoyles said, 'or if it is particularly bad and directed at someone in particular, he could be brought off court.'

In the Dent match, as in earlier rounds, McEnroe made little effort to control his quick-fire anger. Against the 13th-seeded Australian, whom he'd lost to in the men's singles in Paris in another five-setter, he blew his top in the second-set tiebreak, vigorously protesting when a serve was called out, flinging down his racket then letting loose a stream of invective at a linesman. Boos rang out around No.1 Court. 'At times he looked like an embryonic Nastase,' the *Morning Record* noted. 'But unlike Nastase, his temper seems to be a help to his game rather than a destructive influence,' the *Montreal Gazette* remarked. Despite his conduct, McEnroe, after losing that second set and the next, staged a superb reply to complete a three-hour victory and add the experienced 27-year-old to his list of victims.

He was asked about his abrasive on-court behaviour. 'Well, I don't think I'm too shy,' he explained. (Associated Press journalist Robert Jones called this 'the understatement of Wimbledon's centenary tournament'.) 'If I don't like something, you'll know it.' *The Observer*'s Ronald Atkin saw him as 'a highly charged competitor'. The *Montreal Gazette,* 'an excitable youngster'. McEnroe described himself as 'very intense', though added, 'but I've controlled myself here'. 'He has always been that way,' said his mother, Kay. 'Ever since he was a little boy, he grimaced and made faces playing tennis. He always looks like he's so pained.' She told reporters, 'He likes Bjorn Borg and would like to look like Borg. I wish he'd be as quiet as Borg.'

Wearing a Borg-style headband around his curly mop of reddish hair and almost an exact replica of his Fila-sponsored outfit, McEnroe might have patterned his appearance after the Swede, but was showing signs of growing up to be another James Scott Connors. 'He is so cocky and such a showman, people are already calling him the next Connors,' wrote Ted Green. 'Partly because he's outgoing, outspoken, and at times even outrageous. Partly because he treats every tennis match like a war instead of a game. Partly because he plays from the baseline and partly because he's left-handed and built just like Connors. He is not tasteless, as Connors often was before he mellowed. And he does not exceed the boundaries of good sportsmanship, as Ilie Nastase sometimes still does. Just call him, say, involved.'

Meeting Connors and playing on Centre Court for the first time, McEnroe was certain he could give a good account of himself though acknowledged that 'if it turns out I beat him I'll probably drop dead on court'. As it turned out, McEnroe did put up a fine show, playing with fire and no little finesse beyond his years. The No.1 seed faced far more difficulty than most people expected. Connors had looked well below top form when seeing off an overweight, free-stroking Byron Bertram – the first South African since Cliff Drysdale in 1969 to reach the last eight – his grittiness digging him out of trouble time and again. And against McEnroe, blowing hot and cold, he was made to earn every point.

The tournament's biggest surprise didn't quite have enough in his armoury, however, to spring another shock. Although virtually matching Connors stroke for stroke, McEnroe had problems with his serve in the first two sets – each decided by one service break only, and each time McEnroe bringing about his own downfall by double-faulting – and despite his taking the third set 6-4, to the delight of a crowd solidly behind him, it was only a scare for Connors. The fourth set hinged on the seventh game when the more senior man broke to establish a lead he didn't relinquish. McEnroe's dream was put to bed. He was 'a nobody', he admitted, when he played his first-round match. No one was going to forget his name now.

Connors knew he'd been in a scrap. 'If I'd played like that at his age, I'd be proud of myself,' he said generously about the newcomer. 'He tries for shots from impossible angles – and sometimes he makes them. I think he has a very good future if he works at his game.' The journalist who began his semi-final match report by saying that 'Connors came face to face with the future on Centre Court today' can really have had little idea just how prescient that line was.

Connors played the match with a thick white bandage on his fractured thumb but stressed after that the hand 'felt good enough. I can handle it for one more day.' One more day meant Saturday and the final. It was almost ironic that the man who'd got off on the wrong foot with the authorities for not being on Centre Court at the start of the two weeks should end it by stepping out on to the court at the tournament's conclusion. There was no doubt on whose side most of the gallery would be once the showdown got underway. Connors's copybook was still blotted; Wimbledon's tennis lovers hadn't fully forgotten or forgiven. They might clap politely a Connors triumph but were fervently hoping for a Borg victory.

This was the players' very first meeting on grass. Billed as the unofficial championship of the world, with the game's two leading figures facing off, it was a fitting finale for Wimbledon's 100th anniversary. As one journalist put it, 'the world's best film director could not have produced a better scenario'.

Will Grimsley termed it a 'fire and ice matchup', a clash of completely contrasting characters. 'Jimmy Connors paces the backline of a tennis court like a restless caged bearcat,' he wrote. 'He tugs at his shirt sleeve. He slaps a hand against his hip. He digs his toes into the ground in the fashion of a fractious thoroughbred. He counts every string on his racket and, head bowed, bounces the ball four times before every serve. He looks like a bundle of energy seeking to flee its fetters. Strike a match to him and he would certainly explode.'

Borg, on the other hand, Grimsley wrote, was 'a stoical Swede. Tornadoes swirl all around him, the ground shakes and the sea gets turbulent but he doesn't bat an eyelash. Blond, bearded, blue-eyed, he is the unflappable Viking. Batter him, bend him, test every stanchion of his steel and he remains as frigid as a winter's day in the Alps.'

Connors hadn't done himself justice thus far. The scrambling win against McEnroe hardly inspired confidence. Yet the American maintained he was a better player than when he'd captured the crown three years earlier. 'I can mix my game up much more and I think I have a few more shots on grass,' he said. The final would lift his standards; he would 'psych up' himself to win, he boasted. Nonetheless, William Hill quoted Borg odds-on favourite at 8-11. It had been a long time since Connors had entered a match as an underdog.

Despite the dissimilarities, Pancho Gonzales, the man who succeeded Jack Kramer as the world's top professional at the start of the 50s and was the fiery king of the courts for most of that decade, saw a commonality. 'Each [player] is different in his approach to the game but the same in his remarkable physical assets and grim determination,' he said. Borg and Connors were both 'gut fighters. They are of a single mind – a flaming desire to win.' Gonzales forecast that the final would be 'fought inside the head and stomach – it's a battle of invincible wills'. He couldn't have been more accurate.

On a perfect summer day – the capital's warmest of the year so far, with temperatures topping 79°F – both players came out in the scorching cauldron of a packed Centre Court trading blows, slugging it out, 'testing one another like heavyweights in the first round of a 15-round championship bout', according to the *Sunday Times*'s John Ballantine. The pace was furious, the hitting ferocious. Early on, it was Borg whose shots had the greater impact. In the third game, he had three break points, and only Connors's ability to counterattack under severe pressure saw off the Swede's challenge.

Bjorn Borg surrounded by fans at the All England Club in 1973. The Swedish youngster was almost instantly the subject of hero worship from the Wimbledon teeny-boppers.

On 4 July 1973, during his quarter-final with Roger Taylor, Borg pleads vehemently to linesman Mr Alf Fulston after the British player's service on match point is deemed good. The official's decision was quickly reversed and a 'let' was played.

Escaping his fans at Wimbledon sometimes called for Borg to take drastic measures. Here, in 1974, the Swede is forced to jump out of a hotel window to avoid a crowd of young admirers.

In 1974, as July began, Borg's Wimbledon ended. Here, the young Swedish star walks off court shaking the hand of his conqueror, Ismail El Shafei. He was easily tamed by the Egyptian player.

Borg and Arthur Ashe
enter the Centre Court
arena for their quarter-
final in 1975. By the end
of the clash, the young
Swede was virtually
limping out of Wimbledon.

Borg's injured stomach
muscle receives a blast
of pain-killing spray
during a break in one of
his matches en route to
victory in 1976.

On 3 July 1976, fresh from sealing his first Wimbledon men's singles title after defeating Ilie Nastase, Borg takes a well-deserved drink before collecting his prize.

In his 1977 quarter-final against Borg, Nastase was at his argumentative worst. Here, in the second set, he continues what amounted to a running battle with umpire Jeremy Shales. Shales had occasion to caution the Romanian player several times during the match.

America's Vitas Gerulaitis in action against Borg in 1977. Their five-set semi-final was hailed as one of the greatest encounters ever seen at the Wimbledon championships.

In 1977, in his very first Wimbledon, John McEnroe made it all the way to the semi-finals as a qualifier. He was eventually beaten by Jimmy Connors. Here, the two Americans leave the court after Connors's 6-3, 6-3, 4-6, 6-4 win.

A moment of sheer ecstasy. At the end of his epic five-setter with Jimmy Connors in 1977, Borg looks to the heavens above Centre Court as he wins Wimbledon for a second time.

In 1978, Guillermo Vilas stands at the umpire's chair on Wimbledon's Centre Court chatting to actor Dean Paul Martin during the making of the film, Players. The Argentinean won the fictional final, but never really found his finest form when it came to the actual championships.

Fred Perry congratulates Borg in 1978 after the Swede equals the former Wimbledon champion's record by winning the men's singles for a third year in a row.

A moment of contemplation for Vijay Amritraj during his second-round match against Borg in 1979. The Indian player had the defending champion in all sorts of trouble but eventually succumbed to a five-set defeat.

Taking time out from the tennis in 1979, Borg and his fiancée Mariana admire a waxwork of the Wimbledon champion at Madame Tussauds in London.

Handshakes at the net for Borg and American tennis player Roscoe Tanner at the end of the 1979 final. Against the Tennessee Thunderbolt, the Swede was taken to five sets for a second time in four years before securing a 6-7, 6-1, 3-6, 6-3, 6-4 triumph.

John McEnroe takes a tumble during the monumental 1980 final, which saw Borg take the title for the fifth consecutive time. The American might have lost the match but he won a lot of friends with his gutsy performance and exemplary behaviour during the defeat.

The Golden Boy with the golden trophy. After beating McEnroe in 1980 to win his fifth title on the bounce, Borg celebrates with a kiss for the cup.

The 1981 Wimbledon finals are remembered as much for John McEnroe's tantrums as his tennis. Here, Mac the Strife gets into one of his many conflicts with the umpire during the semi-final success against Rod Frawley.

Launching himself with vim and vigour, the American sought to seize the initiative but his control was lacking. But at three games all, Connors began to assume command. His low, flat approach shots gave Borg little chance to get his high-kicking topspin working. Whenever a ball landed short from the champion – sitting in midcourt and begging to be hit – Connors capitalised. Feeding like a vulture off any bad length stroke, he gorged himself. In the eighth game, Borg, at 3-4 down, lost his service to love, a first double fault giving Connors the break he needed, and the No.1 seed then held in authoritative style to take the first set, 6-3.

He was still dictating matters at the start of the second. The exertions of his strenuous semi-final were clearly affecting the Swede. But Borg, trailing 15-40 on serve in the third game, saved one break point by forcing Connors to chase a low forehand, which he netted, then levelled at deuce with an ace. And after fending off four break points in a five-deuce game, unleashing huge first serves at the American, he kept ahead 2-1. 'If he had broken me then, I would have gone,' Borg was to say later.

After Connors held to make it 2-2, the whole complexion of the match altered dramatically. Instead of giving Connors the speed and the angles he so relished, driving every ball with the same pace, Borg changed his tactics. 'Trading brawn for brains, Borg played David to Connors's Goliath,' wrote Brian Mossop, 'his slingshot being a mixture of teasing gentleness and forceful persistence.'

The Swede now found the secret to success. Slow looping returns were guided carefully into the back corners; there were chips and slices to the middle of the court. As longer rallies developed, the American's vulnerability was exposed. Eagerly and impatiently going for winners off almost every ball, Connors paid the price for his uncompromising style. Mistakes evident throughout the fortnight crept back in. Backhands went astray. Forehands found the net or floated over the baseline. To the biggest cheer of the afternoon, Borg broke in the sixth game, and then the eighth, and after a 35-minute set, he levelled with a 6-2 win.

It was palpitating stuff. 'I have scarcely seen better tennis than in the first two sets,' enthused Bill Brown, 'when these men, almost literally like the cavemen of old, battered at one another with tennis strokes that were out of this world.' An enormous crowd watched enthralled. Now, Borg became more aggressive, a sustained assault in the second game of the third set cracking Connors's service for the loss of only one point. Varying his attack, often lowering the trajectory of his strokes, Borg reduced the sting of his opponent's deadly backhand drive, and in the sunshine the American's early brilliance dimmed further.

The buoyant Swede served out the next game for a 3-0 lead, then broke again, to love, for 4-0. There was a strange silence from the direction of the Connors supporters in the competitors' stand. A 'Jimbo Rules OK' banner was now in hiding. Connors stopped the rot with a break in the fifth game, but Borg then broke for the third time and served out the set, hitting two clean aces, to take it, 6-1, in only 23 minutes.

For three sets Connors had been, wrote Bill Brown, 'like a George Foreman coming at Muhammad Ali with all fists going and little reckoning for what might happen if the other man was not knocked off his reach'. In the fourth set, his wild swinging continued. Connors still attacked every ball as if his fate hung on it. But never finding any real consistency in his groundstrokes, both the American's forehand and backhand betrayed him repeatedly, as Borg maintained his momentum, keeping Connors hopscotching about the court with some fine play.

At 3-2 up, though, with the help of a service return net cord and a relatively simple smash put wide by Borg, Connors broke, and while his opponent instantly clawed back, then levelled at 4-4, Connors refused to lie down. With two break points against him in the ninth game, he looked to be out for the count. But, typically, getting to the net at every opportunity, he punched his way out of trouble.

Leading 6-5, with Borg serving to take the match into a potentially Championship-winning tiebreak, Connors hit two rasping cross-court forehands and, after Borg had double-faulted for a third time, the top seed left the Swede marooned with an inch-accurate lob that landed on the baseline and, as the *Albany Herald* correspondent put it, 'must have had eyes'. It was now two sets all. While Connors sent a clenched-fist signal to his mother in the stands, Borg, wrote John Ballantine 'dropped over his racket on the baseline like a gut-wracked marathon runner crossing the finishing line and collapsing'.

His legs had begun to look heavy, his movement more hesitant. But in a final that the *Sunday Times*'s man said had 'more subtle twists and turns than an Agatha Christie thriller' there was yet another development. Borg, summoning strength in his aching body, led a most unexpected charge. He won the first four games of the decider. At 40-30 up on Connors's next service game, he was within a single point of a 5-0 lead and almost certain victory. Connors, however, ran in behind a deep drive and volleyed his way to deuce. Again Borg got to break point, but Connors this time showed a master's touch with a delicate drop that caught a bemused Borg completely unawares. A smash by Connors and a blazing backhand return that dropped over abruptly after hitting the net cord gave him the game, the American standing, almost insolently wiggling his hips at his opponent.

It soon became 4-2. Despite an ace – his eighth – Borg was pegged back further as a running forehand pass, two netted backhands from the Swede, and a volley with Borg in the wrong court earned Connors a break. And then it was 4-3. Borg was watching his lead being whittled away. In the eighth game, Connors broke through again – once more with the benefit of a fortunate net cord on a return of service dropping dead on the

Swede's side. He sealed the game by taking a Borg forehand on the run and volleying back a winner into a vacant court. Now it was the turn of the Borg followers to fall silent. While Connors, shaking his fists, slapping his thighs, exhorted himself to 'Go, baby, go', Borg hung his head, seemingly demoralised.

Connors looked set to pull off an act of escapology to rival Houdini. With a sharp backhanded volley at the net he went to 15-0 in the next game. But then, as Peter McFarline wrote, 'for reasons not even known to his mother', he double-faulted. 'The God-awfullest double fault you ever saw,' as Connors called it later, was only his third of the match but what an expensive lapse.

At 15-15, Borg suddenly sniffed an opening. Coldly, methodically, he settled to receive service, shifting from one foot to the other, obsessively twiddling his racket, and raising a hand to his mouth, as was his curious ritual. A perfect forehand stop volley took him to 15-30. Then, as Borg came to the net, Connors put a backhand far too wide and followed up with another backhand that cleared the baseline by a few feet. 'The American,' wrote Ronald Atkin in *The Observer* 'was broken, in all senses.'

Serving for tennis's most coveted prize, Borg responded faultlessly. A bullet-like overhead smash, a careless forehand into the net by Connors and a scorching service that Connors could barely reach gave the Swede three Championship points. When a searing backhand skidded high off the frame of Connors's steel racket as the American at full stretch made a desperate lunge at the ball, it was the end of 192 minutes of the highest drama. Borg, standing, threw his arms wide and aloft, his head back, and looked skywards. In the competitors' box, his mother and father, sitting alongside Bergelin and Mariana, could finally breathe.

The two players could not have delivered a more perfect birthday present. It was, described Peter McFarline, 'a cinemascope production if there ever was one featuring everything that has made tennis what it is over 100 years'. Fellow Australian Brian Mossop declared it 'a marathon worthy of a place in Wimbledon history, if not for the quality of the tennis, at least for the courage of the beaten Connors. Like him or not, he had to be admired as he picked himself up from the floor.'

Borg, too, had given a heroic performance at the death. Connors's fifth-set rally would have broken most. But the Swede, when he could so easily have knuckled under, urged on his weary limbs to rake in the last points, his phenomenal capacity to control the match through the crisis times and his massive willpower seeing him home.

Clutching the trophy, Borg smiled for the cameramen. But those smiles barely masked an overwhelming fatigue. As he'd neared victory, Borg, bent over, had panted for breath between points; he seemed ready to drop. And an hour after the final, having delayed a news conference for 40 minutes to shower and rest, the still-exhausted-looking Swede sank wearily into a chair and said what everyone in Centre Court had guessed for themselves: 'I have never been so tired on a tennis court before.'

Stroking his 'lucky charm' – the three-week beard and moustache that Frank Keating of *The Guardian* suggested made him 'look like a maudlin prep-school Hamlet' – Borg was asked how he was going to celebrate. By shaving it off was the answer. 'I only grew it for this tournament because I wore a beard when I won last year,' he said. He was, he told reporters, 'a bit happier at winning this year than last', so very badly had he wanted to beat Connors. The win, Borg believed, entitled him to be given the world No.1 ranking – 'for the moment' anyway. Connors, unsurprisingly, disputed the claim.

At 21, Borg looked formidable enough to dominate men's tennis for years. 'The future stretches golden and inviting,' reckoned Ronald Atkin. Keating called him 'a stupendous player with a stupendous temperament.

Already he stands head-high in the Hall of Fame.' Just the fifth champion since World War II to successfully defend his singles title – only Australians Hoad, Laver (twice), Emerson and Newcombe had accomplished the feat during that period – Borg was the youngest-ever player to win back-to-back titles.

The Swede, though, was even now looking ahead. Having become part of a very select company, he had his sights trained on joining an even more exclusive club. However, it would be another 12 months before the opportunity arose for him to do so, when only Borg himself could determine whether he was worthy of becoming a member.

26 June – 8 July 1978

ADORNING THE front cover of the 24-30 June 1978 issue of *Radio Times*, a headshot of Bjorn Borg – the stubby beginnings of his annual beard surrounding only the faintest trace of a smile; his warm, pale blue eyes bashfully meeting the camera pointed at him – was topped with a headline, 'Third time lucky?' As one G.A. Green of Derby observed in the magazine's Letters page a little while later, the question didn't seem quite appropriate regarding the young Swede's prospects in the forthcoming Wimbledon. 'Perhaps the caption, "Three wins in a row?" would have more neatly fitted the bill,' the letter writer suggested. His/her argument had been that the former expression was used when a contestant competing for the third time may be successful after failing on the two previous attempts. That certainly hadn't been the case with Bjorn Borg at Wimbledon.

In 1936, when Fred Perry beat Baron Gottfried von Cramm, the German whom Perry had defeated in the previous year's final as well, the Briton didn't just win his third successive Wimbledon men's singles title but set up one of sport's most venerable records. Now, 42 years later, it was in danger of being matched as the 22-year-old Borg lined up to beat the world's best again at The Championships. The almost angelic magazine portrait belied a burning ambition within the Swede to equal Perry's feat.

'Winning Wimbledon a third time is all that matters to me,' had been Borg's battle cry virtually since the moment the tension-filled five-setter with Connors in 1977 was over. On the cusp of the new Championships, nothing had changed. 'I don't mind to win it ten times,' he told reporters. Behind the clumsy phrasing of his normally excellent English was an almost frightening truth. Borg in all probability wouldn't win ten Wimbledons, but he was going to take some stopping. 'He is at his best age now, mentally and everything,' said Lennart Bergelin.

Adaptable, immensely strong and fit, he was a proven winner on a variety of surfaces. Of the 20 tournaments he entered in the 1977 season, Borg won 13, posting a 16-3 win/loss record against the world's top ten players and, albeit for one week only before Jimmy Connors reclaimed the position, on 23 August 1977, the Swede sat on top of the ATP rankings for the first time – becoming only the fourth player to hold the top spot since the rankings were established in 1973. Although a shoulder injury suffered whilst water skiing had forced him to retire (at 6-3, 4-6, 0-1) during his round-16 match with Dick Stockton at the US Open, Borg swiftly overcame that disappointment by claiming five consecutive titles – in Madrid, Barcelona, Basel, Cologne and London.

Connors, beaten in the final at Forest Hills by Vilas (losing the decisive fourth set 6-0 and bolting from the stadium afterwards stating that his title had been 'stolen' because of rude crowd behaviour and bad line calls), had bettered Borg in their thrilling three-set final of the Colgate Grand Prix Masters tournament in January before a crowd of 17,150 at Madison Square Garden. But, weak with a virus, the Swede wasn't fully fit and, after another tournament success (on carpet in Birmingham, Alabama), he'd exacted quick revenge on Connors to take the Pepsi Grand Slam in Florida. A torn stomach muscle had then required Borg to ease his schedule, but since March, when he'd beaten Vitas Gerulaitis to win the WCT $200,000 Tournament of Champions in Las Vegas, the Swede had enjoyed 33 victories in 33 outings, including another success against Connors, this time in Tokyo, the margin in Japan a crushing 6-1, 6-2.

Though forced out of the WCT finals with a hand infection, he'd given ample warning just how prepared for Wimbledon he was; after shunning the dollars of World Team Tennis, Borg's form had brought him the Italian (combating both the intense heat and provocation from frenzied, coin-hurling home fans to beat Panatta in a five-setter) and French crowns (not losing a single set all tournament before humiliating Vilas 6-1, 6-1, 6-3 in the final for his fifth career grand slam title), and his opponents agreed that he was playing better than ever. For a man who had just passed his 22nd birthday he had been at the summit for a long time. And that's where he intended to stay. 'I want to win everything,' he said. 'Maybe other players can go out there without this idea, but it is probably what explains me. It was really, really wanting to be No.1 that got me there.'

It was success in SW19, though, that he craved the most. The pot of gold at the rainbow's end might have grown even bigger – a £19,000 first prize was up for grabs this year – but the money meant nothing. 'It's tradition. It's everything,' Borg said. 'And when you play here you really don't care if you make one dollar, that's the truth.' The *Daily Mirror*'s Peter Wilson reckoned that 'barring physical accidents, earthquakes, civil commotions, activities of the Queen's enemies or acts of God, the men's singles is almost certain to go to one of two, or at most three, men'. Namely Borg, Connors and Gerulaitis, the top three seeds in that order.

In seeding Borg No.1 (for the first time) and Connors second, Wimbledon had cut across the current form on the ATP computer, thought to be all-powerful in the ranking business. In that, Connors was top dog and Borg at No.3, with Guillermo Vilas the man in between. 'The drama of tennis is not in the technicalities of hitting a little white ball,' the former French great Jean Borotra once said, 'but in the clash of personalities, the clash of rivalries, the international element.' No rivalry was more intense than that of Borg and Connors.

Until 1977, Borg had been, as one journalist phrased it, 'content to tread in the American's shadow'. In Curry Kirkpatrick's view, 'a man against the field, a boy against Connors'. Connors had had Borg's measure. And Borg knew it. But the score sheet for their singles now read 8-5 and four of the last five times they'd locked horns Borg had won. No longer intimidated by Connors's power or presence, the Swede, according to Bergelin, had 'lost that respect of Connors. He *knows* he can beat him.'

Connors's overall game was undoubtedly better designed for grass than his rival's, but, as he'd proved, when it came to strength of mind Borg was peerless. 'At times his flawless composure ... can be chilling,' Rex Bellamy said of him. 'Borg never thinks about the point just played, his adversary or the crowd,' ventured another English commentator. 'He is impervious to outside distraction. He puts points away like a squirrel storing nuts for the winter.'

Still, Connors remained the one man who really looked capable of stopping Borg's pursuit of another title. Since winning the Masters he'd lost only three times – to Borg, Californian Jeff Borowiak and Hank Pfister. Only recently, though, he'd been sidelined for five weeks with a blood disorder, mononucleosis, and for eight of those days was in an LA hospital undergoing tests. However, after working himself into good shape on the grass courts of Beckenham and Birmingham, winning 12 matches to capture both tournaments, Connors claimed to be ready. And the 25-year-old had proved his point at Edgbaston the Sunday before Wimbledon when routing Raul Ramirez in resounding style, dropping just six games, to win the John Player Tournament. The enigmatic American looked to have hit his peak at just the right time.

Were he to succeed, it would again be despite the crowd, which always threw away its traditional politeness to cheer his every mistake and seemed to take particular delight in seeing the 1974 champion squirm. While Borg, 'the Swede with the atomic arm', wrote Geoffrey Barker was 'a handsome charmer' whose 'rare combination of skills and impeccable court temperament make him universally loved at Wimbledon', the American was anything but – the Mr Nasty to Borg's Mr Nice Guy was 'unloved by Wimbledon's knowledgeable gallery', according to the Australian journalist. 'The British establishment,' Barker believed, 'will be praying that the awful Mr Connors will be thrashed again by the nice Swedish chappie.'

Presenting the greatest danger to the two favourites was a player from the States who, by contrast, had stolen the Centre Court's hearts. Vitas Gerulaitis, since the classic semi-final confrontation with Borg, had consolidated his place in tennis's elite by winning the Australian Open at the end of 1977 (defeating John Lloyd in a five-set final in Melbourne), then enjoying a superb start to 1978, culminating in a victory over fellow American Eddie Dibbs in Dallas's Moody Coliseum at the WCT finals in May, his third title of the year. Despite losing his Italian crown in the first round to Panatta, Gerulaitis had put himself firmly in the World Big Four. Regularly dubbed 'the eternal second', the 23-year-old now had a taste of winning the big ones – and he liked it.

By his own admission, Gerulaitis was not quite yet a member of what he called 'the Two-Mile High Club' – of Borg, Connors and Vilas. In a spectacular 1977, Vilas, the long-haired, moody Argentinean, had arguably soared above everybody else. Instilled with a new found self-belief, fitter than ever, and playing more clinical tennis under the glowering tutelage of

Ion Tiriac, the South American amassed more victories and more money than any other star on the circuit.

At one point, he registered an astonishing streak of 53 successive victories on clay, a feat no man had achieved since tennis entered the Open era, and only ended when a disgusted Vilas quit in protest in a final at Aix-en-Provence, France, after losing the first two sets to Nastase, who was using the 'spaghetti' racket that had just been barred (although the prohibition took effect the day after the tournament ended). There were 145 victories in total over the whole season, including Davis Cup matches, and a record 17 tournament successes. In the regular-season Grand Prix race, Vilas finished No.1.

But after a break of several months from tour tennis early in 1978 (he'd damaged his ankle at the Masters in January where Borg beat him in the semis), Vilas – the man they called 'Willie' – had had difficulty finding his old form. He'd won the German Open but then tamely surrendered his French title to Borg, and his fourth-seeding was really only the result of the vagaries of the ATP computer; Vilas's record on grass, a surface on which he appeared to lack sufficient conviction, was fairly lamentable. The Argentinean, now 25, seemed to have a mental block when it came to playing on the stuff in SW19.

Of the other main contenders, it was foolish to write off fifth seed Brian Gottfried, who'd beaten Borg once the previous year, while No.6 Tanner couldn't be overlooked either. But one notable absentee from the list of probable challengers was Ilie Nastase. The Romanian had won only one secondary tournament all year, an event in Miami, which most top stars skipped (though Borg had participated and lost in the quarter-finals to the man Nastase would overcome in the final, Tom Gullikson), and, having, as Will Grimsley put it, 'lost to humpty-dumpties unworthy to tote his racket case', had skidded out of the world's top ten rankings. Seeded only ninth and, at 33-1 one of the longest shots in field, the man who'd won the US Open in 1972, captured the French and two Italian crowns, twice been runner-up at Wimbledon and won four Grand Prix Masters, emblematic of the tour championship, was now, in Grimsley's view, a tennis also-ran.

Quoted at 6-4 by bookmakers to carry off the jackpot, Borg was a firm favourite but, as David Irvine noted in his *Guardian* preview, 'in a competitive arena which is increasingly being tailored to the slow-clay specialists, grass remains the surface on which it is least safe to draw assumptions'. History also took a rather less favourable view of the Swede's chances. Since Perry, five men – the American, Don Budge, plus the four Australians – had won the men's title in successive years but for a variety of reasons had been unable to make it three in a row. And only on three occasions since The Championships went Open ten years prior had the No.1 seed taken the crown.

Borg was well aware of the size of his task. Asked by David Hunn who he feared the most, the Swede told the *Radio Times* journalist it was whoever he was drawn against in the first round. Nobody was more likely to beat him than that man, when Borg was at his most susceptible: still uncertain of the face of the courts, what his form was going to be like, and making adjustments to his basic hard-court game.

There were at least 75 players in the draw, Borg said, that he would prefer not to meet in his opening examination. 'If Victor Amaya was not top of the list when the match started,' wrote the *Glasgow Herald*'s Reginald Brace, 'he certainly was at the end.'

At 6ft 7in and 15½ stone, the dark-haired, high-cheeked 23-year-old from Holland, Michigan was, height-wise, the biggest man in US tennis. The imposing stature of Amaya – 'Victor Huge-o' Curry Kirkpatrick wittily dubbed him – meant he sometimes had to answer to the rather unfortunate nicknames 'Lurch' and 'the Incredible Hulk'. Brace wrote that Amaya looked 'like an all-American quarterback, with his padding still in place' and played tennis 'like a squadron of B-52s'. And at times in the traditional curtain-raiser for the titleholder Borg didn't know what had hit him.

'So, here's the golden boy then ...' Dan Maskell announced as the defending champion presented himself on Centre Court at two o'clock precisely (the opening day's play beginning, weather permitting, at that hour according to the command of the All England Club since 1919). But it was Amaya who was soon grabbing all the attention. Coming unseeded to Wimbledon with only the humble recommendation that he was 31st in the US rankings and winner of the Adelaide title the previous year, plus a semi-finalist in Rome, the giant left-hander almost engineered a major upset.

In bitter, blustery conditions, with the ball skidding low on the greasy turf, Amaya disturbed the clinical calm of the slow-starting Swede from the off. Borg's very first service game of The Championships was broken. And although he broke back immediately, in the face of Amaya's raw power the top seed was unable to settle into a steady groove, mistiming the bounce of the ball and repeatedly depositing half-volleys into the net or out of court.

Blessed with a booming service, which rivalled anything on the pro circuit, the American launched his 135mph rockets on the slick, spongy surface frequently forcing Borg into powder-puff returns that Amaya, barrelling in to cover the net like a large statue, then mashed into corners with crisp backhand volleys. His towering frame and a frighteningly long, octopus-like reach made him almost impossible to pass. Peter Wilson likened him to King Kong standing on the roof of the Empire State Building smashing planes out of the sky.

Nonetheless, after games went to eight-all, Borg looked to have the first set guaranteed when striding to a 5-2 lead and then 6-4 ahead in the tiebreak. At set point, though, he lost concentration, serving a surprising double fault and after Amaya levelled with another of his crunching serves the American went on to seal a 9-7 triumph; after 51 minutes he was one set to the good.

Within a quarter of an hour, Borg was back on course. He broke Amaya when the left-hander netted a backhand, and held his next service to love to lead 4-1. When Amaya double-faulted and was broken again, Borg claimed the set on his second set point after double-faulting on the first. And normal service seemed to have resumed.

But Amaya made certain he wasn't going to fall under Borg's spell. Instead, it was the champion, again unable to cope with the severity of Amaya's huge serve, lobbing short and volleying feebly, who was hypnotised. Amaya broke in the fourth game and again in the sixth to lead 5-1 before four crashing services that gave Borg no chance completed the third set most emphatically. The king of Wimbledon was looking, Peter Wilson wrote, like 'a second-class monarch'.

Two sets to one behind, when Amaya led 3-1 in the fourth set with game point on Borg's service, the Swede's reign appeared perilously close to a startling, abrupt end, and 'the champion wore a Strindberg gloom' noted Geoffrey Green. Only once in Wimbledon's history had the top-seeded man been knocked out in the first round – Charlie Pasarell ambushing the defending champion, Manuel Santana, in 1967.

At 30-40, Borg's first delivery was lashed into the net; a fault. His crown looked now even wobblier. The Centre Court clock stood at a quarter to four. The 14,000 crowd was hushed, numbed by Borg's unexpected vulnerability. As Borg prepared to serve again, Amaya inched in intent on whacking his return and smothering the net once more.

However, the boldness of Borg's second serve at such a desperate moment caught him off guard. The Swede hit the ball hard, fast and viciously spinning deep down the middle; it kicked up menacingly, exploding at the onrushing Amaya who, running in to clip a forehand down the sideline, could only hit the top of the tape with his return and the ball fell back. Deuce. 'I couldn't believe it,' an incredulous Amaya said later. 'Here is the ultimate percentage player and he nails me with that gamble.' When Borg went on to hold, he looked to be out of jail. Not yet. Amaya went 40-15 up in the next game but made an error before Borg hit two remarkable backhand returns to take advantage then put away a volley to break.

Now nearer his usual self, Borg at last got the hang of Amaya's serve, and his groundstrokes into full working order. With some splendid needle-threading passing shots in the brief rallies and several lofty lobs, the Swede paralysed his opponent. After another crucial break in the eighth game he clinched the set 6-3, Amaya on the final point taking a volley clearly heading out. And though the American led 3-2 in the final set, he couldn't halt Borg's final surge of four consecutive games, as the match slipped away from his massive clutches.

The champion's willingness to take a risk in the face of peril had been pivotal, but it was a tenuous victory. Amaya had almost shut the door completely and Borg, all his resources taxed to the limit, barely squeezed through. He was, he admitted, 'lucky to survive'. Every aspiring Wimbledon winner supposedly appreciated getting a really testing match under his belt in the early rounds. The Swede didn't sound too sure. 'I'm glad I've got that one off my chest,' he said. 'It can't get much more difficult.'

For Amaya, there was no solace in defeat. Having, in the words of the *Washington Post*'s Barry Lorge, 'caused the tremors that almost turned into shock waves on the slippery grass of Centre Court', the American was left only to reflect on what might have been. 'I will kick myself later,' he told reporters. With size 15 feet, it was bound to hurt.

On that first damp and chilly Monday, when the breeze had a Siberian bite and intermittent drizzle curtailed the bulk of the day's programme, more than two-thirds of the scheduled 60 matches in the men's singles weren't completed. Despite the nearly wintry weather, record numbers – 29,886 – showed for an opening day. The following day, another grey, overcast, and nippy one, even greater numbers – 33,552 – streamed through the turnstiles. By the end of it, some had seen the first major surprise sprung.

After his giant-killing run in 1977 had seen him jump from obscurity to instant fame, John McEnroe was seeking to enlarge his growing reputation as 'a youngster with a rosy future', as one commentator put it, rather than his status as an enfant terrible. The 19-year-old New Yorker, in only his second week as a professional, after a year's attendance at Stanford University, had come to the tournament on the back of an appearance – and defeat by Tony Roche – in the final of the Queen's Club tournament and, seeded No.11, much was expected of him. But after the glamour of his Centre Court semi – McEnroe got to see the other side of the Wimbledon coin – he was conquered out on No.7 Court and, in an ironic twist, by a player who had had to qualify himself: 26-year-old Californian Erik van Dillen.

In a match that see-sawed wildly, while McEnroe, the player the British press had dubbed 'Superbrat', began shouting and swearing, van Dillen, a former US Davis Cup player known almost exclusively for his doubles play, kept his nerve, gradually chiselling away at his opponent's power game and after three hours and ten minutes and five pulsating sets, McEnroe, as a last forehand drive went long, snatched off his headband in defeat and was on his way home.

His wasn't the only unforeseen disappearing act. Arthur Ashe, who'd been out of the game for almost a year after surgery on his left heel, was on court for five hours before being summarily dismissed by relative unknown 6ft 5in Steve Docherty, a 28-year-old Australian. The 1975 champion had never lost before the third round in ten previous Wimbledons. French Open semi-finalist Dick Stockton's defeat to the tall, angular, moustachioed Australian John Marks, whom he'd beaten heavily in Paris, completed a hat-trick of first-round exits for seeded Americans.

Even the top-seeded US players had their troubles before advancing. Connors made a meal of beating New Zealand's Russell Simpson, Gerulaitis was taken to four sets by Heinz Peter Gunthardt of Switzerland, as was Brian Gottfried by England's blue-eyed boy John Lloyd, in a rain-punctuated battle, while Roscoe Tanner had to come from two sets down to beat Ismail El Shafei.

On Wednesday, all four won their second-rounders, only Connors finding himself really pushed, overcoming a powerful challenge from 26-year-old Australian Kim Warwick, the big Sydney-born right-hander with a telescopic reach taking the third set 6-2 to strong applause from the Centre Court before Connors prevailed. Connors admitted afterwards it was a scrap. 'The little ones [matches] are the toughest,' he said. 'The big ones I can handle.'

Encouraged by the first warm afternoon of The Championships, an estimated 20,000 people were waiting outside when the green gates opened at noon that Wednesday, mile-long lines snaking their way along arterial roads leading to the courts. By late afternoon, spectators were still flowing in and officials briefly closed the turnstiles to ease the crush. But the crowds or the sun didn't witness the defending champion. Due to play his second-round match with Peter McNamara last on No.2 Court, Borg earned an unscheduled extra day's rest when a long three-setter in the women's singles and failing light meant that proceedings were halted before the two players got on court.

That rest was extended even further. On Thursday, the sun was smashed out of court again as Wimbledon's big foe struck in deadly fashion, a daylong downpour meaning that for the first time since the 1972 finals day an entire afternoon's schedule was a complete washout. Around the water-soaked courts, raincoats and stoicism were the order of the day. Optimists hoped against hope for a let-up but were disappointed. The liveliest action was a throng of schoolgirls, huddled under multi-coloured umbrellas outside the players' tearoom, chanting: 'We want Connors. We want Borg.' They erupted into screams and shrieks whenever one of them waved from the windows.

On Friday, they finally got to see Borg in more vigorous action. McNamara, victor over Frenchman Christophe Roger-Vasselin in four sets in his first match, wasn't expecting to put the Swede on his deathbed. 'As long as I get a few games off Borg, I'll be happy,' he said ahead of the encounter. The 23-year-old Melbourne man must have left the court – the match eventually took place on No.1 Court – reasonably satisfied. But Borg monopolised proceedings and was little-tested as he rolled past the Australian in a brisk manner, 6-2, 6-2, 6-4.

With conditions at times during the first week more suited to the Winter Olympics than tennis, tournament referee Fred Hoyles faced a mountain of problems. An earlier (noon) start was planned for the Saturday at least. Singles matches would have to be played both Monday and Tuesday, if the schedule was to get back on track. That Saturday, Borg faced Jaime Fillol, an opponent harder to predict than the British weather. 'You never know about Jaime,' Borg remarked. 'It depends on the day. Sometimes he plays very well, and sometimes …' On this day, under cool, grey skies, the Chilean fell somewhere in-between.

Borg always had enough to beat Fillol, but was hard-pressed all the way and looked distinctly uncomfortable on occasion. In the third and fourth sets his legendary enthusiasm seemed to drain away as he nearly allowed the South American back in the match. He began in smooth, assured and punishing form, banging his first serve deep and hard, unleashing some bullet-like backhands and, wrote Ronald Atkin, 'luring his man forward and passing him with poker-faced ease'.

The Swede led 4-0 and had a point for 5-0. And while Fillol, with some brave net charges, introduced the first uncertainty into Borg's play, after an hour the defending champion was two sets up. When he moved 2-0 ahead in the third set 'the burial ceremonies seemed a formality' reported Atkin.

But Fillol, in Brian Glanville's words, 'rose impressively from the ashes'. In a decisive counterattack, he took the next 12 points to get his nose in front, as Borg's timing went astray and a surprising number of groundstrokes came off the wood. Borg, serving at 6-7, slumped to 15-40 and, though saving one set point with a solid forehand volley, netted the next with a half-volley return, and Fillol was back in contention.

There was even a hint of an upset when the Chilean, a PT instructor from Santiago, audaciously broke Borg again in the fourth set and took a three-love lead. His game at a low ebb, Borg also fell foul of Wimbledon and its mania for tradition; with the weather turning cooler and rain threatening, Borg wanted to slip on his predominantly red tracksuit top, only for the umpire to say no – it wasn't allowed; instead, an attendant was dispensed to the locker room to fetch a suitable white sweater.

By the time the woolly arrived via Bergelin, Borg had warmed up on court, breaking back in the fifth game as the umbrellas went up. After battling to 3-3, heavy drizzle sent the players off for half an hour, and the break proved fatal for Fillol. Upon resumption, Borg grasped the initiative, breaking in the ninth game after a spectacular passing forehand, before ending Fillol's fleeting hopes in the tenth game, a stunning backhand finishing the job to earn the Swede a place in the final 16.

It was perhaps a gauge of Borg's command that he won in spite of his so-so form. But the champion had, as the *Sunday Mirror* put it, 'sprinkled sets to opponents like a wedding guest throws confetti' and, afterwards, he confessed he wasn't playing as well as in 1977. 'Maybe I'm just getting a little tired. I've been playing a lot in the last five to six weeks.' It wasn't simply fatigue. Anxious to make history, the importance of that third title was weighing more heavily. 'I am thinking about it on the important points,' Borg admitted.

He wasn't alone in encountering difficulty in the third round. In a late-afternoon match also interrupted by rain, Connors was on court for nearly three hours and four sets before wearing down 32-year-old Tom Gorman on a damp, uneven and heavily scarred No.2 Court, even taking a nasty crash into the courtside canvas at one point. Gorman, who'd earlier scuppered British prospects by eliminating 34-year-old Mark Cox (and was a player Connors had never beaten in their three previous meetings), said subsequently about the surface, 'I wish I could have changed shoes during the points. The middle was dry, but when I ran to the sides, drowning was a possibility.'

It was a reality for Guillermo Vilas. While Gerulaitis, following a straight-sets win over India's Jayakumar Royappa, downed big Sherwood Stewart in another three-setter to reach the last 16, the South American's hopes were sunk. After showing signs of finally adapting to grass, looking sharp when quickly seeing off Stan Smith, Vilas had then toiled to overcome Britain's John Feaver, taking well over two hours and four sets to beat the recently axed British Davis Cup player.

But against Tom Okker, the No.4 seed had, in his own words, 'trouble with everything'; clearly off form, Vilas extended his exasperating run of exits, bowing out with a whimper in an embarrassing 79 minutes and once more Wimbledon wasn't to see the best of the Argentine virtuoso. The 34-year-old Okker, playing near-faultless tennis, served and volleyed his way to a 6-3, 6-4, 6-2 upset, earning the Dutchman a little revenge for his country's defeat in the football World Cup Final the previous weekend.

A shell-shocked Vilas appeared to be near tears later when he talked about his downfall. He'd put in the hard labour on the practice courts, was playing well and genuinely thought he had a chance of lifting the title. The loss at least allowed him ample opportunity to prepare for another match – the following Tuesday he was due to play on Centre Court against Dean Martin Jr in a celluloid version of the Wimbledon final for a Paramount Pictures movie, *Players*, scheduled for release in 1979.

Knowing he needed to up his game if he were to make the bona fide final, Borg did just that. Geoff Masters, the doubles specialist from Brisbane (who'd partnered Ross Case to the Wimbledon title the previous year), was relatively untroubled in the first week, beating both Bill Scanlon of America then Ove Bengtson in four sets before cruising to his best win, a straight-sets victory over the white-capped Frew McMillan, at the time the world's best doubles player. Bristol-based McMillan, the South African son of a British father, had earlier seen off Buster Mottram, seeded at Wimbledon for the first time.

Borg was an altogether different proposition, however. The defending champion required just one and a half hours to brush past the unseeded Australian. The first two sets were a veritable breeze. Borg, spraying winners at will at the bewildered right-hander, took the first 6-2 in 21 minutes. In the second set, although the Swede's serve began to falter a bit and his whole game fell a notch, he still had enough to outclass his opponent and take it 6-4.

But the tall, aggressive Masters refused to wave the white flag. Exerting more pressure, he broke to lead 2-0 in the third set and, while Borg quickly broke back, in the tenth game Masters, 5-4 and 15-0 up on Borg's serve, needed only three points to extend the match to a fourth set. Any impending crisis was averted; the Swede scrambled his way out, won the game, and, after breaking Masters in the 13th game, held his own service to tie up the victory.

He later called it his best performance of The Championships thus far, though was still unhappy that his form lacked the ruthless authority that marked his two title successes. 'There were times when I am being too careful over certain points,' he said, mixing up his tenses somewhat. 'I know I can do better and I am beginning to get irritated with myself.'

Connors, meanwhile, was oozing contentment. Playing with typical belligerence, the arch-aggressor ditched another Australian, the fast-serving No.14 seed John Alexander, with an easy straight-sets triumph. Described as a 'baby giant' in his early days when, as a precocious teen in 1968 he represented his country in the Davis Cup, the 6ft 3in Alexander had survived a five-hours-20-minute marathon with the even taller Paraguayan, Victor Pecci, in an earlier round. But on this day, against the No.2 seed, the 27-year-old was outplayed in every department. Aside from a smattering of careless shots, Connors barely made a mistake.

Alexander wasn't the sole seeded Aussie to fall. In what he said would be his final shot at a Wimbledon title, John Newcombe, whose 16th seeding was more a tribute to his past grandeur than a realistic assessment of his present winning potential, had nevertheless beaten three fellow countrymen: Dale Collings, Ross Case and Phil Dent. However, a tenacious Raul Ramirez, disproving the theory that he was a lightweight on grass, had far too much for the two-times former champion and Newcombe departed the men's singles for the very last time.

Wimbledon wasn't Wimbledon without some sort of storm involving Nastase. But this year it was one whipped up by his opponent. The Romanian, having cruised past Tom Gullikson, faced Roscoe Tanner who, after his first-round fright, had enjoyed two scare-free victories. At The Championships, Nastase was wearing a scruffy black beard, and if the hope was that it might bring some Borg-like good fortune it seemed to be working. Against the No.6 seed, Nastase's game had everything – he served better than he had for years, while his delicacy of touch around the net often left Tanner trapped in no-man's land.

Two sets to one and 5-3 down in the fourth set, a double fault confirmed Tanner's fate, the American bowing out despite taking the first set of the match. He didn't go willingly. Tanner, insisting his serve was good, protested the linesman's call vehemently for several minutes, demanding to see Fred Hoyles. When the referee ventured on to Centre Court but declined to intervene, 'the man with the homicidal serve' (an epithet from *The Guardian*) shook hands quickly with Nastase, gathered up his tracksuit top and rackets, nodded to the Duke and Duchess of Kent in the Royal Box and – despite the tradition that both players leave side by side and bow – strode off brusquely, with Nastase trotting several yards behind. Still in a huff afterwards, Tanner moaned that tennis was about the only sport he knew where professionals were judged by amateurs.

Perhaps Tanner should have listened to the words of Sandy Mayer. After his opening victory against Czech Tomas Smid on an outside court so poor that, post-match, Mayer called it 'criminal', the No.8 seed had claimed some notable scalps en route to the last eight – brushing past Mark Edmondson, then Marty Riessen before just scraping through a five-setter against Wojciech Fibak after blowing a two-sets-to-love lead. But while the vast majority of players obviously regarded Wimbledon as the blue-ribbon event on the circuit, the 1973 semi-finalist considered it overrated, just one of many tournaments, saying, 'If you think of it that way [as the most important], you can put a lot of pressure on yourself.'

Ahead of his quarter-final with Borg, the American, whose father played in international matches for both Hungary and Yugoslavia and emigrated only shortly before Sandy was born, was talking a good game. In their most recent meeting, the year before, also on a fast grass surface, he'd beaten Borg in Arkansas and was confident of a repeat. 'I believe I have a game that is better-suited to grass,' he said, 'and I have a few ideas how to beat Bjorn again.' Whatever ideas Mayer had, putting them into practice yielded little reward.

It was an entertaining duel. Mayer played bravely and often brilliantly, and brought out the best of the defending champion's tennis. But Borg's best was just too good for the 26-year-old. Hitting bold attacking shots throughout, the Swede swept to a two-set lead, and with rain threatening – rumbles of thunder were heard at the start of the first set and came ominously closer game by game – seemed in increasing haste to finish off his opponent before any deluge.

Mayer didn't make it easy. After a long and arduous job holding his service in the second game of the third set, Borg broke in the next game, the American wilting under constant heavy fire, then, playing with impatient fury, also took the next game to love to lead 3-1. But at 40-0 against service, he was almost pressing too hard. Mayer pulled it up to 2-3. Then Borg, racing into position between points like a man possessed, double-faulted twice, and was suddenly pegged back at 3-3.

That was the end of Mayer's challenge, though. His game 'briskly aggressive, tidy, unfussy', in Rex Bellamy's description, Mayer lacked 'a big shot and a capacity for producing the unexpected'. As the skies darkened and the thunder grew louder, Borg's topspin forehands became all the more explosive and, for all the crowd's roars of encouragement, Mayer was blown away. Borg rushed through the next three games to seal a 7-5, 6-4, 6-3 win. Two minutes after he left the court, the heavens opened and the covers were swiftly spread over the grass.

Mayer might have departed, but that Tuesday the Americans celebrated the Fourth of July by winning two of the last four places: Connors, as effective as a wrecking ball against the No.7 seed Ramirez (notching up a 13th win in their 16 meetings), and Gerulaitis who, after experiencing slight discomfort when removing Hank Pfister in four sets, took four more before finally settling the argument in a three-hour thriller with Brian Gottfried. Gerulaitis said he'd played better in that quarter-final win than in the previous one and a half years.

The other last-eight match pitched Nastase against Okker, who'd thrashed American Tom Leonard in straight sets. Pre-Wimbledon, the 31-year-old Romanian was blunt in admitting, 'I have to face the fact that my days as a top player are numbered.' Against Tanner, nonetheless, he was at his magnificent best, producing a masterly display that, by the end of four inspired sets, had the crowd rising to acclaim him. Even the sour taste left by the odd disputed line decision didn't linger.

But playing the unseeded Dutchman, Nastase's magical return to form was extinguished. His game never quite scaled the heights it had and Okker, always on the offensive, drawing on skills which the seedings committee had overlooked, outmanoeuvred the Balkan firebrand 7-5, 6-1, 2-6, 6-3. After 15 years of tennis frustration, the quiet little family man from Amsterdam finally reached the semis for the first time, revealing afterwards that he liked playing the Romanian because 'He does not blast you off court like other people.'

It was a sad day all round for Nastase. He learned later that the Men's International Professional Tennis Council (MIPTC)* had recommended he be suspended (from Grand Prix tournaments for a year) and fined (a maximum of $10,000) for a series of infractions on the circuit. The council cited incidents in six tournaments, the most recent an alleged use of obscene language and indecent gestures at a WCT event in Houston in April. As it turned out, he escaped the punishment. But in the wake of

---

* The Men's International Professional Tennis Council (MIPTC) was founded in 1974, and had administered the men's professional Grand Prix tennis circuit since then. It was made up of representatives of the International Tennis Federation (ITF, previously ILTF), the ATP and, from 1976 onwards, tournament directors from around the world.

Nastase's capitulation to Okker, Will Grimsley, a vehement critic of the player's persistent pattern of misbehaviour, penned what amounted to an obituary for the Romanian's career.

'He began punching opponents at 14. He drew his first suspension at 17. He has been defaulted in tournaments all over the world,' Grimsley wrote. 'Some critics have urged that his abuses have been so flagrant he should be banned for life. Yet the Mad Romanian carries on – a charmer in the parlour, a veritable devil on the court. In the past, he always said he was sorry and came back strong. Now, at age 31, it's too late. Time has passed him by.'

Not so, Okker. Now regarded as one of the game's elder statesmen, the player called 'the Flying Dutchman' in his more prosperous days had had a very poor year, winning only four matches in previous tournaments. But at Wimbledon he'd made a joke of his 104 world computer ranking, turning back the clock a few years to give some vintage performances and proving the surprise of The Championships.

Okker hadn't been seeded for two years and credited his rejuvenation partly to the unique feeling of Wimbledon's main arena. 'The Centre Court atmosphere gives you a push,' he said. 'It brings back the desire to win.' The prospects of him becoming the first unseeded player to take the title, however, were slim. He and Borg had met eight times since 1974, with the Swede winning six. And, the previous day, in a weather-congested programme, Okker had played no less than nine sets of doubles.

It looked ominous for Okker immediately. Borg broke in the very first game, and throughout the opening set, hitting with brute force and unerring accuracy, was always too much for the Amsterdammer to handle. Borg was leading 5-3 when rain necessitated a 34-minute delay. It was a brief stay of execution. Upon resumption, each player held service and the Swede had a one-set lead.

In the second, he broke in the third game. Okker showed here and there that there was still plenty of spring in his step, as he sped along the baseline hitting some fabulous forehand shots. There were occasional glimpses of beautifully controlled touch-play. But his challenge was only ever fitful. Borg's wonderfully versatile groundstrokes were, Rex Bellamy reported, 'humming with topspin, which is devilishly difficult to attack'. For every Okker winner, he was passed twice by the Swede. At 2-3, Okker had a break point but couldn't convert it and though, at 5-3, Borg failed to take advantage of three set points against service, he then held to tie up the set.

In the third set, Okker was again broken – in the third and fifth games – but with Borg serving for victory at 5-2, the Dutchman elicited a last brave effort. Okker, reaching forward for low volleys and angling them with all the guile of a man who had played Wimbledon 15 times, captured his opponent's service for the first time. On yet another cold day, the shivering crowd were warmed by the underdog's late bite. Okker took the next game too. But Borg allowed no further leeway. Okker collected only two more points as the Swede, balls coming off his racket like bullets, won the last two games with consummate ease. Without ever needing to reach full throttle, 'It always seemed' Bellamy wrote 'that, if necessary, Borg could slip the purring machinery of his game into overdrive.' The champion had done everything he had to do almost to perfection.

In the other semi-final, Connors faced Gerulaitis. The last time the two had met was a few nights earlier at London's 'in' disco, Tramp. They'd checked out around 11pm. 'I can go to a disco any time,' said Gerulaitis. 'I get a chance to win Wimbledon only once a year.' That chance was swiftly over. On Centre Court, it was Connors who had all the best moves.

Before a packed crowd enjoying a rare glimpse of sunshine after ten days of shivering temperatures, Connors, after fighting off a set point in the tenth game of a full-blooded 67-minute first set, then ran away with the match. Gerulaitis, who'd lost ten of 11 previous matches against Connors, his last win six years earlier, in some ways sowed the seeds of this latest downfall. He continued using the same tactics even when they plainly weren't working and as David Irvine summarised, 'Feeding Jimmy Connors with pace is a lot like stoking a boiler. He just gets hotter.' Striking 'a stream of volleys with murderous finality', as one Reuters writer reported, the left-hander bludgeoned his way to a 9-7, 6-2, 6-1 win in commanding fashion.

Hospitalised two months earlier, Connors said afterwards: 'I'm lucky to be here. I didn't think I would be able to play.' There was certainly nothing wrong with his eyesight. The white Slazenger balls were looking 'as big as a basketball' to him, he said. 'I seem to have ten seconds to play every shot.'

With Connors's usual coach and personal guru Pancho Segura not around, instead he'd invited into his entourage as a counsellor and confidant Bobby Riggs, a former player and inveterate hustler. In contrast to Segura, whom Connors said was 'very intense', Riggs, Wimbledon champion in 1939 but perhaps best known for the 1973 'Battle of the Sexes' – an internationally televised match held at the Houston Astrodome in which he was defeated by 29-year-old Billie Jean King – was a relaxed figure whom the American enjoyed having around to talk tennis and play golf and backgammon with.

Connors might have welcomed Riggs's calming off-court influence, but for the man Will Grimsley described as 'a street fighter in knee-high socks and white pants [shorts] and a Little Lord Fauntleroy haircut', every match was still trench warfare – Connors couldn't play well unless he was at fever pitch. The 60-year-old Riggs called him 'the most relentless, ruthless, mean player I've seen since Fred Perry in the 1930s. Perry would hold you underwater – beat you 6-0, 6-0, 6-0 if he could. Jimmy is the same way … He will tear into you. To him, a tennis match is a bar room brawl.'

Borg expected the final to be nothing less. 'Every match we play goes down to the final point,' said the 22-year-old. On occasions during the previous two weeks Borg had experienced misgivings, and doubted he'd achieve his greatest ambition. And now, while Connors was, in his own words, 'loose and easy', with so much prestige riding on the outcome the pressure was still building for the defending champion. 'Maybe this never happens to me again in my life,' he said. 'I have never felt this kind of feeling before.' Saturday's eagerly anticipated clash – the first time since 1965, when Emerson beat Stolle for a second year running, that a Wimbledon final had produced a replay of the previous year – would be, Borg stated, the 'most important of my career'.

If the Swede could succeed in duplicating his feat, Fred Perry declared he would be the first to congratulate Borg and would also throw him a 'two-man party'. But the 69-year-old, now a BBC radio commentator, was making no predictions about the outcome. 'I have never bet on a tennis match in my life,' he explained. 'I certainly don't want to start with this one.' It was far too close to call. 'When two irresistible forces meet,' Perry said, 'the only thing to do is send for the fire brigade.'

On a cloudy, clammy day, on which rain had fallen all morning, it was Connors who warmed quickest to the task of winning. Following two deuce points in a seven-minute opening game, the American – 'blowing out great gusts of air with every serve', observed the *Evening Times's* Bill Brown – held his service then immediately captured Borg's in another deuce game with a glorious backhand volley down the line after a long rally. But from that point on, it was the champion, unrattled as always, who assumed just about complete control.

In the next 14 games he allowed Connors only two. Connors was missing a lot of first services and Borg took full advantage. A double fault in the third game let the Swede in, and, after a series of potent serves drew him level at 2-2, he barely looked back, sweeping through the first set, reported Ronald Atkin in *The Observer*, 'like a forest fire in a drought year'.

As expected, the two players went at it in blood-and-thunder fashion; each point, Brown wrote, was 'contested with white-hot ferocity'. Balls were hit at an astounding velocity as rallies flashed across the Centre Court surface. Some, according to Brown, 'bordered on the unbelievable'. It was Borg, though, who outstayed his opponent on most of them, his piercing forehands and sharply angled backhands constantly prancing past the American's reaching racket; when he ventured to the net he volleyed with a finality he'd rarely shown before. Connors, wrote Atkin, 'was occasionally reduced to the role of a spectator at a firework display'.

Borg, conscious that he had to pin the left-hander to the baseline where he could do the least harm, consistently hit the ball with great depth and pegged Connors back. A prolific use of a sliced backhand (to Connors's forehand), which kept low on the soft grass – 'a shot I normally don't use much', Borg said afterwards – had the No.2 seed in all sorts of bother. Seemingly dumfounded in the face of such an assault Connors's groundstrokes were erratic and posed little threat.

If anything, it was Borg's vastly improved service that really gave him the decided edge. As one journalist put it, in two years it had gone 'from a rifle to a cannon'. He served with shattering power. At times, its sizzling force drew gasps from the gallery. Strings on two different rackets were broken. Not even Tanner, wrote Brown, 'could stir the blood and catch the breath as Borg was doing with services that literally screamed over the net'.

By contrast, Connors's service weakness hurt him. His first serve was ragged and unreliable. His awkward-looking, flapping second, spun into the corner, Borg was able to attack with near impunity. After the top seed broke to lead 2-1 in the second set, the fourth game was key. Connors, firing a salvo of fearsome forehands, came desperately close to breaking back straightaway.

He had four points for 2-2. But Borg, unleashing more colossal serves – one whacked with such might Connors's attempted forehand return flew 20 feet straight up – and flicking a delicious backhand cross-court winner past his fast-approaching opponent, pulled out of danger.

At 5-2 up and serving for the set, Borg went 0-30 down, but two clean aces – his third and fourth – brought him level and, though Connors fought to take his man to two deuce points, with another tremendous cross-court backhand that trapped the American as he charged to the net Borg clinched the game. Two sets up, he was, Brown noted, 'looking like a giant'.

'All the time, Borg's flowing, dancing footwork was a joy,' wrote Rex Bellamy. 'He seemed to be on castors.' Connors plugged away. Every point was bitterly fought for. But after the first six games of the third set all went with service, Borg simply shifted into overdrive again. At deuce in the next game, when two successive cross-court backhands forced Connors to net on both occasions, he made the breakthrough. And though Connors wasn't done yet – he went 40-30 up in Borg's next service game – the irrepressible Swede got out of trouble with a volleyed winner before a wide sliced serve and another down the middle, both of which Connors netted, gave Borg a 5-3 advantage. He was now on the cusp of victory.

Serving to save the match, Connors soon found himself 0-30 down – Borg producing a delicate inch-accurate forehand cross-court pass and a heavily spun backhand blast. The American made it 30-all but Borg, with a decisive volley at the net, earned Championship point. At precisely 3.46pm on the Centre Court clock, when Connors couldn't keep his fiercely hit backhand volley in play, the title was Borg's once more; the long-standing record of Perry – the former champion among the first on court to shake Borg's hand – had been reached.

As that final point was secured, to tumultuous acclaim from the crowd, the Swedish phenomenon tossed his racket aside, dropped down on his knees – 'as though Valhalla had come to Earth' commented Peter Wilson – and then, standing still for a brief moment, pressed his clasped fists to his closed eyes. He was, he revealed later, saying a silent prayer to his parents.

Borg, abandoning his usual phlegmatic disposition, couldn't hide his delight afterwards. His monumental victory was, he said, 'a dream I never think possible'. The awesome performance – 'a display of sheer virtuosity' Wilson called it – had left Centre Court in a state of near shock and Connors more than a little dazed too. Even Bergelin, whom Bud Collins had described in commentary as looking 'as grim as a Bergman movie', could hardly restrain himself. Borg had been superior in a few little matches, the coach said, 'but this is the best big match he ever played'. Despite Connors's assertion that 'I'm never out of a match until I've shaken hands', in truth he'd been a bull dominated by a matador. Borg thoroughly devastated the American according to the *Sydney Morning Herald* 'with all the certainty of a man whose tennis stretches credibility'.

'He's a hell of a player,' Perry said of the Swede. 'He has everything – great size, natural physical assets, speed, lightning reflexes and, more important, excellent temperament. With it, he's a great boy.' What everyone thought would be another bitter, bruising battle was turned into what Perry termed 'a travesty' by Borg's sledgehammer power. 'Everything went Borg's way,' the former champion said. 'If he'd fallen out of a 45-storey window in a New York skyscraper, he would have gone straight up.'

Straight up *is* where Borg had gone. He surely now had a spot among the all-time greats, and could be spoken of in the same breath as Tilden, Budge, Gonzales, Kramer and Laver. Will Grimsley reckoned Borg had been projected 'into an elitist society spoken of by tennis buffs only in reverential terms'. He stood alone at the top of the tennis tower, a long way apart from his rivals. 'All of the men's pro tennis world, unlike Caesar's Gaul, is divided into two parts – young Bjorn Borg and the rest of the 200 to 300 court gypsies who travel the international circuit,' Grimsley wrote. The Swede was 'on one towering tier and you need binoculars to see those just below him'.

He had now gone 40 matches without a loss. In the last six weeks, he'd won the Italian Open (second time), the French Open (third time) and Wimbledon (third time), on top of three matches for Sweden in the Davis Cup. Borg became only the second player since Laver in 1969 to win the French and Wimbledon in the same year, and the first since the Australian to win the Italian, French and Wimbledon in the same season. That he was currently the most complete tennis player in the world was indisputable, whatever the machinations of a little computer in Dallas.

Nothing seemed beyond the supercharged Swede's capabilities. Now reaching towards the tennis firmament, he was, he said, playing for history, for some new achievement. Halfway to adding another chapter to his phenomenal success story, Borg would tackle the third leg of the Grand Slam in the US Open the following month. If all went to plan, he would make only his second appearance in the Australian event in December. 'It gives you something to go for,' Borg affirmed. 'What can you do with all that money? Buy cars and clothes. You only need one car and one pair of jeans.'

Only two men had achieved the Grand Slam before – Don Budge in 1938 and Laver in 1962 (as an amateur) and again in 1969. With two of the jewels already in the bag, and Borg's mastery of his opponents, 'it does not seem so far out of reach', said the Swede. (Connors, of course, would be shadowing him all the way. 'I may follow him [Borg] to the ends of the earth now,' he told reporters in quintessential fashion. 'I'll stay with the s.o.b. until I beat him, and he knows it.')

For Borg, before then, there was a date with a razor. 'Get that horrible beard off,' Perry had told him when they'd met recently in Paris. Borg had agreed to shave, as per his new tradition, once Wimbledon was over. He'd also promised to buy the grey-haired Englishman dinner at the next year's tournament. There, Borg would go for title No.4. Now that he'd equalled it, the aim was to shatter Perry's record. Even Perry, the confirmed non-gambler, must have been tempted to put money on him doing it.

25 June – 7 July 1979

WITH A reported annual income of around $3m, a fabulous house and apartment on the French Riviera (as well as owning a chain of 11 islands in the Baltic Sea, off the east coast of his native Sweden), plus a nearby sporting goods shop, which his parents ran for him, Bjorn Borg was a very wealthy young man. Reputedly one of the world's five richest sports stars, he'd relocated to Monaco in 1974, not just to enjoy the warmer climes in the Mediterranean but also its tax-friendly status. But now, what 'the Monte Carlo millionaire who struck gold on the tennis court' wanted, wrote Neil Wilson in the *Glasgow Herald*, was 'something not even his riches can buy'. 'My dream,' Borg declared on the eve of Wimbledon 1979, 'is to be remembered as one of the greatest players in the game.'

The long-limbed Swede had already taken giant strides towards realising the ambition, and his desire was gathering momentum. Only the month before, a panel comprising Fred Perry, Lew Hoad and Don Budge had selected Borg as the first official 'World Champion'. Winning Wimbledon for a fourth time in a row, the first man to do so since New Zealander Anthony Wilding completed his streak in 1913, was the next step. 'By mortal standards, Borg is already a tennis god, a modern appendix to Scandinavian mythology,' wrote Wilson. 'But by his own standards, he is still a fortnight away from greatness.'

Borg was acutely conscious of what a victory would mean. Prior to 1922, when Wimbledon discarded the system (and moved from its original location at Worple Road), the reigning champion played only a single Challenge Round match against the winner of the all-comers tournament. But those were the cosy, far-off days. It was all very different now. A fourth consecutive title for Borg would be unprecedented. Were he to be successful, he said, 'I can be sure people all over the world will know I have achieved something no other man has done before.'

The previous autumn, another dream had been sabotaged. In September 1978, on the hard, rubberised asphalt court at the USTA National Tennis Center in Flushing Meadows, the US Open's new home after 62 years in leafy, affluent Forest Hills, Jimmy Connors, with what Curry Kirkpatrick termed a 'nearly perfect 6-4, 6-2, 6-2 dismantling of Borg', had exorcised the ghost of his Wimbledon humiliation, and a trip to Kooyong in Australia was taken off the Swede's travel itinerary again.

For Connors, it was a fifth straight year in the finals of the Open – and his third victory (all on different surfaces) – though Borg, hampered by a blister on his right thumb that required an injection, paid little heed to the result because of his injury. Right after the match he 'forgot about it', he later said. The pair were seeded to meet yet again at Wimbledon – but not in the final. With the American at No.3 seed, lurking this time in Borg's half of the draw, if the form charts went according to plan, he and the defending champion would clash at the semi-final stage. Instead, it was another brash competitor from the States whom Borg was likely to come face to face with over the net on 7 July.

John McEnroe, since abandoning a law course at Stanford University to hit the pro circuit in 1978, had gained so much stature over the next few months, he had climbed to No.3 on the ATP computer rankings and now even leapfrogged Connors into the No.2 seeding for Wimbledon. ('It should be the other way around,' McEnroe said with perhaps surprising modesty.) His prodigious talent had blossomed rapidly. As well as helping the US regain the Davis Cup, winning his two singles matches over the British by the most one-sided scores in the 79-year history of the competition, he'd taken the Grand Prix Masters title in New York, the premier prize of the pros, after fighting off two match points in the final against 35-year-old Arthur Ashe, then overpowered both Connors (thrashing him in straight sets) and Borg, 7-5, 4-6, 6-2, 7-6, to capture the World Championship Tennis crown in Dallas in May.

Such was McEnroe's advancement, some fellow pros saw the player known as 'Junior' on the tour, 'The Kid' to his fans, as already a notch above his closest rivals. 'He has a more complete game than either Borg or Connors,' said Roscoe Tanner. Sandy Mayer called him the 'only one true genius in the game'. Australian John Alexander, who'd enjoyed a recent win over Borg in Milan, believed that 'McEnroe is the equal of anyone I've ever played.'

Now, as the world of tennis focussed on the All England Club again, much of the talk in the build-up to The Championships centred on McEnroe's credentials as a potential Wimbledon winner. Having already made the front of *Time* magazine, *Radio Times* had the 'Whizz Kid' on their cover; 'America's brightest young tennis hope' ran the headline. Standing 5ft 11in tall, exactly the same height as Borg, McEnroe was a brilliantly inventive player brimming with innate ability, a rare combination of stroking power and touch, of speed of thought and action. Court-smart beyond his years, his awareness, always knowing his opponent's position, was tremendous. In November 1978, in the semi-finals of the Stockholm Open, the Irish-New Yorker had met Borg for the first time – and beaten him (inflicting a first defeat for the Swede by a player younger than himself). He now held a 3-2 lead in their head-to-head matches.

No one questioned his natural, instinctive flair, or doubted that he'd matured immeasurably as a player. But, whenever he took to a tennis court, alongside his immense quality, McEnroe's temperament always shared equal billing. Never known for keeping his cool under difficulty, the 20-year-old, all unsmiling intensity and pained contorted features – 'He has a different but equally twisted face for each call,' wrote author Paul Theroux, 'like separate chunks of malevolent putty' – had left lines people and umpires the world over nervous wrecks with his on-court edginess. McEnroe's unbridled irritability had attracted an extraordinary amount of criticism in the previous few months. He was castigated by the press and regularly vilified by his hometown crowds. Still, the young American vowed not to let it get in his way. 'I don't want any distractions at Wimbledon,' he said. 'If you get distracted here, you lose.'

McEnroe's warm-up had gone well. Whereas Connors hadn't done his Wimbledon cause much good, only playing one tournament – the French Open – in six weeks since May, McEnroe had tuned up nicely with victory on grass at the Queen's Club, beating big-serving Victor Pecci in the final. It was the strong, agile 6ft 4in 24-year-old Pecci, christened 'the Leaning Tower of Paraguay' by Bud Collins, who'd surprisingly beaten Connors in the semi-finals in Paris before taking Borg to four sets in the final.

Defeat in the warm springtime of Dallas aside, Borg had enjoyed a decent year. Tournament success in Richmond (where he survived eight match points in a semi-final with McEnroe) was followed by a third straight Pepsi Grand Slam title in February, Borg registering a sixth win over Connors in their last nine meetings in the final. He'd also won the Monte Carlo Masters, defeating Gerulaitis 6–2, 6–1, 6–3, and followed it up, a week before the WCT finals, by again beating Connors, in Las Vegas, in the Alan King Caesars Palace Tennis Classic.

After capturing a fourth French title early in June, Borg's preparations had travelled – superstitiously so – the precise same path as recent years. He'd practised in seclusion at the same north-west London club (the Cumberland), played (and won) the same exhibition match there for its members against Vitas Gerulaitis, and accommodated himself, Mariana and Bergelin at the same out-of-town hotel, the Holiday Inn. The growth of facial fuzz, part of his psyching-up process, was once more in place.

'Just to feel you have the chance to do something nobody else has done is a tremendous responsibility,' Borg said ahead of his latest quest for a place in the record books. As always, he would find his path strewn with traps, dangermen looking to trip him up, especially in the vulnerable early rounds. Even more so if the courts were wet underfoot. Roscoe Tanner identified the weather at Wimbledon as a possible chink in Borg's armour. 'If the grass became damp and slippery, and he was unable to move about so quickly,' the American said, 'half his game would be gone.'

Fast footwork, creating time to posture himself perfectly to make his shots, was such a key ingredient to Borg's success. 'The most important thing about my game is my legs,' he would tell *Life* magazine's Christopher Whipple in 1980. 'I move well. I prepare myself. I always arrive in the right position.' Borg was no slouch over longer distances, either. In a December 1976 heat of BBC's *Superstars* in Vichy, France – in which the Swede won six out of the eight events – he even outpaced Olympic 110m-hurdles gold medallist, Guy Drut, in a steeplechase.

Whatever the conditions, after his struggle at the same stage the previous year, Borg had every reason for a nervous case of short-sightedness about his immediate future – a meeting on Centre Court with the tough American veteran Tom Gorman. In 1970, at his first Wimbledon, Gorman, an elegant stroke-maker, had been an immediate favourite with the Centre Court crowd when he lost an attractive match with Ken Rosewall. The following year, after ousting Rod Laver, he'd reached the semi-final where he was bettered in a memorable battle by Stan Smith. Gorman, at 33, ten years Borg's senior and suffering from an inherent back weakness, was in the twilight of his career but insisted he wasn't going into the match with the Swede to be 'cannon fodder'. He'd beaten Borg once before and, he said, 'That helps my confidence.'

It was a typical Wimbledon opening, with the 11-acre All England Club festooned with thousands of freshly planted hydrangeas and new coats of the club's colours, green and mauve. And, just as typically, a quota of nail-biting moments for Borg's supporters. After the customary 2 o'clock start was delayed by 15 minutes because of the damp, Borg set off in the wrong gear. 'It takes time to get used to the Centre Court, the atmosphere of the tournament,' he said before the match. Here he was soon providing the proof. Cautious and tentative because of the wet turf, and finding Gorman's service more than he could handle, Borg fired on too few cylinders. Trailing 4-3 when the players took shelter from the rain, after a 63-minute break he lost the first two games upon resumption to fall a set behind.

Playing on Centre Court for the first time in five years, the tousle-haired Gorman, with competent, confident tennis, was making some superb shots. He had chances in the second set too. The defending champion, though returning much better and more certain of his footing, had two break points against him on his own service in the ninth game but survived with a lucky net cord before levelling the match, 6-4.

The crucial juncture came in the third set. This time Borg was broken in the ninth game to fall 5-4 behind. But, helped by a pair of double faults by the American, one at break point, Borg broke back immediately and, seemingly hyped up by that vital turn, he played with refreshed assuredness. The seasoned campaigner from Seattle double-faulted twice more in his next service game as well. 'After that,' Gorman said post-match, 'it was just like facing a steam roller.' He won only one more game for the rest of the contest, as the Swede sealed a 3-6, 6-4, 7-5, 6-1 victory. 'To let Borg off the hook,' remarked the *Daily Mirror*'s Peter Wilson, 'is as dangerous as landing a shark and failing to kill it at once.'

While the biggest giant of them all was unsteady on his feet, on an opening day on which, according to Neil Wilson, 'rain and high winds made the mightiest merely mortal', three Goliaths suffered catastrophic blows. Arthur Ashe, who'd predicted the weather would wreak havoc with the seeding, became the first victim himself, the No.7 seed slumping to a straight-sets defeat on No.2 Court to little-known Australian Chris Kachel, a former bank teller who saw well out of only one eye and was a qualifier for the third year running.

Ashe, who'd beaten the 24-year-old convincingly just two weeks earlier at the Queen's Club, was philosophical in defeat. 'When you're young and you have a bad day, they call it inexperience. When you're in your late twenties they call it the law of averages. And when you're older they call it old age. It's just bad days,' he said.

No.2 Court, graveyard of so many favourites in the past, also saw the end of one of this year's. All the pre-tournament sparring in practice sessions with Borg didn't help Vitas Gerulaitis who became the victim of the first major upset, the fourth seed losing a rollercoaster three-hour-ten-minute five-set marathon to fellow American Pat DuPré – that, despite DuPré being guilty of 28 double faults.

Gerulaitis, who won the Italian Open beating Vilas in a five-set final, had been working hard both on his game (with a newly fashioned, open-stance serve) and on losing his reputation for fast-living. The New Yorker had acquired the nickname 'Broadway Vitas' due to his well-known love of the high life. Still under the shrewd management of Fred Stolle, he'd adopted a new spartan lifestyle and agreed to an early-to-bed regime. Against DuPré, a Belgian-born 24-year-old raised in Birmingham, Alabama, it 'seemed he had forgotten to wake up as early', wrote Neil Wilson.

On a rain-slowed court the balls were heavy and the flamboyant Brooklyn man was hampered in his movement. DuPré, a Stanford University economics graduate who later described himself as 'a horrendous grass courts player', took the first two sets and although the No.4 seed came to his senses to level, DuPré, who had outranked Gerulaitis ten years earlier when the pair were America's top juniors, was not to be robbed of his glory. Amid tense excitement in the fading evening light, DuPré bagged a prized scalp, Gerulaitis storming from the court at the end and refusing to meet reporters.

No.10 seed Fibak, to lowly ranked American Bruce Manson, who hauled himself back into the match after dropping the first two sets, and Italy's 16th-seeded Corrado Barazzutti, beaten by Andrew Pattison, were others brought down by relatively unknown Davids.

Gerulaitis's leading compatriots fared much better. On nearby No.1 Court, sharing the dual honour with Borg of opening the tournament, McEnroe disappointed the thousands who hoped to see some of his theatrics, barely raising an eyebrow in anger when breezing past Connecticut-born Terry Moor. He even gave them a touch of comic relief. At the start of a rain shower McEnroe slipped his shirt up over his shoulders to cover his head. 'We're all going to sink,' he protested to the umpire. Meanwhile, Connors, despite losing the second set on a tiebreak, won in straightforward style against Frenchman Jean-François Caujolle.

Borg, against the unseeded Gorman, had fully lived up to his reputation as a notoriously slow starter, but also the man with the enviable temperament for any potential crisis. The American, according to Bud Collins, an extrovert, enthusiastic and extremely knowledgeable TV commentator in the States, 'tied Borg to the railroad tracks … but the Swede didn't even bleed when the train rolled over him'. However, when the next engine came along, Borg found himself in mortal danger.

It arrived in the form of Vijay Amritraj. A player of cunning and guile, Amritraj, one of three tennis-playing brothers who'd learned his game near the cricket pitch and its flower-bordered pavilion at Madras, had beaten the Swede twice in their previous four meetings including a five-set classic the last time the two had met on grass, in the second round of the US Open five years earlier. And on Wimbledon's No.1 Court he came so very close to pulling off a repeat success. On a muggy Wednesday afternoon, Borg edged Amritraj 2-6, 6-4, 4-6, 7-6, 6-2 in two hours 44 minutes, but at one point in the fourth set the alarm bells were ringing so loudly for the champion that, as he confessed later, 'I thought I would lose the match, for sure.'

Bent on not playing a stereotypical serve-and-volley game, the classy, creative Indian offered up an intelligent variety of serves. His alert returns of Borg's thunderous serve and anticipation of his attempted passing shots appeared to perturb the Swede. Hitting some superlative shots, he won the first set in 25 minutes. And while Borg replied by winning the second following a break in the ninth game, Amritraj, keeping his opponent guessing with his deftly positioned strokes, then took the third set with a break in the final game, which included a rare Borg double fault.

Two sets to one ahead, the 25-year-old broke Borg's serve for a 3-1 lead in the fourth and, although Borg scraped back immediately to 2-3, in his next service game, as Bud Collins put it, he 'again found himself hanging in trouble with Amritraj stomping on his fingers at 0-40'. Passed three times by the inspired Indian, Borg was close to disaster. It was then that he hit a shot that proved a pivotal moment.

Gunning a serve to Amritraj's backhand, the Swede flew to the net ready to volley, when the Indian stroked a monumental return down the sideline. It was 'as good a backhand as I ever hit', he said later. Borg, lunging, stretching, lurched to his right, and over 7,000 customers jam-packed into the court sucked in their breath. 'Low volleys aren't his smorgasbord,' wrote Collins in his match report, 'but he probed down around his ankles, twisted his wrist as he made contact, and dumped the ball cross-court where it died safely out of Amritraj's reach.'

Somehow Borg not only got his racket to the ball, but lifted it up, where it hung tantalisingly on the net cord before dropping on the Indian's side. Amritraj's 'blackjacking stroke [was] transformed into a dribbling survival volley', as Collins saw it, and the match was turned on its head. From 15-40, Borg then blasted an untouchable ace. Amritraj missed a backhand return of service and the score was deuce. Two outright winners later, the game was the Swede's.

When the set went to a tiebreak, Amritraj, who had an 80 per cent record in tennis's penalty shoot outs, claimed the first two points with a spectacular ace and a passing shot. But Borg rallied brilliantly to take it, 7-2, and Amritraj's opportunity slipped from his hand. After coming close to capsizing, Borg enjoyed much smoother sailing from thereon. The deciding set went his way from the start. At 2-5, the Indian managed to save seven match points before netting an easy volley to finally confirm Borg's narrow escape.

Borg admitted afterwards he'd nearly walked the tightrope once too often. Amritraj had, in Collins's words, 'pushed Borg off a precipice … only to watch the champion bounce back'. Borg believed that the gentle, smiling Indian, at 3-1 in the fourth, 'got a little nervous when he realised how important it was'. But much of the post match talk was about that one shot. 'I passed him, I tell you,' said a still-disbelieving Amritraj, 'I think even Bjorn would admit that forehand was a little lucky.'

He did. It was, Borg said, 'a lucky topspin forehand volley' and 'not exactly a shot you use much'. 'That forehand wasn't lucky,' contested the distinguished American columnist, Mike Lupica. 'It was [just] Borg. It seemed for a moment [as] if he'd hit the ball with his championship plate.' Amritraj described his opponent as 'an absolute genius' for the way he snatched victory from the half-closed jaws of defeat. No one played the pressure points with greater decisiveness. 'Borg seems to be able to switch on the adrenaline like you or I can switch on a water tap,' marvelled Peter Wilson. 'Maybe we will never know what stirs this dispassionate Swede,' Lupica wrote, 'what icy reservoirs he calls upon when things look worst. But those reservoirs are there: he is a remarkable athlete.'

Borg, of course, didn't go out deliberately to run his matches so close to the wire. 'I don't design it that way,' he insisted, 'I'd rather be ahead, but this is what happens – I don't know why.' His early tournament traumas, though, were becoming, wrote Morley Myers, a UPI sports writer, 'almost as much of a Wimbledon tradition as strawberries and cream'. The trouble with Borg as a prospective victim was, the heftier the odds against him the more he became relaxed. 'When I see the match slipping away, then I take chances,' he said. He went for winners or tried to hit the lines and was usually successful. 'I feel I am a better player when I am down a break than when I am level or in front,' he said. Both Gorman and Amritraj had, in Bud Collins's words, 'taken their best shots at him, causing Bullet-Proof Bjorn to issue his usual deathbed statement on each occasion: "For sure, I think I'm gone." Gone where? Eventually to the shower with another victory ... at the Big W.'

Marty Riessen was another echoing the consensus about the Swede. 'He has a knack,' the American veteran said. 'If you get out of tight spots like he does, you just have to be good.' The 37-year-old, who'd first graced the Centre Court 14 years earlier, had himself had another of the favourites in some bother. In Riessen's second-round clash with Connors, at one stage it looked as if the No.3 might join the swollen ranks of favoured casualties; Riessen took the first set from his fellow countryman on a tiebreak. Connors, however, showed his habitual resolve; he recovered to take the next three sets in a row.

McEnroe also endured a bumpy ride, dropping the first set to an adventurous Buster Mottram, a player he'd thrashed in the Davis Cup final in Palm Springs, before going on to win 6-7, 6-2, 7-6, 6-2. Britain's bad boy, controversial because of his avowed right-wing politics, Mottram hadn't been that complimentary about Wimbledon. 'Playing on grass is like Russian roulette,' he complained after his first-round win over Richard Lewis. 'I hate it. There is no strategy.'

For other big names on the international scene, their gambling days were done for another year. No.13 seed Manuel Orantes (sent packing by little-known Frenchman Gilles Moretton in five sets) and José Higueras (knocked out in four by American John Sadri) were both put out to grass. And joining them on the sidelines was Guillermo Vilas.

The pundits rarely mentioned the powerful but stylish South American as a serious Wimbledon contender any more. 'A superb athlete,' according to Will Grimsley, 'who handles a racket the way a musician might a violin', the Argentinean had never been able to transfer his abundant gifts to the verdant greens in SW19. Vilas had won the Australian Open in January – the top seed beating John Marks in the final – and, as usual pre-Wimbledon, had pronounced himself mentally and physically prepared to go all the way. But, having swamped Roger Taylor in his opening match, the No.6 seed as usual quickly hit a road block.

This year it was a fresh-faced 19-year-old from North Carolina, Tim Wilkison. Big, strong and agile – on two occasions he was even able to hit the ball over the net for winning points after falling – Wilkison, after losing the first set, lobbed his fellow left-hander to death to earn 'definitely the biggest win of my life'. And just two years after mastering all he surveyed, a dejected Vilas found Wimbledon beyond him once again. The sensitive Argentine, 'his strong Latin features reflecting strain and his sweaty black hair hanging in strands to his shoulders' wrote Will Grimsley, looked a broken man afterwards, unable to hide his disappointment. 'It is tragic to see such marvellous talent go to waste,' Grimsley stated.

Meanwhile, after battling manfully to save his crown, Vilas's old friend had no plans to abdicate yet. Though while others might have thought that Borg's rule would carry on in perpetuity, he himself acknowledged it was getting harder every time to preserve his unparalleled record. 'This [year's] is the toughest Wimbledon draw I have ever had,' he said. His foes were showing Borg little respect, 'roughing up' the defending champion, Collins called it, and 'trying to roll him out of joint like just another Swedish meatball'.

Next to take a pot shot, due to meet Borg that Friday, was Hank Pfister, a 6ft 4in hard-serving right-hander from Bakersfield, California. But Borg also faced another threat to his title hopes. Troubled with a recurrence of a nagging pain in the back of his left thigh he'd suffered playing in Hamburg in early May, which had forced him to default from the German Open against Eliot Teltscher and kept him out of tennis for a spell the previous month, the Swede had looked unusually sluggish at times during his marathon with Amritraj, his feet not obeying his natural reactions.

Post-match, the strain not only required heat treatment at Borg's London hotel – from a new electronic machine, owned, apparently, by harmonica star Larry Adler – but had both Borg and his coach concerned about the player continuing his campaign. Bergelin gave his charge only a 25 per cent chance of fulfilling the third-round clash. 'You saw the way he moved,' said Bergelin. 'It's not something you can repair in a few days.'

Sceptics noted that there had been much the same talk in Paris three weeks earlier – and Borg had won the French Open title. Although Borg had genuinely suffered major ailments in big events, Swedish journalists knew that any prognosis on an injury usually came from his coach – and tended towards the pessimistic. 'Borg never complains. It is always Bergelin who is telling us that Bjorn has physical problems,' one reporter said. 'Most of the time they don't prove accurate.'

So it turned out. On the Thursday morning the champion, though moving stiffly at first, practised for more than an hour at the nearby Cumberland Club and, according to a committee member, 'he ran like a hare'. And against the American, not showing one twinge from his much-publicised injury, Borg raced about as ferociously as he ever had on the All England Club courts and – more animal similes – 'romped to victory like a spring lamb' in David Irvine's words.

The lanky Californian, a bull of a man with a fast serve and formidable forehand, had played Borg in Tokyo and in Las Vegas, taking him to a final set both times. But on this occasion, he was totally outclassed. It was a vintage Borg performance. 'He served with accuracy, he volleyed, he passed, he manoeuvred Pfister like a pendulum,' reported John S. Radosta of the *New York Times*. 'Pfister shared the problem common to all of Borg's opponents: will Borg's deceptive double-fisted backhand go left or right? Usually he came up with the wrong answer.'

The American, a little nervous on Centre Court, changed his racket in the opening game and probably wished he could have swapped opponents, too, as Borg produced a stream of rasping passing shots down both lines. One UPI journalist summed up Pfister's task as 'like trying to chase shadows in a blackout' as Borg whacked winners almost at will.

After struggling to save his first three service games – which all went to deuce – Pfister was finally broken when Borg lobbed superbly to lead 4-3. He held on to his advantage to take the set. From then on it was a landslide. With a trademark display of awesome power and clinical precision, Borg allowed his adversary only the third game in the second set – Pfister having to survive a break point to win it – before making short work of the third set. By the end, wrote Morley Myers, the unfortunate American was reduced to 'the role of a bemused sparring partner with nowhere to hide'. Pfister was walloped 6-4, 6-1, 6-3. He 'looked as though Borg had pulled a gun on him. And used it,' Bud Collins concluded.

After his glittering exhibition, Borg revealed that only when stretching backwards did he even feel the thigh injury 'and if it is like this in my next match, I'll be very satisfied'. Ice and ultrasonic treatment plus cream massage had worked their magic. Borg's play led some journalists to question if the Swedish star was playing 'possum'. 'Would it be ungallant for me to ask if you feel you have conned some people?' said one British newsman in the post-match interview. Borg looked confused. 'Do you know the word?' the reporter queried. Borg shook his head. The question was rephrased. Bergelin, standing in the wings, broke in to answer.

It was he, he admitted, who'd raised the prospect of Borg possibly forfeiting his title, though denied he had exaggerated the player's condition. Bud Collins wasn't convinced. If you believed 'the Virtuous Viking', as Collins called Bergelin, 'poor, crippled Bjorn Borg' had about as much chance of getting through his match against Pfister 'as Camille did of going beyond the third act. His muscle pulls were worse than hoof-and-mouth disease.' As it happened, Collins reported, 'the only things critically pulled were the legs of those who listened to Bergelin'.

However bad the strain might have been, rivals hoping Borg would quit on his stool were soon put right. 'Some day I am going to lose,' he told reporters. 'But I will not lose on the tennis court. I will be dead.' His fellow big guns boomed on too. Connors hammered Johan Kriek of South Africa, while McEnroe hit his way past Tom Gullikson. But the singles continued on its unpredictable course. After Friday's third round, just six of the 16 men's seeds remained – though most of the players who caused earlier upsets were gone and forgotten; as quickly as the tournament created a new giant-killer, so another was consigned to the role of yesterday's hero.

Kachel had already departed, beaten by Ove Bengtson, in the second round. Now, Tom Okker abruptly ended the glory of Wilkison (whose 'carriage turned back into a pumpkin' wrote John S. Radosta). As yet more seeds were consigned to oblivion, new names came roaring into the limelight. While his brother, Sandy, was ousting John Sadri, Gene Mayer rubbed out No.11 John Alexander. No.8 Victor Pecci, who'd had a tremendous year – the Paraguayan's serve leading even Borg to predict he would be dangerous on Wimbledon's grass – crashed out to 20-year-old Australian qualifier Brad Drewett. Brian Teacher, ranked 14th in the US, toppled another Brian, No.9 seed Gottfried.

And it was Teacher that Borg faced next. It proved a taut encounter, one which elicited the tennis of Teacher's life. The 6ft 3in Californian from Beverly Hills, a year older than Borg, had run the Swede very close the previous autumn in the final at the Seiko World Super Tennis Tournament in Tokyo. At Wimbledon, with his huge serves, stinging volleys and excellent overhead shots, he did everything but pull a knife on his opponent. After losing a narrow first set 6-4, the unseeded American took the second 7-5 and continually gave Borg plenty to worry about. The Swede, mostly from the baseline, was forced to fight grimly throughout.

But each time Teacher had him at crisis point, the champion raised his game to a completely different class, pulling out his best shots as required. As he strove to edge ahead in the third and fourth sets, the American went to the net and was erratic; missed volleys cost him vital points. Borg, dishing out another lesson in cut-throat tennis, punished him. The American could do little with two of Borg's passing shots in the fourth set but stand back and admire them. Hotly pursued all the way, the top seed eventually won the last two sets 6-4, 7-5. 'I'm not mad that I played so well and lost,' Teacher said afterwards. 'I'm mad that I played the whole damn tournament so well and had to meet up with *him*.'

At times, in all his matches, Borg had seemed to coast along then suddenly put his game into overdrive – then none could touch him. One American who definitely wouldn't be getting close was McEnroe. 'Never mind talking about a McEnroe-Borg final, or a McEnroe-Connors final,' the No.2 seed had quipped before The Championships started, 'a McEnroe-anybody final will do just fine.' But a day after downing twin brother, Tom, McEnroe faced 15th seed Tim Gullikson, whom he'd beaten in the finals of Stockholm and Wembley the previous year, and was vanquished in straight sets.

The 27-year-old, ranked a surprising No.16 on the ATP computer despite no grand slam or major title to his credit, swept to a 6-4, 6-2, 6-4 victory in two and a half hours. The stocky right-hander, who for ten years had practised against his brother, was used to playing 'lefties'. And it showed; everything Gullikson hit was magic as, in the chill of a summer evening, Wimbledon reached a peak of high drama.

The Saturday duel, fought in cool, windy conditions, transfixed the capacity crowd on No.2 Court. Fans were virtually hanging from the rafters to watch it. Several times the umpire had to call for spectators to be removed from behind the canvas backdrop, and afterwards police formed a wedge to take both players safely to the sanctuary of the dressing rooms.

McEnroe, suffering from a cold and playing with his left thigh heavily strapped, a legacy of a muscle strain, was generous in defeat, acknowledging that Gullikson – who'd played 'a smart match' – was a deserved winner. But he'd not felt 100 per cent fit nor, he said, had he prepared himself well enough; he'd had trouble warming up because of the weather, and by the time he had, the match was virtually lost.

It was one full of frustrations for the 20-year-old. McEnroe had not just Gullikson but a chattering gallery to contend with, plus a crowd of excitable Italians screaming and yelling for their hero, Adriano Panatta, victorious on the adjoining court against Sandy Mayer. As early as the first set, McEnroe shouted at spectators who were moving about, and complained about the noise. Then later, in the third set, he was spoken to sternly by the umpire after skirmishing with a linesman who called a foot fault.

Fully behind Gullikson, the crowd cheered every point won by the twin, and jeered McEnroe. In a feverish atmosphere that had the hallmarks of a football game, at times their antagonism towards the younger player was intense. 'I am not blaming the hostility of the crowd for my defeat,' McEnroe said, 'but they sure didn't help me. I could feel they didn't want me to win. I also think it is a personal thing with them and me. They want to see Borg in the final every year. Perhaps the only answer is to be a great guy.'

One American writer proposed that McEnroe personified for the British all that was worst in his countrymen. Over the years they'd held much the same opinion about Jimmy Connors. In his own fourth-round match, the No.3 seed met the sole British survivor, 35-year-old Mark Cox. In 1968, Cox had won a place in tennis history by being the first amateur to beat a professional – Pancho Gonzales – in the world's first Open, at Bournemouth. Now a part-time Surrey farmer who admitted his tennis ambitions were long since dead, Cox had reached the last 16 for the third time in his extensive career, just edging Gilles Moretton after surviving six match points in an exciting five-setter. But in Connors he found a man in a hurry; the American dropped only four games in a brisk execution of the Briton.

With Argentina's José Luis Clerc going down to Roscoe Tanner, only four seeds remained as the quarter-finals approached. Those holding

Centre Court seats for the final were reportedly already trying to sell them off more cheaply to the touts than just a day or so earlier.

Borg insisted that McEnroe's departure 'still doesn't make it any easier for me'. It was largely because of the antics of the lesser lights, eating their way slowly through the heart of the seeding list, that Borg's push towards the greatest achievement in modern tennis had been relegated to the background. But the Swede's relative obscurity was also down to his own hesitant progress: the mechanical plods past Gorman and Teacher; the near-fatal fall against Amritraj. Only against Pfister had he given glimpses of his true class. One Australian journalist even observed that 'Borg always conveys the impression that the best is yet to come.' If he was going to move out of the wings and take centre stage, now was the time.

For the second year running he met Tom Okker, who'd disposed of Gene Mayer in the fourth round. Borg had a 7-2 win/loss record against Okker in his favour, and not even the most patriotic Dutchman fancied their countryman's chances of squaring the ledger. Wisely so. Early in the match the 35-year-old had trouble with the seam of his shorts and his game seemed to unravel just as quickly.

Borg began at breakneck pace, dropping only four points as he twice broke Okker's serve to lead 4-0. And though Okker managed to end a losing sequence of 12 points by holding serve in the next game and again held his next service game, Borg clinched the first set 6-2 with a love game. It took just 21 minutes.

The second set was even more lopsided. The Swede again broke Okker's opening serve and, punching passing shots down both lines with machine-gun accuracy and throwing in inch-perfect lobs whenever Okker tried to attack from the net, he never gave his opponent a chance to mount a serious challenge. After leading 2-1, Borg knocked off the next four games to take the set, again in 21 minutes.

The pattern was disturbed slightly in the third set. Showing greater resistance, Okker stayed level for the first four games, but the Swede made a break to lead 4-2, went to 5-2, and while Okker was allowed the eighth game as a consolation when Borg made some inconclusive returns, that was his last joy. Borg served at 5-3 and won on his first match point when the Amsterdam man drove out. All the wind was knocked out of the Flying Dutchman's sails in just 67 minutes. 'I didn't even get time to get tired,' Okker joked afterwards.

Okker, who'd been playing Wimbledon since Borg was an eight-year-old, faced an impossible task. Even his court-covering wizardry was of little help against the Swede's mobility and strength. The Dutch touch artist was made to look, Peter Wilson wrote, 'like a man roller-skating over cobblestones'. Borg was always there at the end of any rallies to pocket the point. 'He [Borg] could do all kind of things with the ball because he got to it so quickly,' Okker said. After yet another stroke of magic from his racket, in the third set, even Borg had looked slightly embarrassed with the ease of his victory; after a shrug of his shoulders he raised his hands in an apology to his opponent.

Borg seemed to have timed his tournament perfectly. He was homing in on a fourth title, wrote Aussie journalist Peter Stone, 'like some computerised laser beam'. It was Connors who, as expected, now stood in his path. In the last eight, the No.3 seed had met 22-year-old Texan Bill Scanlon, who'd seen off Brad Drewett, with a 3-0 record in his favour. He made it 4-0 but only after Scanlon, ranked 37th in the US, had extended the 1974 champion to four sets. Connors committed errors throughout and Scanlon wasn't overly impressed by his fellow American's form. 'If Borg has the chances that Connors gave me,' he said, 'he will take Jimmy in three sets.' As forecasts went, Scanlon's was almost spot on.

Ahead of their clash, Borg termed it 'a pity the draw has worked out so that I meet Connors [in the semi-final]'. The American's seeding had rebounded on the organisers, who clearly hadn't foreseen the young pretender, McEnroe, suffering a fourth-round upset. 'No self-respecting Hollywood mogul would have allowed it to happen; showing the climax before the last reel hits the screen is bad box office,' moaned Morley Myers.

Connors was making no predictions – in fact, he was saying nothing at all, maintaining the silence he'd kept since the tournament's start. Having apparently taken the hump at his seeding, he'd declined the All England Club's standard invitation to attend post-match interviews and news conferences. Throwing a shroud of secrecy over himself, the 26-year-old hadn't spoken a word to the media throughout.

The match began at a predictably frenetic pace, both players rallying, as an Associated Press writer put it, 'as if two howitzers were bombing away at each other from close range'. Leading 2-1, in the fourth game Connors had two break points but the Swede was free in an instant, saving them both before levelling. In the next game, a magnificent lob that left the American rooted to the spot gave Borg three break points. This time, Connors saved them all. But when he rushed in behind his forehand to attack and Borg passed him with a searing backhand down the line, and then he netted what should have been an easy half-court backhand, Connors's first really bad shot of the match cost him dearly.

It was a green light for Borg. After playing more soft shots earlier on, with Connors applying great pressure, Borg began hitting through the ball and getting more depth on both sides. His explosive power snuffed out Connors's southpaw counterattacks before they were launched. The American was totally unable to counteract Borg's arrow-like accuracy and drive. 'His best shots were as pebbles thrown against a wall,' wrote Neil Wilson. And though each of the next three games also went to deuce, it was the 'Angelic Assassin', as Bud Collins dubbed Borg, who always showed the lethal touch. The Swede won them all to take the opening set.

Play continued to be closely fought. When Borg served two aces to win to love in the second game of the second set it broke a sequence of seven deuce games. Borg's service was unmerciful. The ball came off the racket with brutalising force. He fired 11 clean aces all told. His looping topspin forehand and two-fisted backhand, Will Grimsley described as 'deadly guided missiles'. Connors simply lacked the weapons to combat the continual bombardment. And after breaking in the seventh game with the score at 3-3, Borg gave Connors no chance to get back. At 5-3 down, the American for the first time showed signs of weakening, 'his ego now clearly bruised by the battering he was taking', Wilson noted. Borg gained another break in the ninth game to take a two-set lead.

Connors, sniffing at a nasal spray during breaks, found hay fever the least of his worries. The sweltering Centre Court was a minefield for him. One false step and viciously struck drives flew past the American whenever he tried to make the net. When Connors stayed back, scrambling along the baseline, Borg either outlasted him or produced crisp, angled shots that left the 1974 champion stranded. Peter Wilson in the *Daily Mirror* compared Connors's plight to 'like trying to fight a man-eating tiger when you have only false teeth'.

In the opening game of the third set, he glimpsed a faint ray of light. When Borg failed to reach an arcing lob, then put a loose backhand into the net, the Swede was broken for the first time. But, as Neil Wilson saw it, 'it was the last shout of a dying man'. Borg's careless lapse was brief. After holding to lead 2-0, Connors's hopes were ruthlessly dashed. Unveiling his whole repertoire, mixing scorching passing shots with delicate drops and deft lobs, Borg won every remaining game. Connors, strangely lacking his usual intensity, appeared to lose interest in the last two games. Save for an occasion when he slammed a ball in the direction of a linesman who he felt had made a bad call, the American hardly hit a shot in anger.

His lack of fire was never more evident than in the seventh game of that last set when, with Borg serving at 40-15, the Swede lashed a backhand to the baseline that Connors merely stared at and made no attempt to return as it landed at his feet. That point gave Borg a 5-2 lead, and he wrapped up victory in the next game by breaking service to love. The final point was bizarre. Borg hit a return off the wood of his racket and Connors, with the whole of his opponent's court to aim at, swiped the ball wildly out to the side. The match, virtually a carbon copy of the rout 12 months earlier, was over in 106 minutes, three minutes faster than the 1978 final.

After a brisk, perfunctory handshake, Connors stomped off court. 'Let's get out of here,' he shouted to his mother, Gloria, after telling an All England Club official where he could stick his 'goddam' tournament. Just four minutes after the match ended, the American, hair dripping with sweat, unshowered and still in tennis attire, leaped into a private, chauffeur-driven Mercedes with his mother as well as his practice partner, Lornie Kuhle, and fled the premises.

He'd even extended his self-imposed non-communication rule to his opponent, failing to congratulate Borg after the crushing defeat. 'What did Jimmy say to you at the end of the match?' Borg was asked. 'Nothing,' he replied. 'We did not speak.'

When his remark as he hurried off was widely quoted in the press, the surly American found himself on the front page of many Fleet Street newspapers once again. The *Daily Telegraph* called Connors's exit 'an ungracious farewell' then dug the knife in deeper. 'But one could sympathise with his chagrin,' sneered Lance Tingay. 'It is hard, to say the least, to have claimed to be the No.1 player in the world, as did Connors with a good deal of justification, and then in the spectacular setting of the world's greatest arena be made to look not much better than a beginner.'

Connors's cold-shouldering of his long-time rival drew condemnation from a compatriot too. Will Grimsley suggested that 'it would have been a nice gesture, don't you think, Jimmy, if … you'd have put a friendly arm around the young Swede's shoulder and said: "Nice match, Bjorn." Even fighters who spend 15 rounds knocking each other's teeth out accord each other that little courtesy, win or lose.'

Against what David Irvine termed 'the relentless onslaught of a man whose genius sparkled like a fistful of diamonds', not even playing up to his optimum was enough for the American. Connors, according to Neil Wilson, 'had drawn on all his old skills and found them insufficient'. He was out-served, out-thought, out-manoeuvred. After years of battling with Borg in search of undisputed supremacy, it appeared that Connors was now finding it hard to keep abreast. The victory on Centre Court was Borg's eighth in their last 11 meetings.

In the view of Ted Green (in the *LA Times*), the competition between the Swede and the American was 'now more revelry than rivalry, and Borg is having all the laughs'. 'They are not contests any longer,' Grimsley opined. 'They are mere warm-ups.' In a match that was supposed to reduce the final to a mere showpiece Borg enjoyed his easiest romp. 'It was like watching Muhammad Ali punching the small bag in the gym,' Grimsley wrote. 'It was John Wayne against the Apaches. It was a thundering freight train going head-on against a runaway rabbit.'

'I just hope I am playing as well for the next four, five, however many years,' Borg said afterwards. He could 'work on some things' he said, like his serve-and-volley game, 'but to improve them even more, that would be difficult.' 'Some of us believe he is wrong,' wrote Neil Wilson. 'It would be impossible.'

The next player to get a chance to tug at Borg's cloak of invincibility was Roscoe Tanner. Having crushed McEnroe, Tim Gullikson faced the

No.5 seed in the quarter-finals, a third meeting with his fellow American, whom he had beaten twice, including a win on grass at Nottingham in 1977. In beating three unseeded players on the way to the last eight – the American Van Winitsky, and Peter McNamara and Ross Case of Australia – Tanner didn't drop a set. He'd only surrendered one in his fourth-round victory over Clerc. And against Gullikson, despite losing the third set on a tiebreak, Tanner was almost always in control, roaring to the finish line in the fourth set to blot out the challenge of the No.15 seed.

It set up a semi-final with Pat DuPré. A long shot few had fancied to get past the first round, the little-known DuPré, after upsetting Gerulaitis, had continued to make a name for himself. America's 28th-ranked player had since beaten Carlos Kirmayr of Brazil, France's Yannick Noah (a 19-year-old) and American Bob Lutz before emerging victorious from an exhausting three-and-a-half-hour cliffhanger with Adriano Panatta.

In the final set with Panatta – who was seeking to become the first player from Italy to reach the last four since Nicola Pietrangeli in 1960 (before losing to Laver) – raucous outbreaks from a couple of hundred voluble Italians in the Centre Court crowd chanting for their favourite fellow countryman forced referee Fred Hoyles to take to the court and appeal for silence. The yelling went on, but the Roman playboy they called 'the Pasta King' began to tire after leading 2-1 in sets and DuPré outlasted him. For the third successive year an unseeded player reached the last four.

There, the rank outsider's fine run came to an end. DuPré was bidding to become the first unseeded player to make the men's final since West German Wilhelm Bungert finished runner-up to Newcombe in 1967. But the Belgian right-hander, once on the same winning 1973 Stanford University tennis team as Tanner, gave the Tennessean few problems on the day. DuPré was cut down, 6-3, 7-6, 6-3.

Ranked in the world's top ten for several years, Tanner was exhibiting the best tennis of his career. The most impressive weapon in his armoury, his serve – once recorded at 153mph – always made him dangerous, but he'd upped his all-round game dramatically over the previous 12 months. Gone, wrote David Irvine, was 'the single-minded determination to blast everyone into oblivion'. His overall play was far more consistent. The key, Tanner outlined, was 'better movement, concentration and confidence'. He wasn't letting the little things bother him anymore, but playing each point on its own merit. His role model: Borg. 'He has the right attitude,' Tanner said of the Swede. 'He never complains and he keeps playing.'

He kept playing and he kept winning. For two days before the final, Tanner's ears were filled with talk of how unbeatable Borg was. The masterful manner in which the defending champion quashed Connors only hardened opinion that he would be far too hot for Tanner to handle. At odds of 6-1, the American was given little chance of pulling off an upset. If past records were anything to go by, the 23-year-old Swede would walk all over the two-times losing semi-finalist. In 11 meetings in eight years with the left-hander, Borg had lost only three (the last time, in the US Pro Indoor 18 months earlier). He'd also won their three previous encounters.

But Wimbledon finals paid little heed to form charts. Neither did the 27-year-old Tanner. For the player nicknamed 'Scoe', facing the Swede held few terrors. His underdog status, he felt, might even work to his advantage. 'All the pressure will be on him [Borg],' Tanner said. He certainly wasn't going to go out thinking he couldn't win. 'If that was the case I might as well take the plane home and send my regards on Saturday.'

Tanner's coach, Dennis Ralston, the US Davis Cup captain since 1972, was also confident of a surprise. 'There is no way that Bjorn Borg is invincible,' he said. 'No man has ever been *that* good.' Ralston, a Wimbledon singles finalist himself in 1966, losing to Manuel Santana, was convinced that Tanner had the arsenal to inflict damage upon Borg. Inevitably, it was that 'now you see it, now you don't' service – 'hard enough to drill a hole in opponents' one American journalist observed – that he and most experts cited as being significant. Tanner would go after Borg, in Bud Collins's words, 'on a lightning serve and a prayer'. With the Centre Court grass harder and drier than at any time in the fortnight, and with several bald, brown patches to exploit, Tanner at full pace was liable to prove more than a handful.

The overwhelming favourite shrugged off suggestions that the result was a mere formality. 'I know some people felt that my match with Connors was virtually the final,' Borg said, 'but it [playing Tanner] could be more difficult than they think.' Prophetic words indeed. On Saturday, 7 July 1979, Leonard Roscoe Tanner the third, grandson of a Tennessee mountain man, came within a few tenuous points of pulling off one of the great upsets of Wimbledon.

In his first Wimbledon final, the blond American, his usually straight hair permed into a tightly curled mop, looked perfectly at home. Showing no nerves whatsoever, the left-hander, in the opening game, outlasted Borg in two rallies, passed the champion with a running forehand, and then delivered a piledriving ace to go 1-0 up.

But Borg, aside from a double fault, was equally impressive in his own first service game and, in the early exchanges, games followed a similar blueprint: both players experiencing little difficulty in holding; if either had to dig himself out of a hole, an almighty serve usually did the spadework.

Knowing that attack was the best way, Tanner threw all he had at Borg. A blazing delivery, a sprint to the net and a crisp volley was a formula he put into practice throughout. He forayed to the net even on his second serve. But it wasn't all wham-bam-thank-you-ma'am tennis; Tanner mixed things up, taking risks that often paid off. 'You can't just pull in everything and play safe against Bjorn,' Tanner said later, 'because he's better than anybody else at that.'

Tanner's tactics put the champion under immense pressure. But Borg gave as good as he got. A capricious, gusting wind made it hard for him to use the lob as a weapon but, with his usual terrific power, he probed relentlessly for an opening. As each player strove for mastery, an all-action encounter of extreme athleticism and hard-hitting developed. Rallies in the real sense were non-existent. It certainly wasn't tennis for the purists.

At 4-5 down and 0-30, Borg was grappling to save the first set. But three big serves and an overhit forehand from the American came to his rescue, and in the next game it was Tanner who ran into even deeper trouble. A magnificent forehand pass that hugged the line gave the top seed break point at 30-40. Tanner, though, provided a prompt and forthright solution: he struck the fourth of the 15 aces he was to project past the Swede and eventually held with a finely anticipated backhand volley.

Taken to deuce on his service for the first time, Borg held in the 12th game but in the tiebreak*, after leading 4-3, the Swede was surprisingly swept aside as Tanner reeled off four successive points. At 4-5 down, Borg volleyed long a fierce service return to hand Tanner set point, and with a perfectly executed forehand lob at which Borg flailed his racket in vain and could only stare sadly at as it glided over his head, the American had drawn first blood. The set took 43 minutes.

If Borg was disturbed, inevitably it didn't show. 'His concentration is so profound that it is almost visible,' wrote Hugh McIlvanney, 'like an insulating cloud around his head.' After the first two games of the second set were exchanged fairly routinely, the Swede took his next service game to love and then, riding on a wave of passing shots and jumping all over

---

* From 1971 to 1978 the 13-point tiebreak was adopted at Wimbledon at eight games all in every set except the fifth in men's matches and the third in ladies' and mixed matches. From 1979 onwards it came into force at six-games-all in all sets except the last.

Tanner's second serve, broke to lead 3-1 as the American balanced another crashing ace with a double fault. Often breaking away from the baseline and beating Tanner at his own volleying game, Borg, now at his regal best, then pocketed the next three games at a cost of only three points and, at one set all, the Centre Court crowd breathed a collective sigh. They had, after all, come to see history being made.

Between sets, Tanner looked at a little notebook at his courtside chair. Dennis Ralston had written down some strategy. Referring to the battle plan did the Tennessean some good. Still recovering after the flurry of Borg punches, after fighting off three break points in the first game with some punishing serves, Tanner took the initiative. In the next game, he broke Borg for the first time before racing to a 3-0 lead.

His serve found its snap again. His volleys were sharp and decisive. Looking fresh and hungry, Tanner came within a point of making it 4-0. Borg saved himself with a typical forehand pass before a volley at the net and an acutely angled cross-court saw him register his first game of the set. But despite having three break points in the seventh game, at 4-2 down, Borg spurned his opportunities; a resolute Tanner held on, and when the next two games went with service, the Swede was behind, two sets to one. History had been put on hold. Amidst the Borg element around the court there was almost a stunned silence.

In *The Art of Lawn Tennis*, another of the books written by Bill Tilden, the former American great stated that, 'The primary object in match tennis is to break up the other man's game.' With a service whose speed Tilden would have admired – on serve, the ball was said to have left Tilden's racket at an astounding 163.6mph – and rapier-like volleys, Tanner was as close to upsetting Borg's rhythm as anyone had in the past four Wimbledons.

An Associated Press journalist likened the left-hander's gallant challenge to 'trying to pull the plug on a computer'. Yet it didn't come out.

Instead, Borg, back on programme in the fourth set, proceeded to disturb Tanner's game, clobbering his second service and extracting unforced errors as the American's play became edgier. The crucial break came in the fourth game. Borg, 40-15 down, fought back to create three deuces before finally taking it when Tanner half-volleyed two consecutive dipping forehand returns out of court. Five games and no breaks later the Swede evened the match.

Looking for a quick advantage in the final set, Borg got it. Serving at 30-40, Tanner moved forward but failed to put away a smash, sending it straight to Borg who, from behind the baseline, whipped a backhand past his opponent for a winner. It was soon 2-0. Tanner had three break points but Borg, spinning deliveries to the American's backhand, staved him off, and the Swede, playing before his parents for only the second time at Wimbledon, appeared to be sitting pretty. He had another good opportunity in the third game when he three times reached break point, but this time Tanner repelled the threat.

Games stayed with service. The tension and emotion mounted. As the crowd roared after every point, the umpire Paul Alderson repeatedly called for quiet. It was imperative for the American to break back. In the eighth game, he came desperately close. Leading 40-15 on Borg's service after a lovely touch volley, his big chance was there. But first, with Borg trapped at the net, Tanner sent a courageous forehand passing shot wide, and then he netted a backhand volley. When the stocky 27-year-old hit an approach too long then was passed by a forehand cross-court, the likes of which only Borg could hit, the Swede finally salvaged the game and led 5-3.

He was obviously tired. His body language betrayed him. 'If he [Tanner] had won that game, there's no way I would win the match,' Borg said later. But after Tanner held, Borg, serving for the Championship, now had history firmly within his grasp. When he reached 40-0 with a backhand pass, he was so moved he forgot the habits of a lifetime and actually slapped his thigh. The occasion's momentousness, though, even got to Borg. The man who, according to the *Sunday Mirror*'s Ken Montgomery, had 'stalagmites where other people have mere nerves' faltered. His knees trembling, his racket arm shaking, he lost power and control. Tanner, with a fine backhand then a volleyed winner, fought off two match points. When Borg made a hash of a forehand volley, it was deuce.

But Borg righted himself. A swinging first serve forced Tanner into a bungled return, and it was match point again. And when Tanner sent a backhand flying wildly beyond the line, the spectacle was at an end. In the competitors' box, Margarethe and Rune fell on each other's shoulders. As noise hit him like a thunderclap, their son knelt on the ground, his arms in the air. Having been, as Mike Lupica put it, 'knocked all over this classy ring called Centre Court' for nearly the entire two hours 49 minutes match, it was perhaps more in relief than joy.

After the euphoria of his win, Borg admitted that the final was his most difficult ever. In those last few points, he'd felt his legs turning to jelly. 'I was too scared to come to the net,' he said. So tense was he, in fact, he could barely hold his racket. 'In that fifth set, all the years of Wimbledon seemed to descend on him, slowing his legs, shortening his groundstrokes,' reported Lupica. 'Borg was like a heavyweight champion, knowing he is ahead on points, barely, trying to hang on, clutching and dancing, trying to keep from being knocked out by a challenger fighting the fight of his life.' The Swede was almost willing himself past Tanner at the end.

Borg modestly proposed that 'Today, maybe, fate was on my side.' But it had taken far more than providence to prevail. 'Borg had to reach down one last majestic time and find the rare ingredients of a champion,' Lupica wrote. 'He had to search for everything, call for it all: guts and heart and nerve and steel. He had to be better than fear at the very end, in the last few games, when he was on the threshold of his singular achievement.' The 23-year-old was once again able to bring these special qualities to bear.

'When I won for the first time in 1976, I never imagined I could do it four times running,' Borg told the press gathering. 'This is the biggest thrill of my life.' When pressed to think of a modern sporting achievement to match his, Borg nominated Belgian cyclist Eddy Merckx and his five wins in the Tour de France. Curry Kirkpatrick suggested that 'probably the Swede's awesome streak in London stacks up more realistically somewhere between the stunning longevity of Muhammad Ali and the instant legend accorded Olympians Bob Beamon in Mexico City and Mark Spitz in Munich'. (Borg was actually due to have dinner with the world heavyweight boxing champion, Ali, as part of a celebration of his latest success.)

Men's tennis had never been so competitive, so deep and rich in talent, yet Borg stood now as a true giant of the sport. 'To be so far ahead of that generation that you are in a class of your own must make Borg unique in the history of tennis,' opined Neil Wilson. The Swede, nonetheless, recognised that he wasn't infallible. The Championships fittingly saved its greatest contest for the finale, but one or two points had made all the difference in a match that arguably hinged on that eighth game of the fifth set. 'One of these days I am going to lose these points,' Borg acknowledged, 'and then …'

Until that eventuality, there were still goals left. Most immediately, another tilt at the grand slam. There was talk of wanting 'to win a lot of big titles and set more records'. One of those he would target at the 1980 Wimbledon. Borg had now won 28 straight matches at The Championships. The following year he'd be seeking to better Rod Laver's record of 31, set by the Australian between 1961 and 1970 (there was a five-year gap in Laver's successes when Wimbledon was closed to professional players). And, of course, looking to extend his sequence of titles to five. The appetite for success was far from satiated.

23 June – 5 July 1980

AS THE halfway point of the first year of the new decade approached, Bjorn Borg was, without doubt, the king of the world of tennis. A man for all seasons and all surfaces, he held superior head-to-head records over all his rivals and, even though he occasionally showed he was only human – suffering the odd shock defeat in a minor tournament – the Swede was just about unbeatable in top competitions. The statistics were staggering. Of the 80 singles matches he'd played since his triumphant leave-taking of Centre Court on 7 July 1979, Borg had lost only two. He hadn't been beaten by a right-hander since 1977. Borg's awesome shadow loomed so large that, as Rod Laver pointed out, 'many of his opponents feel beaten before they start a match against him'. He seemed now to be at the very apogee of his powers.

'What is it that makes this shy, athletic young man such a formidable competitor?' asked John Barrett, now an established BBC television commentator, in a *Radio Times* preview of the 1980 Wimbledon. 'Never in the 103-year history of championship tennis has a man achieved so much so young as Bjorn Borg.' Borg was blessed with that intangible something that sets apart the very best in any sport. 'Nobody has found out what it is,' said Fred Perry. 'Guts, fitness, concentration, determination. Apparently, it's a gift.'

No player had been studied more closely. An eminent Boston surgeon, Dr Carter Rowe, had even written about him in the venerable *New England Journal of Medicine*. The Swede, he concluded, was an almost flawless athlete who used nearly every muscle in his body, harmoniously, on virtually every shot. 'If a computer were asked to design a perfect tennis player,' wrote Reuters correspondent Jon Henderson, 'it would almost certainly come up with a man like Bjorn Borg.' Borg, he said, 'possesses a blend of temperament and skill that has enabled him to come closer than any other player to turning winning tennis matches into an exact science'.

With his astonishingly low regular pulse rate – in Henderson's view, 'perhaps the most significant clue to why Borg is able to confront a crisis on the tennis court with such languid calm' – and blood pressure of 70 over 30, Borg was undeniably a physiological phenomenon. 'If it wasn't for his slightly hippy appearance one could almost think that Bjorn Borg was a reject humanoid from the latest Hollywood sci-fi spectacular,' purported a writer of an article about the Swede in *Saab Scene* entitled 'The Million Dollar Man'. To Thomas Boswell of the *Washington Post* a creature from Greek mythology sprang to mind: Borg's close-set eyes, he wrote, 'must make him seem like a Cyclops to opponents'.

His fellow stars on the touring circuit attributed extraterrestrial qualities to the super Swede. 'He must have come from outer space,' said José Luis Clerc. 'He cannot be of this world,' agreed Spaniard José Higueras. Never mind Borg hailing from a different galaxy, to give everyone else a chance Nastase suggested 'they should send him away to another planet!' We play tennis,' the Romanian said. 'He plays something else.'

Borg's on-court strategy was straightforward. He wanted his opponent to make the mistakes. 'My style of play is based on one simple principle –

elimination of error,' he said. 'I always try to play a safe game, to make the other guy take the risk.' There were no stupid strokes or miracle shots. If you saw the ball dance dangerously on the sideline or baseline after leaving his racket, it was a mishit, he claimed. The Swede was 'like a pawnbroker', according to Nastase. 'He doesn't give any points away. Never.' 'When he's playing badly, he'll just hit the ball a little higher and shorter, but it's always over the net,' Vitas Gerulaitis said.

Against all types of opponents, the bedrock of Borg's tennis – his exaggerated but totally dependable topspin groundstrokes – was essentially the same. On slow-bouncing clay and fast grass alike, Borg was usually content to slug away from the backcourt. 'It sounds like a contradiction,' said Ion Tiriac, 'but what makes Borg so tough is his lack of diversity. He knows two things – backhands and forehands. He can't get confused wondering when he should serve or volley or attack.' 'The reason Borg is No.1,' offered John McEnroe, 'is that he says, "This is the way I play. Come and beat me if you can." He's not going to change his game and he's not going to beat himself. That's part of the mental aspect of being a champion.'

Only when he was behind did he really gamble. 'I say, "I am going to lose" and I start hitting out more,' Borg explained. 'This native daring unnerves opponents,' argued Boswell. 'Since they think of Borg as essentially defensive and patient, it stuns them to see him attack wildly and successfully. They sense that they have unwittingly pricked the lion's paw.' In those rare but inevitable moments when he had to go for broke, rather than become paralysed by anxiety, Borg displayed an almost casual manner. 'Maybe that's the way he combats nervousness, with nonchalance when he's in danger,' McEnroe proposed.

In tiebreaks and other key games, too, Borg had the uncanny knack of lifting his game on the most important points. When others crashed,

Borg soared. 'I think probably I was born with that,' said the Swede. Lesser mortals were overawed by his tremendous belief in himself. There was a total refusal to consider defeat. 'My greatest point is my persistence,' he said. 'I never give up in a match. However down I am, I fight until the last ball. My list of matches shows that I have turned a great many so-called irretrievable defeats into victories.'

In the *New York Times*'s Neil Amdur's opinion, it was the concentration, more than any other factor, which was 'the key that unlocks Borg's treasures'. Another writer likened it to that of 'a grand master chessman'. Borg, in *My Life and Game*, revealed that the question most asked of him was: how did he remain so impassive on court and never seem to get upset or flustered over bad calls or if he felt an opponent cheated? It was, of course, an act – one he'd been perfecting since his early teens. 'You know,' he'd told Jay Teitel in 1978, 'they're always saying, "He's not emotional, he has this ice in his veins." But inside I feel it. I feel excited or nervous, or angry, sure.' Yet somehow he still preserved an inscrutable air. Behind the granite face his feelings stayed hidden. He had 'a special talent for masking them', stated Vitas Gerulaitis. 'I've never seen him change his expression in all the matches I've watched him play.' Finding him impossible to read, his foes were all the more intimidated.

'I still wouldn't say he's invincible,' Roscoe Tanner had declared in the aftermath of the Wimbledon final. That autumn under Flushing Meadows' floodlights, the American backed up his belief, wreaking a swift revenge for his loss by knocking out Borg in a dramatic, hard-fought quarter-final at the US Open before he himself was eliminated by Gerulaitis who went on to lose the final to John McEnroe. Another Grand Slam dream had been quickly quashed.

Borg did break his New York jinx, though. In January 1980, playing on the indoor carpet courts at Madison Square Garden, he claimed a first

(Colgate) Grand Prix Masters title from the strongest and most select field ever assembled. It was acclaimed as one of the great performances of the past decades. In five days of round-robin matches, he saw off Tanner, Connors, Higueras, McEnroe and Gerulaitis, a merciless Borg and his explosive topspin doing a 6-2, 6-2 demolition job on his practice partner in the final. According to Gerulaitis afterwards, there was no longer tennis's big three. 'There's the rest of us,' he said. 'Then there's Bjorn.'

In May, a month before the French Open, Guillermo Vilas, winner of his second Australian Open earlier in the year, had upset Borg in the Nations Cup on clay in Dusseldorf, West Germany. It was the Wimbledon champion's first defeat in 50 consecutive singles matches. But in Paris, where he turned 24, Borg left yet another indelible mark in the record books. After routinely ripping apart Gerulaitis again – scoring a 6-4, 6-1, 6-2 victory in the final – Borg, winning for an unprecedented third straight year, became the first player to be crowned the French Open champion five times, surpassing the record of Henri Cochet, victorious on four occasions since the tournament became international in 1925. It was Cochet, now 78, who presented the Swede with the trophy. Asked if the former champion had any congratulatory remarks, Borg replied, 'Well, he didn't look too happy. He said, "Well done", that's all.'

Even though 17 of the world's top 20 players were competing, including eight of the top ten and all of the top five, Borg, just as in 1978, had taken the top prize – around $53,000 – without losing a set. Only two players got as many as four games off him in any one set. American journalist Ted Green argued that, in some respects, Borg's achievements at Roland Garros were more amazing than his record at Wimbledon because 'there are no cheap points' in the French Open. 'Every rally is a potential marathon.' Whatever the surface, another American writer, Tom Loomis, had a clear message for anyone who questioned Borg's position at the top of the tennis tree. 'When are they going to admit that the Swedish stylist will win 19 of 20 matches if they play them on the deck of an aircraft carrier?'

According to Thomas Boswell, 'for a tennis player to be the best on Earth on both clay and grass might be comparable to a track man being able to win the 100-metre dash and the 1500-metre run in the Olympics'. Yet, with his unrivalled prowess on the hot, red Parisian clay and a similar invincibility at Wimbledon, Borg was just that. It was his incomparable mastery at the All England Club, nonetheless, that was all the more intriguing to the writer. 'Perhaps the most puzzling brain teaser in tennis,' Boswell wrote, 'is why Borg has had his greatest triumphs, has built the cornerstone of his reputation as perhaps the greatest player in history, in the one place, and on the one surface – grass – that should suit him least.' With its attack-favouring bounce, grass was the surface on which Borg, with his 'ingrained preference for counterattack' really should have been most vulnerable.

Year after year, his peers, too, were amazed that he could build such an incredible streak. 'Most of us thought it was a kind of fluke the first time he won Wimbledon in 1976,' said Arthur Ashe. 'Hell, nobody in 30 years had been able to win on grass from the baseline hitting topspin the way he does.' Yet under conditions that seemed to Boswell 'antithetical both to his style of play and his basic temperament' Borg had outshone them all and made Centre Court what Boswell termed his 'personal celebratory kneeling ground'.

Now, at the first Wimbledon of the new decade, after four years of majestic rule, the Swede was aiming for a royal flush last achieved at what an Associated Press writer called 'this ancient grass-court extravaganza' by Laurie Doherty between 1902 and 1906. Compared with the Englishman's success – Doherty's first was in the year after Queen Victoria died when gentlemen in white flannels played a very different game and tennis was but a polite diversion for ladies and gentlemen, his five successive titles encompassing only a ten-match winning run – Borg's would be a feat almost defying comprehension. Borg never needed motivating for what he regarded as the greatest championship of all but, as someone who thrived upon statistical ambition, he was very mindful of the milestone another success would see him reach.

The four-times champion had turned the esteemed event, Ted Green wrote, into 'his own private lawn party', an 'annual Bjorn Borg Invitational', and 'you wouldn't blame the 127 other players for wishing that Borg would spend the next two weeks someplace else. Maybe in Sweden. Or in traction.' On its June 1980 front cover, *Time* magazine called him 'The Incredible Tennis Machine'. Could anyone put a spanner in the works?

Of all the 'stop-Borg candidates' (as Green called them) McEnroe still seemed the most well equipped. Borg himself considered the American left-hander's hard, skidding serve as 'the best' in the business but knew that McEnroe possessed many more threats. 'He is incredibly fast,' he wrote in *My Life and Game*. 'Great power volley plus touch with a flipping wrist. He can drop volley on both sides. It sounds strange but he has more touch than Nastase. He is a master of the unexpected. I can never anticipate his shots.' McEnroe, Borg said, was the only pro who possessed 'radar eyes'.

After his last two Wimbledons, McEnroe had perhaps yet to show he could cope with the demands of a two-week major tournament, but in September he'd cleared that hurdle by taking the title at Flushing Meadows, the local boy making good when dispatching his Queens neighbour Gerulaitis in the final. (It meant a lot to McEnroe. Gerulaitis, like Borg, had been an inspiration to him – they'd grown up close together – and McEnroe viewed Gerulaitis as a 'cool' figure, a tennis rock star he sought to emulate.) In 1979, in total, McEnroe won ten Grand Prix tournaments.

However, 1980 hadn't been that successful thus far. He'd already lost 12 times, including a third-round defeat in the French Open to the vastly improved Australian Paul McNamee, using his new two-handed backhand, in what was regarded as the best match of the entire tournament. McEnroe was susceptible to injuries – he'd had problems with his wrist and ankle in Paris – and, some said, his serve had deserted him.

But the American had served clear notice that he was more than primed for the forthcoming 12-day assault course on Wimbledon's grass, blazing through the Queen's Club tournament without dropping a single set as he easily defended his title. Rather than taking things gently, McEnroe regarded remaining in that competition as long as possible as the ideal Wimbledon tune-up. 'So I figured the best thing was to win it,' he said. Even his temper had been under control. Knowing it could only enhance his prospects, he was once again making a determined effort to live down his 'Superbrat' image. 'It'll have to be a really bad call before I complain,' McEnroe promised.

Fate seemed to be favouring Borg as Wimbledon began. With Vilas out of action, recuperating from an appendicitis operation, and Harold Solomon and Yannick Noah, seeded 11 and 12 respectively, missing through injury, the obstacles between the defending champion and the Holy Grail of five titles on the bounce were reduced. None of Borg's early opponents looked capable, as one British observer put it, of making him 'soil a sweatband'. The top five seedings were the same as the previous year, but McEnroe, Connors and Tanner were all congregated in the other, bottom half of the draw where what Randall Northam in the *Glasgow Herald* called 'the sound and the fury' would mostly be. 'That they will bash each other into submission before they come up against the serene Swede seems very likely,' predicted Northam.

Connors, as Ted Green put it, 'hasn't beaten Borg in a month of Sundays and doesn't seem to believe he can any more'. He'd had mixed fortunes ahead of Wimbledon. After convincingly beating McEnroe to take the

WCT final in Dallas at the beginning of May – without Borg's attendance –
he then lost to Vijay Amritraj a week later in the Tournament of Champions,
a competition he was expected to win. The title went to Gerulaitis who beat
McEnroe in the final. Of Borg's main rivals only Gerulaitis, who'd recently
lost to Kim Warwick, and a freak wind in the semi-finals at the Queen's
Club, featured in the defending champion's half of the draw, and Borg had
crushed him 16 times without one loss.

'There is no reason why Borg should lose,' forecast Rex Bellamy in *The
Times*, 'unless it be illness, injury, or the exciting distraction of his wedding
arrangements.' On 24 July 1980, Borg was set to face up to another challenge
in his young life: marriage. After four years together, he and Mariana, his
devoted globetrotting companion, were to wed in a brief civil ceremony in
the Bucharest town hall followed by a private religious ceremony for 200
family and close friends at a small church, Caldarusani Monastery, outside
the Romanian capital. The following day, they would leave for Monaco, and
elaborate re-enactments for business acquaintances and more casual friends
at the famed *Regine's* in Monte Carlo, a commercial venture, and Marbella
(where he maintained an apartment). Borg was, he said, trying to put his
upcoming nuptials to the back of his mind, but confessed that Mariana
'reminds me all the time [about it]'.

The Swede's razor had been superstitiously put away and the customary
stubble was sprouting on his chin, although Mariana wasn't too keen on an
unshaven fiancé – 'She does not like it,' Borg told reporters, 'but she has no
choice' – but his preparations had, by his own admission, been less thorough
than in the previous four years, rain having cut into his fortnight's practice.
So, it was little surprise that the still-single man approached the 'gentlemen's
singles' (as it was known in Wimbledon's precise and proper parlance) on the
back of his traditional speech that he feared his opening two matches having
not yet had a chance to accustom his game to the tricks played by grass.

Radio Times's David Hunn acknowledged Borg's Achilles heel. 'Never mind the final,' wrote Hunn, 'it is the first day that provides the giants of Wimbledon with their most critical test. Then, in those green and early hours, the axes of the eager young woodsmen are likely to fell the mightiest of trees. None is safe.' The eager young woodsman confronting the Swede this year was not so tender in years.

In 1974, Ismail El Shafei, the man whom an 18-year-old Borg said he was 'killed by', had been a talented opponent with a penchant for playing well against the world's best. 'But,' Rex Bellamy wrote, 'whereas Borg's precocity has improved like a good wine, [El] Shafei's is no more than a few fading pages in a family album.' Now 32, nearing semi-retirement and looking portlier than in the past, the Egyptian, who'd been playing Wimbledon since 1963, had even had the indignity of needing to qualify for the first time.

Nevertheless, El Shafei was still considered as one of the most dangerous 'floaters' in recent years, and while initially stunned when he learned that Borg would be his opening opponent – 'He's the last man I wanted to meet' – ever the professional, he soon struck an optimistic tone. 'I am not without hope,' El Shafei said. 'Borg has always had trouble in the early rounds, and he doesn't like left-handers like me.' His half-full glass would soon be empty.

A match Borg might have feared proved to be an ideal nerve settler. The Swede was seldom at the top of his game but, in truth, didn't need to be. Borg handled the conditions and his adversary with assurance, easing to victory with scarcely a concern. What was surprising was not the outcome but the style with which it was achieved. Deciding that the grass was too soft and slippery underfoot, rather than setting up camp on the baseline, Borg turned himself into virtually a serve-and-volley specialist – a highly accomplished one. 'The passing shot had to be perfect and the ball was staying low, so I came in more,' he explained afterwards.

Before a sell-out crowd, with all seat reservations booked up four months in advance, it took Borg just 20 minutes to take the first set. At 3-2 ahead, the Swede made the first break in the sixth game, the Egyptian failing with a low volley at 0-40, and then proceeded to wrap up the set with the loss of only three points on his own service. It began to look, reported Randall Northam, 'as if El Shafei would be brushed aside like a Cairo bluebottle'.

But light, irritating drizzle was falling through most of the play, and when it grew heavier as the set ended, the umpire called a halt. The restart was delayed by over two and a half hours. When play resumed, Borg seemed less sure of himself, toiling to hold his service in the early games of the second set. A relaxed El Shafei showed some delightful touches. Still, he wasn't able to string them together. Only when he got his first service in did he look capable of extending the match. One whiplash serve in the opening game of the set saw Borg's racket practically disintegrate in his hands, shattered into five pieces as he took a roundhouse swing at the ball. 'I have broken rackets before, as many as ten in a match, but never like this,' he said later. It made little difference. The champion swapped his splintered weapon for a new one – one of 30 spares that he carried around – and though the Egyptian mounted a positive challenge, with Borg battling through five deuce points to hold his service in the second game, he threw away any chances to break with more sloppy volleying. Borg escaped each time and having worked the cold out of his muscles took a 3-2 lead by breaking El Shafei's service with a glorious backhand return.

Now smoothly into his stride, hitting with precision, from that point on Borg raced away, not faltering until 5-2 up in the third set when he dropped service for the only time in the match, uncharacteristically netting four consecutive volleys. At 5-4, after wasting two match points, he served out the match to complete a 6-3, 6-4, 6-4 victory. Rain apart, the gentle exercise took him an hour and 29 minutes.

On a rain-ruined opening day, with no play until the early evening on all but the two main show courts, only a handful of the men's matches were completed, but all four top seeds were among those that beat the inclement weather – all enjoying clear-cut wins. McEnroe, a long-standing ankle injury taped up (only 'so I don't turn it over') easily overcame what on paper looked like a tough assignment, routing the rugged 6ft 4in power-serving Californian Butch Walts. Connors stampeded over Richard Lewis on No.2 Court, conceding only four games to the Briton, while Gerulaitis had little difficulty sweeping past Sweden's Stefan Simonsson. Of the seeds, only Victor Amaya, seeded 14 this year, was a first-round faller.

The biggest winner of the first day was the weather. One downpour followed another. When play resumed for a time later in the afternoon, many with Centre Court tickets had already gone home early, giving up hope of seeing more action. On the outside courts, sturdy souls sheltered under umbrellas and Mackintoshes, unwilling to abandon their front-row places. For those who put up with the appalling conditions there was consolation in the traditional Wimbledon fare: strawberries and cream, champagne (in a bottle or a glass), smoked salmon sandwiches and hotdogs. But little tennis. Ticket touts flourished as always.

On the second day there was no let-up. It was downright soggy. Fits of showers wreaked havoc with the schedule. A heavy backlog of matches soon built up. Many began but it was only a matter of time before players had to seek refuge. 'It's damp, dreary and depressing,' moaned Brian Teacher from the players' restaurant as he stared up at yet another huge threatening black cloud overhead. Schoolgirls gathered outside, hoping to spot a famous face or two or grab a scribbled autograph. 'There's even a saying among Britons here,' mused an American newsman, 'that to have "Wimbledon weather" means blue skies and sunshine.' In recent years, though, with The Championships losing more and more days to rain, 'Wimbledon weather' was becoming the sort more suited to ducks.

It rained so much for the first two days that, by Wednesday when the sun showed its face at last, briefly, half the first-round matches were still to be completed. One witty journalist suggested a new name for The Championships: 'Swimbledon'. The tournament was experimenting with the latest in gadgetry. For the first time at Wimbledon – in place on the Centre and No.1 courts only – a 'magic eye' was being used, an electronic line monitor, there to help linesmen decide if a service was in or out. The device's multiple black boxes bleeped a 'fault' warning into the linesman's ear when a serve landed outside the service box. But with all the foul weather, the fault detectors were threatening to gurgle instead of bleep.

On Thursday, with play moved up to noon, the weather got even worse with thunderstorms, lightning and even hailstones hitting SW19 – a capacity crowd scattering in the mad dash to find cover when the storm broke, with several spectators fainting in the crush – and much of the play drowned out once more. The possibility of the tournament being forced into a third week became very real. The last time it had happened was in 1963 when the men's singles final was held over to a Monday.

Before the hailstorm, Connors, looking in a menacing mood, destroyed doubles expert Sherwood Stewart, losing just three games to the durable if unexciting fellow American. After scowling his way to the semi-finals the previous year, refusing to give interviews, Connors was exhibiting a far more relaxed air off court, giving freely of his time to both fans and media. 'Last year was difficult for me,' he admitted. An uptight Connors had been 'a bit edgy' in 1979, 'worried about my wife and the baby she was carrying'.

In October 1978, Connors had married Patti McGuire, a former *Playboy* magazine centrefold, in Japan. Their son, Brett, was born on 1 August 1979. The responsibilities of fatherhood, the 27-year-old claimed, had made Connors a gentler, more patient man. However, the firebrand had no intention of cooling down on court. 'I let out my emotions, sure,' he said, 'but I relieve my tensions that way.' Borg and he had 'different ways of approaching things', he said. 'I do not tick the same way.'

With the Thursday rain, Borg didn't have the chance to tick at all. One of the 75 casualties was his second-round match with the virtually unknown Shlomo Glickstein. Glickstein, described by Philip Howard in *The Times* as 'a large, solid kind of player, with legs like the cedars of Lebanon', had spent barely 12 months on the tennis circuit after serving three years as a sergeant in the Israeli army. He'd taken a set off McEnroe in Stockholm. Grass courts, though, were 'as familiar to him as a sandy desert would be to an Eskimo' wrote Associated Press journalist Geoffrey Miller. He'd only played on the surface six times before.

Glickstein had earned his unexpected date with the defending champion after causing a minor upset against former world top-ten-ranking Raul Ramirez the day before, saving two match points in the fourth set to battle back and defeat the Mexican in a 53-game five-setter – an event that led a reporter from the *Jerusalem Post* to leap from his seat crying, 'We have waited 2,000 years for this day.'

The first Israeli to win a major singles title, having captured the Australian Hard Court Championships, Glickstein outlined his long-term ambitions: 'I want to win as many matches as possible, play in as many countries as possible, and be a good ambassador for Israel,' he told reporters. He saw the forthcoming match with the Swede as 'a great opportunity' but feared the worst. 'It's a dream, which will turn into a nightmare,' he predicted. 'I feel I am going to the scaffold.'

The adverse weather gave Glickstein a reprieve, but his escape from the noose was only temporary. The following day, after almost four days of enforced idleness, a typically clinical Borg eased his way to a 6-3, 6-1, 7-5 victory, his ice-cool character lifting him through a tricky third set when the Israeli held service against three break points to go 5-4 up at one point.

Games went with serve in the first set to three-all, when Borg, in Howard's words, hit a patch of 'the sort of thunderous tennis that Thor plays in Valhalla with skulls for balls'. Glickstein won only three points in the next six games. Borg struck three aces in one game alone. In the third set, Glickstein, playing some delicate strokes, particularly stop volleys that left even Borg stranded, had several opportunities to break. He engaged Borg in some enchantingly fast rallies. But the champion's class and power ultimately told. 'He played well, and will surely improve,' the Swede said of his opponent.

That Friday, after four days of more splashes than smashes, the sun came out – and stayed out. But on a damaged and still slippery No.3 court, McEnroe walked a tenuous tightrope against Sydney-born Terry Rocavert – and nearly toppled from the tournament. The blond, handsome Rocavert, primed by a five-set first-round conquest of Roger Taylor, almost didn't make it to the court on time – the car sent to pick him up went to the wrong address – and he only arrived (via a taxi from Bayswater) ten minutes before the match without any time to warm up. It didn't show. The talented 25-year-old, who'd given Connors and Vilas tough matches in the past, found himself two sets to one up and came within three points of ousting the No.2 seed in the fourth set, McEnroe serving to stay in the match at 4-5 and 5-6.

As the going got rough, the American, looking, wrote Australian Lenore Nicklin, 'rather like a sulky cherub', reverted to some of the belligerent behaviour he'd become famous for, but eventually grabbed his chances and scurried home, finally seeing off the plucky Aussie 6-3 in the fifth set. The self-effacing Rocavert, ranked 112th in the world, had been so certain of losing, instead of letting his wife Kay watch the match, he sent her to buy his airline tickets for a Saturday flight. He was undone, he lamented, by his own lack of belief in his ability to win.

McEnroe was just relieved. It was 'certainly not one of my best days', he admitted. The variable bounce on a surface more like clay than grass had been a chief reason, McEnroe almost required a shovel rather than a tennis racket to dig himself out of trouble and the American argued that 'Borg might have a lot tougher time if he had to play on the outer courts.' 'I am not complaining and I don't want it to sound like sour grapes,' McEnroe stressed, 'but I would be happy if he played outside [the show courts] occasionally.'

The men's event continued to go according to expectations. All 15 of the remaining seeds made the third round, though Gerulaitis experienced problems on the infamous No.2 Court (now with seating extended to ground level) in getting past Sashi Menon of India in four sets. Surprisingly, one of the names still in the hat was that of Ilie Nastase. The stormy petrol of tennis, absent in 1979 through injury, actually came to Wimbledon harbouring hopes of making a bid for the title; he'd even put in several weeks of practice on grass beforehand. 'Too bad I do not work this much when I am young,' he said after defeating Britain's John Feaver in three sets in the first round, when both his artistic strokes and his clowning delighted the watching crowd.

But trouble still followed Nastase around. Hounded all week by the British media about his impending divorce from Belgian wife Dominique – the tabloids had splashed the breakup of their eight-year marriage all over the front pages and posted photos of the player appearing at the tournament one day with Miss United Kingdom, Carolyn Seaward – as Nastase completed a two-day rain-interrupted victory in five sets over Dick Stockton, the combustible Romanian exploded. Rushing from No.1 Court, a news reporter, John Passmore of the *Daily Mail*, pursued him.

There was a brush resulting in Passmore's spectacles falling to the floor and losing a lens before Nastase's bodyguard, a 17-stone Italian nicknamed 'Bambino', quickly stepped in to defuse the situation and hustle the player back to the locker room.

Nastase declined to comment on the incident publicly but told intimates that Passmore had been pressing for an interview – even at the player's hotel (the fashionable Gloucester Hotel, where many of the top stars were staying) – and he had merely gestured to the reporter to leave him alone. 'I didn't say anything to him,' Passmore insisted. 'He pushed his hand against my neck and I reeled back.'

Whatever the truth, the incident gained added importance because Nastase was involved. For all his tantrums and tirades, the Romanian, who once said he'd paid more in fines that he'd taken in prize money, could still be an exciting performer. Sadly, reminders of his more successful past were infrequent. A virtual washout on the pro circuit for a few years, Nastase had gone steadily downhill on the performance ladder and was now a lowly 64th in the rankings, just another journeyman player. 'Erosion of his magnificent game,' wrote an Associated Press journalist, 'has been one of the real tragedies of sport.'

Nastase's love life at least offered some glamour in a week of what was otherwise very glum news. The highest unemployment figures since the war were announced; the pollen count was up and the rain kept coming down in buckets. It was the wettest June in Britain in 101 years. The shopkeepers in the nation of shopkeepers were even starting their summer sales early.

It was on another cold, dark and wet day that Borg played his third-round match, against the big-hitting Australian Rod Frawley. A 28-year-old from Brisbane, Frawley had once given up tennis for four years – teaching in Frankfurt during that time – dismayed at how little was being done for young Australian players by the Lawn Tennis Association of

Australia. At Wimbledon, he'd eased past Borg's compatriot Per Hjertquist though only made the third round after taking the fifth set of his match with American Tony Graham, 13-11.

Having watched Borg when playing for Australia with John Alexander in the Nations Cup – studying the angles of the Swede's serve and strokes – Frawley had given a lot of thought to his game plan for their encounter. It worked quite well at times. In the fading light on No.1 Court, the player ranked 53rd in the world became the first player to take a set off Borg all week.

Frawley, in the first set, struggled to hold serve but fought on and only lost it after an unlucky net cord gave Borg an advantage. In the second set, he broke Borg to love with a final forehand pass on the run to lead 4-2, but immediately lost his own service, and when trailing 5-2 in a tiebreak after games went to 6-6, seemed doomed to a swift defeat. It was then he played his finest tennis. After saving set point at 7-8 with a backhand half-volley played inches over the net, Frawley took the set 10-8 with a backhand pass.

But it came at a price. 'That tiebreak took a lot out of me,' he said later. After his moment of agony, Borg roared back to take the third set, 6-1, and, at 5-4 in the fourth set, served for the match having made a critical break in the seventh game. The suspense was prolonged a little longer; the Swede dropping his serve to 15, as Frawley passed him, Borg double-faulted, and Frawley followed up with two more winners to level at 5-5.

But Borg, calmness personified, came right back. Three passes – one Frawley could only volley into the net – earned Borg three break points and though Frawley saved two, Borg then produced a fourth pass that the Australian stretched in vain to retrieve. It was the champion's ability to place his shots in a foot-wide space between player and line that really made the difference. The top seed then served out to love and a testing workout against an opponent who refused to surrender ended 6-4, 6-7, 6-1,

7-5. Borg, never prone to overstatement, admitted that the two hours 51 minutes battle had been 'very, very hard'.

It was a Saturday of fine Australian achievements. Though Paul McNamee failed in a brave attempt to control a rampant Roscoe Tanner, who'd earlier put out Czech Jiri Hrebec and John Fitzgerald, Phil Dent beat No.8 seed Victor Pecci while 35-year-old Colin Dibley won against tenth seed Ivan Lendl (the 20-year-old from Prague whom Borg had stated 'could be the next best player' to emerge from the ranks of rapidly rising young stars).

All top seven seeds advanced but others came to a full stop. Americans Stan Smith (No.15) and Pat DuPré (No.9), and 16th-seeded José Luis Clerc all saw their dreams perish, their exits leaving only eight of the original 16 seeds in the last 32. Nastase's Wimbledon was over too. In an absorbing clash on No.1 Court against seventh-seeded Peter Fleming, a 6ft 5in blond from Chatham, New Jersey, he displayed patches of brilliance but ultimately the 33-year-old's artistry was subdued. Nastase was knocked out in a dramatic four-setter.

Fleming's doubles partner also progressed. After getting the fright of his young life in the second round, McEnroe, his serve working as regular as clockwork in the first and third sets, had a far less terrifying outing, dispatching Tom Okker 6-0, 7-6, 6-1. Against the slightly built Dutchman, aside from a second set that eventually went to a tiebreak, and during which the American's temper grew shorter the longer it went on, McEnroe's chief worry was the intermittent light rain. Several times the umpire ordered the players to continue despite appealing gestures by the second seed.

The delays and interruptions in the week had been unsettling. 'You sit around waiting all the time, and you don't know when you're going on,' an inconvenienced McEnroe grumbled. 'I know Wimbledon is considered a great tournament along with the US Open, but who wants to play tennis in the wet?'

With matches squeezed in on successive days, it meant a heavy slog for most players. Connors, a round behind the rest of the men, complained about the match scheduling, arguing that 'they could have put a men's best-of-five match [his] on at the start of the day and a women's best-of-three later … But what do I know about scheduling? I just play tennis.' When he did get down to just playing tennis, the American had to overcome dogged resistance from Heinz Peter Gunthardt, losing an opening tiebreak before emerging from a tangle in four sets.

The second week began with a backlog of 70 matches. Both the men's and women's singles were down to the last 16 rather than the quarter-finals, which would have been normal, and those survivors that had battled through had done so on damp and treacherous courts. Borg now had a new record in his sights. With his win over Frawley, he'd equalled Laver's record of 31 straight victories at Wimbledon. He'd set his heart on eclipsing it. The obstacle in his path was Balazs Taroczy.

Normally a clay-court player with a patient, disciplined game, the right-hander, Hungary's top-ranked performer since 1973, had adapted well to the grass and set up the fourth-round meeting with Borg by beating young Ramesh Krishnan, son of Ramanathan Krishnan, a semi-finalist twice in the 1960s. The Indian, who'd emulated an achievement of his father's by winning the Wimbledon junior title in 1979, had disposed of Mark Cox in the second round, which, with the defeats of Buster Mottram and Andrew Jarrett at the same stage, meant that no British male made the third-round draw.

However, Borg's date with destiny was delayed. Scheduled to be the fourth match on Centre Court, the 24-year-old's clash with Taroczy fell victim to yet more rain, which washed out the second half of Monday's programme and then most of Tuesday's also. When it eventually went ahead, on a greasy, slow No.1 Court, Borg, undeterred by the cool, misty rain, looked in a hurry to get history-making; he raced through the first set in just 17 minutes. At 5-4 down in the second, he appeared to be near a faltering point but, before the watching journalists had time to worry about how to spell the Hungarian's name, the Swede laid such notions to rest, serving superbly to blitz through the next three games.

Under the darkening clouds, Taroczy's challenge dimmed. Borg went 5-1 up in the third set and though, in the seventh game, the 26-year-old from Budapest survived a match point at 30-40 on his serve, Borg earned his unique place in Wimbledon folklore in the next game, holding for victory and given a standing ovation as he cracked Laver's record.

Goals remained a vital part of Borg's tennis life. 'I always put something in front of me,' he explained. 'Then I try to achieve it.' Supplanting the man in the history books that he regarded as one of the greatest players of all time gave the Swede enormous satisfaction. 'When I was nine and started playing tennis, Laver was my idol,' Borg said in an impromptu testimonial. 'Until I was 15, everybody was talking about Laver. To beat this kind of record, especially when Laver is involved, is why it means so much to me.'

Borg's 6-1, 7-5, 6-2 stroll, over in just 90 minutes, wasn't one to live long in the memory but it was good enough to carry him into the quarter-finals. There he was joined by 21-year-old McEnroe, and Connors. McEnroe had faced yet more frustration with the British climate. On Monday, in a serve-and-volley duel with few rallies, he took the first two sets against Kevin Curren, the South African qualifier playing only his third tournament on grass. But heavy rain meant that when McEnroe sewed up victory, twice taken to a tiebreak by the 22-year-old with the dynamite serve who'd earlier blitzed Brian Teacher, the match ended 26 hours after it began. And the weather was still miserable. 'I have played in worse conditions but not in a major tournament,' McEnroe said. 'It was raining pretty hard at times and I began to wonder what I was doing out there. We'll probably have snow next.'

Connors earned his passport to the last eight after edging Hank Pfister in four sets but another American's progress came to a juddering halt. Taken to four sets by Bruce Manson, Vitas Gerulaitis was surprisingly beaten in a five-set thriller by 13th-seeded Wojciech Fibak. In the first round, Fibak had been two sets and 5-1 down, saving three match points, before squeezing past Mark Edmondson. And against the No.4 seed, the Polish doubles expert again staged a remarkable recovery, making up a two-set deficit before finally securing a major upset 8-6 in the fifth set. Gerulaitis, who'd beaten Fibak in five sets in Paris, double-faulted 12 times as he went down.

Gene Mayer provided Borg's next hurdle. In October 1978, a fall from a horse in Hawaii had left the 6ft-tall American bedridden for weeks and nearly ended his career. But despite that and a string of injuries – 'He seems more accessible to bodily harm than anyone since Chevy Chase,' wrote Curry Kirkpatrick – Mayer was one of the most improved players on the circuit in recent months and he'd jumped into the world's top ten. Playing together with his brother, Sandy, whenever their schedules permitted, he was also part of one of the game's stellar doubles partnerships. In 1979, they won the French Open, which Gene had won the year before with Hank Pfister.

Seeded sixth at Wimbledon, Mayer was regarded as a good outside bet, his forehand considered by some of his fellow pros as being one of the strongest in the game. Among his victims were Adriano Panatta and Colin Dibley (Mayer coming from 2-1 down in sets against the veteran Aussie). But there was to be no Wednesday surprise. In all three sets, Borg appeared to have trouble slipping into top gear, especially after taking a tumble in racing to the net in the first game of the second set when he immediately served two double faults to drop service. But after Mayer broke the Swede's service to jump to 2-0 leads each time, the 24-year-old New Yorker faltered. Borg overcame the sluggish starts to break back and forge ahead, eventually chalking up a 7-5, 6-3, 7-5 triumph.

Playing with an oversized Prince racket, Mayer, two-fisted on both sides of the court, cost himself valuable points by failing to put away volleys and not getting his first service working. Dainty drop shots saw Borg sprinting from his baseline to pick up and consistently win the points. Although there were few glimpses of his true mastery the Swede was always able to pull out his finest form when it mattered most. In the third set, 5-3 and 40-30 down with the American serving, Borg hit a great backhand return for the point and, as he said later, 'from that point I start to play really well. The best I have played in the tournament.' Borg struck a purple patch with sizzling cross-court shots to break back and take the next three games.

Afterwards, he talked of the difficulties he faced every time he stepped on to a court. 'The pressure? Sure I'm under pressure,' he said, 'and that isn't always comfortable.' The way Borg saw it, it was always his opponent, with nothing to lose, who had the edge. 'It worries me sometimes,' he confessed, for once letting his Iceman mask slip a little. 'Maybe the other guy doesn't care and plays out of his mind. If I have a bad day, that is it.' Those bad days, however, were few and far between.

'When you play against Bjorn Borg, you don't play a man, you play an institution,' said Ion Tiriac. The former star of the Romanian Davis Cup team and long-time doubles partner of Nastase – in Will Grimsley's description, 'a dour, sinister-looking hulk of a man with the beetle brows and Fu Manchu moustache ... who came from the same Romanian village that produced Count Dracula' – could well have been 'talking about the pyramids, the Sphinx or the Rock of Gibraltar,' according to the American writer, for the implacable Swede 'might fit any or all of these unmoveable, unemotional landmarks'.

'There just seems to be no one with the steel, the stamina and patience to take him,' Tiriac said. 'If you hit 20 balls at him, he will hit the 21st. If you hit 40, he will hit 41. The man is amazing the way he can break you with persistence.' As Borg's semi-final opponent was soon to find out.

Brian Gottfried's career had undergone a major slump the previous year but after a lengthy indifferent patch he'd bounced back. Following success at the warm-up Surrey Grass Court Championships at Surbiton, downing Sandy Mayer in the final, the 6ft-tall, strapping American, unseeded for the first time in four years, had enjoyed a fine run at Wimbledon, the only player still in the competition not to have dropped a single set in any of his five matches.

After seeing off two Chris's – Kachel (Australia) and Lewis (New Zealand) – Gottfried had thwarted the hopes of Stan Smith then won through to the quarter-finals with a 6-1, 6-2, 6-2 victory over Phil Dent. There, the hard-serving Maryland man's precise strokes proved far too solid for Fibak, and Borg acknowledged, 'he is playing with a lot of confidence and that is the most important thing'.

But, like so many before him, Gottfried found Borg in impenetrable mood. The 24-year-old Swede raced through the first set in 28 minutes. And though, to the astonishment of the Centre Court crowd, Borg surrendered the second set in the tenth game by playing probably his worst game in a major tournament for years – he double-faulted twice, mishit on the next point and fluffed a simple forehand volley – it was a momentary aberration. Borg merely shrugged his shoulders and proceeded to rip through Gottfried's serve-and-volley game with a dazzling display down both lines.

Racing about the court and reaching every drop shot and placement Gottfried could offer, for the next two sets Borg assumed full command. From 3-2 in the third set, the Swedish ace, launching a barrage of passing shots, reeled off nine successive games – finishing the match with a meteor-like service – for a comfortable 6-2, 4-6, 6-2, 6-0 victory in one hour 57 minutes.

Gottfried played remarkably well, but 'Borg, up there in the clouds, played some game of his own', wrote Rex Bellamy. 'He got better and better while I got worse,' was Gottfried's honest assessment. 'That is what a good player does. He waits for the opportunity then takes it. Finish!' Gottfried had fought manfully but, echoing Tiriac, declared that 'It's hard work playing against Borg. So many balls come back.' The American added, 'It's like taking too many body punches. You are tired by the end.'

On that Thursday, as Borg guaranteed his berth in another final, Connors still a round behind, was engaged in a last-eight match, facing Roscoe Tanner, a fourth-round winner against another American, Nick Saviano, conqueror of Buster Mottram and Pat DuPré (both in four-hour five-setters). 'I will either be in great shape or dead,' Connors had hypothesised at the prospect of matches on consecutive days – Thursday, Friday and Saturday – if he made the final.

Against Tanner his Wimbledon hopes very nearly expired. Tanner, back to the straight, wet look this year, hammered home 16 aces and was up 2-1 in sets. But with the 28-year-old's service steadily losing its sting, Connors took advantage; he kept slamming winners off Tanner's second deliveries, and the 'Tennessee Express', unable to match the greater depth and all-round versatility of the 1974 champion, was derailed. The No.3 seed who had beaten Tanner 18 times in their 22 meetings made it 19, winning 1-6, 6-2, 4-6, 6-2, 6-2.

The following day all Borg had to do was wait to see which of two volatile American southpaws would be on the other side of the net in Saturday's final. Connors squared up to McEnroe, against whom he held a 10-4 win record. In his quarter-final, McEnroe, on opposite sides of the court for once to his doubles partner, had routed an off-form Peter Fleming, winner against Luis Clerc's vanquisher, Onny Parun.

Perhaps it was just as well that McEnroe won – after the last occasion Fleming beat him, they didn't speak for three days. However, the 1980 version of McEnroe, a far cry from the arrogant youth who alienated crowds and officials on both sides of the Atlantic, was in serious danger of becoming the new idol of Wimbledon. He'd even been cheered to victory over Fleming. It couldn't last.

'I hope,' Borg deadpanned ahead of the Americans' semi-final clash, 'they will have a long match lasting several hours.' As it was, the two were on court for 186 pulsating minutes of non-stop aggression. But in a predictably fiery confrontation it didn't take long for tempers to get over-heated. Serving at 4-2 and 40-15, McEnroe produced what looked like an ace, only for a 'net' to be called. The New Yorker's next serve kicked up the chalk and was ruled out. When the umpire Pat Smyth ordered the point replayed, McEnroe's complaints about the officiating saw him given a stern public warning, the first ever issued on Centre Court.

He refused to play on. With the sell-out crowd hooting and heckling, a livid McEnroe demanded – 14 times – the referee be summoned, put a towel over his shoulder and went to walk off the court when Fred Hoyles emerged to meet him. Hoyles upheld Smyth's decision. Clearly rattled, McEnroe lost the next point but, after then clinching the game with an ace, glowered at Smyth, asking, 'How's that, then?' At the end of the game, as the players swapped ends, Connors waved an admonishing finger under the nose of his opponent, saying, 'I'm telling you, keep your mouth shut. Don't say anything out here.' An animated discussion between the two ensued. After the situation was cooled, the match continued – but so did the verbal exchanges.

In the first game of the second set, when McEnroe, one set up, queried a Connors service winner, the No.3 seed chided the younger man with 'My son is better behaved than you. I'll bring him on to play you.' Connors won the set despite intense pressure, saving eight break points when serving at 4-2 and eventually winning a game that lasted 17 minutes and included ten deuces. But McEnroe took control at the outset of the third set and Connors struggled to keep up the rest of the way. Serving strongly – he slammed 12 aces to Connors's one – and volleying precisely, McEnroe sealed the fourth and match-deciding set 6-4 despite being broken twice. Asked afterwards about his relationship with Connors, McEnroe answered wryly, 'We don't go out to dinner together a lot.'

In the final for the first time, McEnroe was in a jovial humour. 'He's won the title four times,' the No.2 seed said of Borg. 'Maybe he won't try tomorrow.' With his semi-final victory at the Masters, the Swede had nudged ahead, 4-3, in their duels, although an ailing McEnroe had carried Borg to tiebreaks twice in that three-set match. The American had been hoping to face Borg on grass for a first time. He was staunch in his conviction that he had just the game to beat him.

Much depended on the New Yorker's vicious, wide-sweeping serve. Sliced to Borg's double-handed backhand (on which his reach was shorter), it potentially took the Swede way out of court, and McEnroe, at the net in a leap after delivering, was capable of dominating any match from there. McEnroe looked, in the description of the often bitingly witty critic Clive James, 'as if he is serving round the edge of an imaginary building'. Each serve's wind-up involved a bizarre ritual that seemed to take an age: there was his odd posture – standing sideways to the baseline, parallel to the net, legs wide apart, body bent over, torso leaning forward from the waist 'rocking back and forth like a broken toy' (according to Frank Deford of *Sports Illustrated*) and racket nearly touching the ground – before finally McEnroe swung into a twisting delivery. John Karter in *The Times* described its slow build-up as 'somehow hypnotic, like watching a cobra uncurling before its lethal strike'.

In the early stages of the final, it was venomous. So had the reception been for McEnroe as he entered the legendary arena. He was roundly booed as he walked on court. It didn't seem to bother him. In those first exchanges, it wasn't just the American's serve that was deadly. With an exquisite range of volleys, backhand and forehand cross-shots, slices and lobs, McEnroe dictated play, toying with Borg as if he were on a string. McEnroe's slashing volleys cut like a switchblade; some of his groundstrokes seemed like blasts from cannons.

He won the opening three games, using a fine offensive lob to break Borg in the second game. And though Borg scraped a service game to make it 1-3, McEnroe, playing more exemplary shots, broke again in the sixth game, then won a deuce game on his own serve – registering a first ace – to wrap up the first set, 6-1, with an ease that shocked the crowd. It took just 27 minutes.

Borg, from the outset, struggled to impose himself. On his own serve, he seemed undecided whether to stay back or come in. He tried both, neither very successfully. McEnroe's serve constantly left him floundering. The American's speed around the court made Borg look almost slow. With McEnroe moving so smoothly about, the ball flowing from his racket, the Swede was largely kept locked on the defensive. His play was nervy. Too many of his shots were sub-par. Groundstrokes were netted, went wide or landed long. When he bore in on the net, Borg's much-publicised new volleying game was in disarray. In the whole of the first set, he didn't gain a single break point.

At 0-30 in the opening game of the second set, his fortunes were at their lowest. After McEnroe had struck a winning pass, Borg went to serve for the next point and the racket flew five metres away from his hand. He overhit his next backhand way beyond the baseline, and in the seats reserved for players' guests his fiancée chain-smoked as she watched. Nearby, McEnroe Snr sat nonchalantly chewing his gum.

Borg kept clinging on but often only by the fingertips. Several times McEnroe had the Swede off balance only to be let down by a poor shot. In Borg's third service game, there were four deuces and one break point before the champion saved himself with a strong first serve. Displaying the versatility from the baseline and at the net that had marked his meteoric rise to prominence, McEnroe was still the player determining most of the points. His serving was imperious.

At 4-4, the second seed's biggest chance came. Three times in succession he reached break point and Borg looked in mortal peril, but each time a heavy serve kept the Swede alive. Borg finally prevailed after four deuces when McEnroe put a forehand out. At 5-5, Borg held his serve to love for the first time and immediately he performed an act of daylight robbery.

When an errant McEnroe drop volley took the score to 15-all, Borg put his foot down on the accelerator; a winning duel at the net took him to 15-30; a picture-perfect backhand return gave him two set points. Waiting to receive, he swayed and pawed the line ready to pounce. McEnroe saved the first of them. But when the left-hander then fluffed an easy volley, in a flash the match had turned. 'Instead of being in the driving seat, I was fighting an uphill battle,' McEnroe said later. 'This is what Borg does to you,' *New York Daily News* reporter Mike Lupica wrote. 'Bit by bit, he puts dents and chips in your spirit and your game. The mental game is even more strenuous than the tennis.'

His confident edge now blunted, McEnroe began committing unforced errors. His serve became at risk. He lost his touch on the volley. In the second game of the third set, he was broken as Borg, fizzing returns at his opponent, took command. His rhythm fully restored, Borg, Lupica wrote, 'was rolling now, volleying as well as he ever had on grass', pounding his strokes from the baseline with 'a frightening power, a discouraging precision'.

Borg's volleying technique, though, was still inexpert and, when leading 4-2, it nearly cost him dearly. But in a 20-point game, McEnroe spurned five break points, several wild bounces on the chewed-up court hurting the American, and from 0-40 down Borg held his service. Some of the Swede's shots defied belief: on one break point, two of McEnroe's backhands rifled towards Borg's midsection were volleyed back faster than they came, in a manner, wrote one journalist, which suggested 'he [Borg] could catch speeding bullets in his bare hands'. McEnroe held the eighth game to love, but several spotty shots by the American later and Borg had clinched the set, 6-3.

For most of the fourth set, each player held his own service games relatively comfortably. McEnroe's serve-and-volley game was back on the boil. Borg was playing with unconstrained freedom. The score reached 4-4, but at deuce in the ninth game, Borg followed one stupendous backhand cross-court with another, played at full stretch to a wicked McEnroe first serve; it dipped sharply and trapped the American as he came in and Borg seemingly had the title sewn up. Serving at 40-15 in the next game, he held two match points and fans around Centre Court were on their feet prepared to salute the Swede's moment of triumph.

He became too eager, however. Borg charged the net on both points and McEnroe threaded a backhand needle down the line for a winner and then knocked off a running do-or-die forehand volley from midcourt to bring the score to deuce. When the US Open champion forced Borg to net a forehand, the American had the advantage. A tremendous backhand service return swept across the court and he'd broken back. Pure instinct had bailed him out.

Two love games later, it was 6-6. The ensuing tiebreak became a compelling drama filled with scintillating moments. 'The two scratched at each other like jungle cats,' reported Will Grimsley. Both players were wholly committed, lunging, stretching and sometimes sprawling on the scarred turf for shots. Neither would yield. It was all-out attack, cutlass versus cutlass. Fatal blows were missed only by inches. Borg had another match point at 6-5 – with agility and in-a-flash reflexes, McEnroe reached a Borg forehand return and volleyed to win the point – then more at 7-6, 10-9, 11-10 and 12-11. McEnroe, with one magical drop volley and a series of backhand passes, saved all of them in brilliant, aggressive style, though twice was rescued by shots that hit the top of the net and miraculously crawled over. Commentating for NBC, Bud Collins called McEnroe 'the reincarnation of Harry Houdini – in short pants'.

The American himself wasted six set points. The tension was unbelievable. Loud cries from the gallery were followed by absolute hushes. If, as Rex Bellamy wrote, 'each man made terrible demands on heart and muscles and sinews', they made spectators suffer too. Lips and nails were bitten, breaths drawn. Incredulous spectators looked emotionally spent. Mariana could barely watch. Borg, meanwhile, blowing on his sweaty palms, remained, reported John Barrett from the BBC commentary box, 'the calmest man in the place'.

But it was his opponent who won out. When they'd met in the Masters in January, McEnroe had led Borg 2-0 in the tiebreak but wilted. This time there was no bending. On the 34th point, Borg, rushing in, attempted a drop volley off a hard McEnroe topspin forehand return, and the ball fell from his racket, 'tumbling off it like a cracked egg' wrote Frank Deford. Borg afterwards dismissed it as 'a stupid shot'. The No.2 seed had taken the tiebreak 18-16. It lasted an astonishing 22 minutes, as long as many sets.

Reeling with disbelief that he'd spurned so many match points, the thought that he might well now lose crossed Borg's mind, he revealed later. 'But I didn't give up,' he would say. 'I just tried to say to myself [that] I have to forget them.' 'Another man would have seen his will crumble, and perhaps his game with it,' wrote Mike Lupica. Not Borg. Urging himself, 'Let's go again', he did just that.

Given a second life, McEnroe went blazing into Borg's first service game of the fifth set and fired two winners. But he only won one more point off the Swede's service for the rest of the match. Borg, mining seemingly inexhaustible reserves, once more found all the qualities of a champion. With a shining display of courage and determination, his ability to meet the highest tests of nerves and skill revealed itself yet again. Serving with regal authority, he held service game after service game, then always threatened to break. 'It was a picture of relentlessness and grace,' Lupica wrote.

He didn't have exclusive rights to bravery. Each time Borg seemed on the verge of putting him away, McEnroe raised his own game to Olympian heights. Twice – in the second game and the eighth – McEnroe had to fight back from 0-40 to hold service. At 3-4 and three break points down, his cause looked lost but he came back again with a series of mighty serves including an ace, his tenth of the final. The toll of Friday's singles against Connors and an early evening doubles semi-final (surrendered to avoid further physical strain) was telling, though. McEnroe was oozing fatigue. The Swede charged on as powerfully and as positively as ever.

Borg went to 7-6 after serving another decisive love game, and at last the roof fell in for the American. At 15-all in the 14th game, Borg ran around McEnroe's second service and drove a crashing forehand return down the line for 15-30. Next, he stood up to a cannonball service and when McEnroe volleyed Borg's low return the Swede flicked a backhand across the court that McEnroe anticipated but could only net with a forehand. It meant an eighth match point for Borg and this time he made it count.

When a good first serve to Borg's forehand was returned, McEnroe drilled a fine volley wide to the backhand but Borg scorched a whistling cross-court double-handed pass at which a lunging McEnroe flailed his racket in vain. As the ball bit into the grass a foot inside the sideline, the Swede dropped to his knees in exultation, arching his back so far that his long hair brushed the balding grass.

Rising to his feet and looking quickly up, he saw Mariana in tears of joy and, amidst the crowd erupting in wild elation, even the normally stolid Bergelin, cracking a happy little smile, stood with his hands up in triumph. It was a full minute before the crowd's exuberant applause subsided for the umpire to announce the final score: 1-6, 7-5, 6-3, 6-7, 8-6. Moments later, the Duke of Kent was extending the golden trophy to the victor, and Borg, to deafening acclaim, held it aloft once more and kissed it.

After a match that the Swede reckoned was 'probably the toughest in my career', he revealed 'a big secret' – he'd been battling through with a pulled stomach muscle, bothering him since the tie with Rod Frawley. 'I have been having treatment every day since then … injections, massage, everything,' Borg said. 'But there was never any danger of my pulling out.' The problem was serious enough for doctors to order Borg to rest at least a month. The Swedish media, somewhat cynically, speculated if he just wanted some relaxation before his wedding day.

Borg's superiority on grass was put to the severest test. 'I have never been so disappointed on a tennis court as when I lost that fourth set,' he confessed. All those missed opportunities, yet, as Barry Lorge wrote in the *Washington Post*, 'even the visions of Paradise Lost that flashed through his mind … could not break Borg's spirit'. Frank Deford propounded that the Swede had actually 'enhanced his reputation, because the character of his performance surpassed the achievement itself. The last man to lose the Wimbledon final after having a match point in his favour was John Bromwich of Australia in 1948, and those who played against Bromwich thereafter say he was never again the same player. One point did him in. And this man Borg blew many such chances. And still he triumphed.' 'You'd think maybe just once he'd let up and just say forget it,' a reverent McEnroe mused. 'No. What he does out there, the way he is, the way he thinks …' McEnroe shook his head. 'I know I couldn't do it.'

What Borg had done in fending off McEnroe's unflinching challenge was, Mike Lupica wrote, 'raise his game to a level that perhaps only Borg can understand'. The Swede was 'playing his tennis in a high place … offering a kind of tennis that other players can only have silly dreams about'. Lupica concluded, 'There are these times when even champions explore new dimensions.'

Borg had gained his deserved niche in history. It was a phenomenal achievement. 'It seems evident now that whoever finally dethrones Bjorn Borg at Wimbledon, if anyone ever does, will need a dagger to the heart,' proposed Barry Lorge. 'Nothing less will do. Surely not a mere tennis racket, even in the hands of a determined man with an assassin's instincts for survival.' With his success, Borg became the first player to win the French and Wimbledon in the same year on three occasions. Laver had done it twice, in 1962 and seven years later.

The victory underlined the Swede's position as world's No.1. But the best-ever? Even in his moment of glory Borg retained the practicality that was so much part of his personality. 'Of course, it is impossible to say just who is the greatest tennis player. You will never know how I would do playing against Laver, or Budge, or Tilden, or Perry.'

According to McEnroe, Borg was 'already one of the greatest, but', he added, 'he might still have a little to prove on hard courts'. Namely, winning a first US Open crown – one Laver had claimed twice. Another crack at rectifying the real flaw in Borg's résumé was next on the agenda.

The following day, stories of the UK economic recession, the climax of Ronald Reagan's bid for the US Presidential nomination, and investigations into police corruption were momentarily sidelined as a sporting event that scaled many of the greatest peaks was propelled from the back pages of the dailies to the front. Newspapers were united in singing the praises of the three-hour-53-minute epic. It was hailed as a classic, long-to-be-remembered, one of the most rousing finals played at the All England Club.

The taut, titanic tiebreak was lauded for its thrills and some of the best tennis the venerable tournament had ever seen. 'In terms of sustained quality there may have been better finals,' wrote David Irvine in *The Guardian*, 'but none, dare one suggest, of such heroic passion or nerve-jangling compulsion fought at a pace so hot that the combatants' rackets must have been in danger of catching fire.'

Across the Atlantic, too, they celebrated. Mike Lupica was in raptures. 'As long as men will pick up rackets and play tennis in important matches, as long as players come to a place called Wimbledon to test their wills and their games and their spirits on the storied grass courts, they will remember the majestic Saturday in July of 1980 … These were Wimbledon's finest four hours.'

There was press acclaim for McEnroe as well, and his gutsy performance. He fought like a terrier but the dignified manner in which McEnroe kept a tight rein on his temper also earned the American plaudits. McEnroe contended that 'it's hard to look good when you play against Borg. He is the epitome of everything good in tennis.' But he managed it. One tabloid had dubbed him 'Mr Volcano' after his eruptions against Connors – which had also seen the BBC switchboards jammed with complaints – but there was none of the churlishness that seemed to have made him Wimbledon's public enemy No.1. 'McEnrot' was now being saluted as 'Mac-nificent'. 'It was a Wimbledon final and I wanted to give the best possible response,' McEnroe said.

Barracked when he swaggered on to the court with that disgruntled slouch of his – 'I was very disappointed I didn't get a good hand before the match,' McEnroe admitted – the 21-year-old received a warm reception at the end, the crowd standing to cheer him as he collected his silver medal. Even the hardened media people, among McEnroe's harshest critics, granted him an ovation when he entered for his post-match interview.

Before the tournament Borg had declared in a magazine interview that 'Sometimes I think I am Superman, and I start to try all kinds of things because suddenly I know I can't miss the ball. I want to show people the most fantastic shot that they have ever seen in their lives. It's like I am dreaming and it's wonderful.' Superman's cape had definitely been stepped on, though. Not only that; in Will Grimsley's view, 'a nerveless kid from the New York suburbs' had proven that 'ice melts and steel can bend'. Borg's grip on the crown had been, according to the writer, 'loosened rather than tightened by his latest victory'.

McEnroe's refusal to succumb peacefully raised self-doubts in the Swede's steel-trap mind, Borg himself disclosing that his renowned concentration had been shaken. 'He found on Centre Court,' wrote Grimsley, 'a younger man who could match him shot for shot and who, under the fiercest pressure, would not buckle but would call upon some mysterious, unshakeable resolve.' The American might have lost a tennis match but he'd claimed a huge psychological triumph. And, from now on, Grimsley warned, 'No matter where Borg journeys in pursuit of new honours, no matter what the surface or the event, there will always be this tough, talented left-hander breathing down his neck.'

22 June – 4 July 1981

AT THE end of the 1980 Wimbledon men's singles final, Fred Hoyles, the tournament referee, approached John McEnroe following the American's defeat by Bjorn Borg and shook his hand. 'You will win Wimbledon one day,' Hoyles told the 21-year-old. McEnroe, too dejected by his loss after stretching the Swede to the absolute limit that July afternoon, uttered little more than a grunt of thanks in reply. The following day, though, a resolute McEnroe flew home to New York promising, 'I will beat the bearded-wonder yet.' Now, almost a year on, the loss fully out of his system – 'I've digested it; it's gone,' he claimed – McEnroe was convinced that 'one day' was about to come, that this could be the hour to unseat the king from his throne.

'Men's tennis is no longer a monarchy,' Will Grimsley stated in the final's aftermath. 'It's a two-way dogfight, and Heaven help the hindmost.' Just a few weeks later, on 7 September, in a glorious resumption of their Wimbledon rivalry, the two best players in the sport fought a second successive 55-game final, at Flushing Meadows, McEnroe fending off a Borg comeback to retain his men's singles crown, 7-6, 6-1, 6-7, 5-7, 6-4, the first man to win back-to-back US Open titles in 20 years. The victory completed an incredible finals weekend for the young American; just the previous evening, McEnroe had come through a stirring five-set semi-final with a bearded Jimmy Connors – another tetchy encounter between the compatriots barely able to conceal their dislike for one another.

For the third time in four years Borg had gone into the championships in the States at less than 100 per cent physically. Already nursing an abdominal strain – the weekend following Wimbledon, he was sidelined as Sweden lost 4-1 to Italy in the Davis Cup European Zone A final in Rome – Borg suffered an inflammation in his right knee while jogging in Sweden, which forced him to default in the final of the Canadian Masters against Ivan Lendl two weeks prior to the US Open.

Having made it through to the showdown at Flushing Meadows, nonetheless, there Borg suffered from a strange crisis of confidence in the first two sets – what he later described as a loss of feeling for the ball – before recovering to draw level, only to surrender a gut-wrenching fifth set as the American found his service game at just the right time. Prior to the defeat, Borg had won 13 five-set encounters in a row dating back to 1976. (Two of those had come in his quarter- and semi-final matches leading up to the final.) After eight tries at the US Open, the duck still hadn't been broken.

After losing indoors, again in five sets, to Lendl in Basel, Switzerland – the Swede's first outing in more than six weeks – then to Bill Scanlon in Tokyo, Borg exacted a little retribution on McEnroe, beating his main adversary 6-3, 6-4, albeit in flat-footed fashion, to win his first Stockholm Grand Prix, the oldest tournament of its type in the world. But he then had to withdraw from a quarter-finals match at the Bologna Indoor through illness, handing Tomas Smid a walkover.

At the Masters in January, Borg confronted McEnroe yet again, overcoming the American (who'd been battling stomach pains, a pulled muscle in his left leg and a chronic sore back) in a deciding third-set tiebreak for the second year in a row. With over 19,000 fans in attendance, Borg won 6-4, 6-7, 7-6, though only after uncharacteristically getting penalised two penalty points for arguing too long with English umpire Mike Lugg over an overruled line call. In the face-off between the eight top tennis players of the previous year, any doubts that Borg was still in a class by himself were laid to rest as McEnroe and Connors plus José Luis Clerc were stopped dead in their tracks before Borg coasted to a 6-4, 6-2, 6-2 win over the 20-year-old Lendl and his second Masters title.

The duels with McEnroe continued. A month after the Masters, at the star-laden $500,000 Molson Tennis Challenge in Toronto, another eight-player round-robin tournament, Borg lost in the semis to the New Yorker, who went on to yield first prize to Vitas Gerulaitis. It was an important psychological boost for Gerulaitis, whose world ranking had slid from fourth to ninth in the previous year. In the third round, Connors had also got the better of Borg, recording a first victory over the Swede since the South American Open in November 1978, a subservience that had lasted 26 months.

Later that same month, there was another Borg-McEnroe reacquaintance, Borg winning two of three matches against his arch-rival, before wrapping up the $100,000 Benson and Hedges Gold Challenge Series in Melbourne with a 2-6, 6-2, 6-4 victory over Gerulaitis. By his own standards, though, Borg was having a terrible year. During a six-week stretch in March and April, the Swedish ace played only three tournaments and failed to advance past the second round in two of them. He lost to the German Rolf Gehring in Brussels then to McEnroe in the final of the Milan championships (both on clay), as well as to Victor Pecci in the first round on Borg's own home clay at the Monte Carlo Masters. Suffering from tenderness in his right shoulder, as well as a virus, he then decided to rest before making a return at the French Open.

Borg arrived in Paris amidst much speculation. There were questions (which he resented) about his health and motivation. Were these mysterious injuries more serious than he was letting on? Was his tenacity of mind still as firm? The rumour mill churned out stories that Borg was growing apathetic and lazy, that he wanted to quit and settle down with his new wife to raise a family. Some even hinted, rather ridiculously, that he was growing senile.

On the slow, killing clay at Roland Garros, Borg gave no suggestion whatsoever that he was faltering. 'A couple of marathon rallies there can take as much out of a man as a whole set on the grass at Wimbledon,' Geoffrey Miller wrote, but Borg, seemingly imbued with renewed power, dispelled any fears about his future to claim a sixth French crown (his 61st title overall). He didn't drop a set until the final. There, he withstood the determined challenge of the dour, unsmiling Lendl, 6-1, 4-6, 6-2, 3-6, 6-1, in three and a quarter hours.

Three years younger than Borg, Lendl, in 1980, had risen from 20th to sixth in the world rankings, and also led Czechoslovakia to its first Davis Cup victory. Once a possible threat on the horizon, the Czech with the adventuresome slingshot forehand now posed a very real danger. His performances in Paris confirmed him as the world's second-best clay-court player. Borg said this was the toughest of his six French finals. Yet after a final set that was decided on a few vital points and was not as uneven as the score indicated, the defending champion, his staying power supreme, emerged from a taxing battle of wits and patience as the master once more.

Borg and tennis history had become, Curry Kirkpatrick wrote, 'as intertwined as satin and lace'. The Swede didn't deny the fact that capturing a first US Open was now the primary objective. Nevertheless, at Wimbledon there were still some very special targets on his radar. He was not only attempting to equal the six consecutive titles of William Renshaw – achieved between 1881 (exactly 100 years earlier) and 1886 –

but to also match Roy Emerson's all-time record of 12 grand slam titles. Statistically the odds against it were astonishing. And, of course, there was that ominous obstacle in his path called McEnroe.

'As with the stars of every era, there comes a time when even the greatest champions of sport must move aside and make way for some younger and hungrier member of the supporting cast,' wrote David Irvine in a *Radio Times* preview. No one fitted the bill better than the young New Yorker. Aside from the royal wedding of Prince Charles and Lady Diana Spencer the following month – they were due to marry on 29 July – McEnroe's prospects were the most prevalent topic of London conversation.

They looked promising. McEnroe's tactical remedy since his heroic Wimbledon loss had been to cut out junk food – he'd slowly shed 20 pounds over the following few months. He was leaner and faster now, and with a year's more experience and a perfect grass-court game – the stinging serve, the sure touch at the net – McEnroe was 'completely certain' that he was the man to put the full stop on Borg's Wimbledon story. 'His day's gotta come,' McEnroe said. 'And I intend to be there when it does.'

Eight days before the start of Wimbledon, he'd tuned up by winning a third successive Stella Artois tournament, without dropping a set, defeating Brian Gottfried 7-6, 7-5 in the final. It was his ninth title of the year. It had long been McEnroe's wish that people overlook his often obnoxious conduct and assess him only as a tennis player. However, despite his continued insistence that he was, as Thomas Boswell put it, 'just a competitor so highly strung that his edge will vanish if he must act civilised and creative at the same time', at the Queen's Club McEnroe showed that he might no longer care as much about British sensibilities as he'd previously professed. During one match he berated a woman umpire then even swatted a ball at her. 'So much for resolutions,' wrote Boswell. 'If it takes bad manners to win against Borg, then bad manners it may prove to be.'

Anyone looking for omens in McEnroe's favour might have highlighted the change in Borg's choice of hotels for Wimbledon. In his first title year, the Swede stayed at the Park Lane and then, for the following four Wimbledons, moved to the Holiday Inn at Swiss Cottage, away from the bustle, in north-west London. This year, along with Mariana (and Bergelin in an adjoining suite), 'home' was on the tenth floor at the Sheraton-Park Tower Hotel in Knightsbridge. On the face of it, the shift seemed relatively insignificant. But routine played such a prominent role in Borg's preparations, particularly at Wimbledon.

During the tournament, he was a creature of meticulous habit. Aside from the beard – started exactly four days before The Championships – there was the insistence that he took the same route to the All England Club, over the Hammersmith Bridge in a car with a stereo radio; there, he always had the same locker, the same number of towels. To string his rackets, at an incredibly tight 80 pounds of tension, he entrusted just one man: Mats Laftman, in Stockholm. And before each match, along with his tennis bag packed just so, ten of those rackets were always lined up in descending order of 'ping'. Each of his compulsive acts Borg called 'a productive stereotype'. These were just a few of them.

His parents weren't without their own quirks. Superstition enveloped the Borg family 'like the shroud of a Swedish winter', wrote Curry Kirkpatrick. During the 1979 final against Tanner when Borg reached triple match point, his mother, chewing candy for good luck in the competitors' stand, spat out the sweet. When Tanner rallied to deuce, Margarethe, according to Kirkpatrick, 'fetched the candy off the grimy floor and put it back into her mouth'. The elder Borgs visited Wimbledon only in odd numbered years – solely out of superstition.

This year, too, their son's practice routine, primarily due to the weather, had shifted from his traditional haunt, the Cumberland Club. Asked whether he thought the changes in habit might affect the Swede, McEnroe replied, 'It really doesn't matter. It all depends if he thinks it matters.' Even so, some customs hadn't altered. For the fourth straight year, Vitas Gerulaitis continued to be Borg's favourite practice partner. And though heavy rain meant their gruelling workouts were largely conducted at the Lensbury Club, an enormous athletic facility in south-west London, on Monday, 22 June 1981, when Borg set off in search of a sixth title, his competitive edge was, according to witnesses, as razor-sharp as ever.

Charged with the tough assignment of trying to blunt it was Peter Rennert, a 22-year-old New Yorker, who'd finished 62nd in the world rankings the previous year, his first as a professional. Friends – McEnroe was a close one (they'd attended the same school and college and Rennert had been acting as one of McEnroe's practice partners) – had encouraged the bearded left-hander by reminding him of the Swedish superstar's previous troubles in early rounds, especially against the big servers. Rennert, on the end of a quick-fire defeat against Sherwood Stewart in the quiet backwoods of Court 13 on his Wimbledon debut the year before, was a good fast-court player and, reportedly, after a soggy spring the skidding grass courts in SW19 were playing livelier than usual this year.

As always, when Borg walked on to Centre Court to lead off The Championships, there was an air of excitement that something special might happen. It was a hot, cloudless day, with temperatures exceeding 80°F provoking some (male) spectators to strip to the waist and the umpire to utter a hushed horrified request: 'Will the people with their shirts off please put them back on.' For the food and drink sellers it was business as usual: half a dozen strawberries with cream cost 85p; non-vintage champagne was £13 a bottle; a glass of Pimm's a quid.

For Borg, too, it was fairly standard fare for an inaugural match. Before a watching Duchess of Kent, wearing a surgical collar because of a slipped disc – thankfully for her, the Royal Box looked straight down the court sparing her any movement of her head to follow play – the defending champion experienced a few customary stumbles before fully finding his feet to advance to the next round.

He made a ragged start. Looking more like the nervous underdog than the titleholder in the early games, Borg's play was peppered with errors. While the slight, wiry Rennert – 'sporting a red bandeau as if to mesmerise his foe into believing him to be McEnroe' Geoffrey Green observed – served consistently and delivered some dainty backhand drop volleys to earn the spectators' cheers, the Swede left them positively gasping when he double-faulted three times in succession in the fourth game, one which went to six deuces and that Borg eventually won after saving three break points.

On one serve in another game he actually lost his racket and had nothing but his foot with which to attempt a return. In the whole of the 47-minute opening set, Borg won only five points against service. Still, for all the shaky moments, the Swede steadied himself when it mattered. When the score reached 6-6, Borg captured Rennert's service on the first point of the tiebreak – anticipating a feathery drop shot before passing the American – then went on to take it comfortably, 7-2.

Finally wising up to the grass's deceptive bounce, in the second set Borg gained his touch with each passing game. Flashes of style shone through. Vicious topspin passes 'left poor Rennert fishing in waters that yielded nothing but minnows', wrote Green. One backhand across his shoulder left the unseeded American shaking his head. Rennert occasionally worked up to the net to surprise the champion but at 4-3 the Swede hit two fine backhand returns and a forehand pass to break for the first time, and that was virtually that.

Rennert's challenge faded rapidly; he won only one more game as Borg ran away with the match, capturing his 36th consecutive Wimbledon victim in one hour 35 minutes. According to David Norrie of the *Glasgow Herald*, at the end of the solid if unspectacular 7-6, 6-3, 6-1 triumph, Borg already had 'the glazed look of success in his eyes'. 'Bjorn is relaxed,' said Bergelin afterwards. 'He knows he can stay out there, all day if necessary, and when you know that, you are able to relax.' Relaxed was not an adjective you could use to describe McEnroe.

The old saying went that Wimbledon never changed, only the champions differed from year to year. But with Borg's virtual monopoly and recent developments at the home of tennis, which had literally raised the Centre Court roof and introduced four new courts, the reverse had been truer of late. Renovations undertaken just after the 1980 Championships and completed earlier that month meant that crowds arriving at the All England Club for the tournament's start found some of the old familiar sights gone. One was the famous ivy-framed flashing scoreboard, shifted from the main concourse where thousands gathered on the macadam walkway to watch the point-by-point progress of the Centre Court match. Millions had been spent on various improvements, including a new restaurant and resting rooms for the players. There was also a new look for No.1 Court. Given a facelift, it now seated 8,500 spectators. And in the warm unbroken sunshine, watching McEnroe face Tom Gullikson, along with their shades they might also have been well advised to wear earplugs.

'The rest of the world becomes lunatic under a full moon,' wrote Thomas Boswell. 'Wimbledon is driven mad by a full sun.' As temperatures soared, so did McEnroe's displeasure. The No.2 seed, 'giving a fair impression of a man in search of a nervous breakdown', Bill Martin reported in the *Daily Post*, beat his fellow left-hander in straight sets but, before the eyes of not just those around the court but millions of television viewers, turned into a raging tyrant and was two penalty points away from disqualification.

All his troubles stemmed from disputed line calls. Having already been warned by umpire Edward James for 'misusing your racket' when, with Gullikson going 4-3 ahead in the second set, McEnroe at the changeover crashed his Wilson Pro Staff against a chair – the racket a replacement for one he'd put his foot on and deliberately broken two games earlier – the American then cranked up the truculence to unprecedented levels. There was insolence: once, when Mr James briskly ordered a point to be replayed, McEnroe turned towards him, stretched both arms to the sky and ceremoniously bowed six times. On another occasion, at the end of a game, McEnroe, his back to the umpire's chair, held up his drink in a mock toast to the official. But far worse was to come.

At 1-1 in the third set, a McEnroe service was ruled out by a linesman operating the electronic 'magic eye' machine, although the ball raised a cloud of chalk. 'You cannot be serious. That ball was on the line,' McEnroe fumed. When James refused to listen to McEnroe's angry protests, he copped the player's full fury. 'You guys are the absolute pits of the world, do you know that?' shrieked McEnroe. James, a Llanelli dentist, coolly announced a penalty point against the American, leaving McEnroe insistent on seeing Fred Hoyles. The referee ventured on to the court, listened to the testimony and upheld James's decision. 'You can't award a point penalty for nothing – that's absurd,' McEnroe snapped, adding his opinion that Mr James was 'an incompetent fool, an offence against the world' in a voice loud enough to be heard on television and throughout the court.

When a four-letter word was also directed at Hoyles at the end of the game – McEnroe telling the referee 'You're as bad as the rest of the shits' – another penalty point was incurred. The docking brought wild cheers from the big crowd. They booed and jeered McEnroe throughout his tantrums, wrote Australian tennis authority Alan Trengove, 'as though the young man from New York was the villain in a Victorian drama'. The love exhibited after the 1980 final was a distant memory. The American was now on dangerous ground. A third transgression would have seen a game docked. Another could have meant disqualification. The displays of rage eventually ended, however, and tennis's Mr Hyde became once again the docile Dr Jekyll, losing only one more game in the match, but, as David Irvine put it, 'the sour taste left by McEnroe's behaviour pervaded the feast like decaying garlic'.

Afterwards, McEnroe maintained that umpire James did 'a lousy job' and defended his right to complain. 'If I play badly, I lose,' he said, 'and if he makes eight or ten bad calls, then he should be replaced.' He did nevertheless show some contrition, labelling the whole thing 'a fiasco, but it was basically my fault'. First-day nerves had played their part. He'd been 'jittery', he admitted. 'I know being a linesman is a thankless task, especially with guys like me around.' The game's most impetuous player willingly accepted that 'all this [unpopularity] is never going to change until I completely change the way I act on the court. But that may take years.'

McEnroe's misconduct earned him a £750 fine from the Wimbledon committee and a warning that further misdemeanours would be regarded as 'aggravated behaviour' making him liable to a heftier additional £5,000 slap on the wrist and suspension. For some, the penalties weren't tough enough. This wasn't just a spoiled child throwing his toys around. 'The Gullikson affair was no ordinary venting of temper,' Alan Trengove noted. McEnroe had acted 'with cold, deliberate malice' and on a main court in front of millions of TV viewers (20 of whom reportedly rang Wimbledon demanding that the American be disqualified).

For a player whose boyhood was spent in the jungle of junior tennis development in the States, his language was rather typical. Bud Collins was among McEnroe's fellow countrymen who argued that his actions were mild compared to what went on in pro baseball, football or hockey.

Another American, Barry Lorge, felt that McEnroe actually behaved better than he used to, and that the British gave him a harder time than he deserved. 'His reputation precedes him and everything gets blown out of proportion,' Lorge said.

Yet this was at what Thomas Boswell termed 'the deliciously elegant and stodgy' All England Club. It was 'not the place' for voicing such anger, said Arthur Ashe. 'There's something sacred about Wimbledon. It's the showplace of our sport.' In July 1979 Ashe had suffered a severe heart attack and underwent quadruple-bypass surgery in December of that year. His playing career had ended. Now 37 and the US Davis Cup captain, his response to what Will Grimsley termed 'McEnroe's reprehensible deportment' was embarrassment. 'I wanted to disappear in my seat,' he said.

Inevitably, on what Boswell called 'this easily outraged island', the press wanted 'the walking outrage to manners' thrown to the lions. They were savage with their criticism. Front pages were filled with comment about the rowdy American under banner headlines such as 'Disgrace of Superbrat', 'Mac the Mouth', and 'The Shame of John McEnroe'. Even *The Times*, the *Daily Telegraph* and *The Guardian* gave McEnroe front-page picture space. An editorial in *The Sun* went so far as to recommend that if McEnroe couldn't alter his ways 'then he should be told to go back home'.

'At age 22, McEnroe should have grown up by this time,' argued Rex Bellamy. 'I think he has chronic psychological problems. He's bad and not getting better.' It was reasonable for McEnroe to object on line calls – 'he can't tolerate injustice and incompetence' – but not to react so contentiously. A complex character and being, as his father called him, 'a tremendous perfectionist' was no excuse. If Borg could channel his fire, why couldn't McEnroe? Borg himself had his own theory. In a 1980 *Life* magazine profile by Christopher Whipple, the Swede had suggested a reason for the American's ranting. 'I think he is nervous on court, so he has to *do* something all the time. Because if he didn't say anything, then he might *think* more, and get more nervous.'

The *Daily Mail* meanwhile called on the advice of the medical profession to help decide 'what makes McEnroe act the SuperYob'. Dr Dougal Mackay, principal psychologist at a London hospital, proposed that most of McEnroe's woes originated from an insecurity in matches that he should win easily. 'It never happens in the important matches against players such as Borg and Connors,' Mackay said. 'If he [McEnroe] knows that he can beat an opponent of lesser calibre, I think he gets bored and needs to cause a fuss to keep his adrenaline flowing.' Like an electric wire that occasionally had to touch water.

A *Sydney Morning Herald* journalist, Frank Crook, was unforgiving, though. 'The very dignity of the world's oldest lawn tennis championship is at stake every time McEnroe takes to the court,' he posited. He then lay in deeper. 'The scowling, pasty, bug-eyed countenance of John McEnroe represents the ugly face of sport in Britain today,' he wrote. 'His tantrums on Wimbledon's opening day were more at home in a down-at-heel seaside theatre or perhaps a freak show.' Crook contested that the organisers were handed a golden opportunity to put McEnroe in his place, but had spurned it. The fine, in Crook's view, 'was nothing more than a fleabite'. A measly and meaningless penalty for such a wealthy athlete. The authorities should have brought the curtain down on him, Crook argued. 'That, at least, may have pulled McEnroe up short and forced him to think about the depths to which tennis has sunk because of him and other money-hungry performers like him.'

A reference to Connors? Quite possibly. Once the 'Peck's Bad Boy' of tennis, Connors had passed the mantle to McEnroe now, but still had his moments. The older American, 'after some 18 months on the temper-tantrum wagon', according to Will Grimsley, had suddenly fallen off. 'This spring, he has been busy bad-mouthing umpires and linesmen and generally making a dunce of himself.' Connors's old tetchiness had broken its chains in Paris when, two sets to one up against José Luis Clerc, winner of the Italian Open, and needing only two points to gain a tiebreak in the fourth, he went 'berserk' over a disputed call, was penalised for arguing the point beyond the 30-second time, blew the game and didn't win another in the match.

Now a cause célèbre after his run-in with officialdom, McEnroe was caught in the eye of a media storm. Ridicule was also heaped upon him. One cartoon showed a middle-aged woman walking away from 'Superbrat' on Centre Court, having just stuck a pacifier in his mouth. 'Thanks a lot,' says the umpire in the picture. 'If only we'd known … all he wanted all these years was his dummy.' A London wine shop soon cashed in on Wimbledon's biggest story, putting a sign in its window: 'Even John McEnroe wouldn't complain about our prices.'

Smarting over his punishment and what he considered the unfair attitude of the press, McEnroe was extremely down according to Peter Fleming, a friend since boyhood. Nevertheless, he remained reasonably light-hearted in public: during a break from the tournament, he posed for photographers at Madame Tussauds, clowning it up by placing a finger over the lips of his lookalike in wax.

While a McEnroe meltdown might have been anticipated, it was a day full of surprises elsewhere. Seeded 13, Yannick Noah, who was born in Sedan in France but grew up in Cameroon, where he was discovered by Arthur Ashe in 1971 during a tour of Africa, was ousted by an unheralded American, Eric Fromm. The 22-year-old New Yorker, from the same Port Washington Tennis Academy that produced McEnroe and Gerulaitis, had never even won a match on grass before and his total preparation on the surface had amounted to 30 minutes. ('They're real generous with practice time here – a half-hour a year,' he said sarcastically afterwards.)

Victor 'Diamond Vic' Pecci, so named because of the trademark stud he sported in his right ear, was left red-faced when, after losing a tough first-set tiebreak to Bill Scanlon, he surrendered the next two sets to love. ('Victor's mind was in the showers after one set,' wrote Paraguay's leading tennis journalist of his countryman, 'and his body was soon to follow.') Tenth-seeded Vilas was another to tumble, his finesse overcome by Mark Edmondson's rugged power.

But the main casualty was Ivan Lendl, the No.4 seed beaten in five sets by obscure 22-year-old Australian Charlie Fancutt, a strapping six-footer whose parents had both played at Wimbledon. The Czech's swift exit was perhaps yet more proof that Wimbledon, with its slickly manicured lawns, required special qualities, and the idea of seeding competitors in a grass-court championship according to their computer ranking largely achieved on other surfaces was rather futile.

With the McEnroe-against-the-world sideshow rapidly becoming the main event, the actual tennis took a backseat. However, on the Wednesday afternoon, Borg returned to centre stage, meeting for a first time the talented young American from Joplin, Missouri, Mel Purcell, who'd eliminated Australian Dale Collings in the first round. On the first rain-afflicted day, their match was one of the few to finish before Wimbledon's traditional enemy stormed the barricades and ended play prematurely.

The 21-year-old Purcell, with his distinctive corn-coloured hair, had had his best success on clay, losing the final of the US Clay Court Championships the previous year to Luis Clerc. In Paris, he'd made the fourth round before succumbing to Connors. Now 27th on the ATP computer standings, Purcell was making his debut on the Wimbledon grass.

The rain interruption failed to unsettle the champion. Playing his usual immaculate baseline game, pumping home powerful, double-fisted backhands and heavy, spinning forehands, Borg was never seriously tested. By contrast with the serve-and-volley game of Rennert, Purcell stayed back much of the time, fatally allowing the Swede to get his rhythm working and approach the net regularly.

With teasing variations of length, pace and direction, the top seed was chillingly impressive. A service break in the seventh game enabled Borg to take the first set, and he ran away with the second, reeling off six consecutive games after Purcell had held his opening serve. In the third set, games went with service until the eighth when the Swede broke through again and then served out for a 6-4, 6-1, 6-3 victory just as the second heavy shower of the day started.

After the drubbing, Borg expressed satisfaction with his game. He was now 'getting used to the grass', he declared. For years that grass had been on either Centre Court or No.1 Court. Not since he faced Mark Edmondson in 1977 had the Swede had to play at the All England Club on what Thomas Bowell termed 'the scruffy, upset-prone outside courts' where surfaces were often soft and bumpy, the bounces generally more erratic. Players labelled them the 'great equalisers'.

Among his fellow pros, Connors and McEnroe included, a feeling persisted that, with the scheduling committee's policy of staging all his matches on the two main courts, Borg was being handed an immense advantage over those used to battling amidst all the noise and bustle outside the stadium. 'People are hanging from the rafters watching McEnroe and I, so why should it be different for Borg?' argued Connors. 'To win the title, a guy should have to play under all the conditions.'

Borg freely admitted how appearing on the show courts – carefully tended and kept exclusively for The Championships – had helped him. 'The ball bounces much better on those courts,' he said. 'It stands to reason. They are not played [on] so much.' But when told that others were suggesting he received favoured treatment, he narrowed his eyes. 'I don't do the schedules, do I?' he said.

Connors soon had a further grievance. McEnroe wasn't the only one upsetting the hierarchy with what emerged from his mouth. Another problem surfaced for 'the staid, stuffy fathers of Wimbledon tennis', as Will Grimsley labelled them: the proliferation of grunts. 'Subtly, these guardians of propriety have passed word down to umpires and players that they would like to see a lowering of the decibel factor,' the journalist reported. The warning seeped down to Connors.

'Please try to hold down the grunting,' the umpire had asked him during his opening match, a devastating 6-1, 6-2, 6-4 victory over compatriot Dick Stockton. Connors – 'one of the pioneers and most unmelodious of the game's noisemakers' wrote Grimsley – had merely laughed, not realising the man in the blazer and coat of arms was serious. 'Default me,' he retorted. 'I couldn't stop grunting if I wanted to.' Barking like a seal on shots since he was a junior, Connors had 'invented the grunt', he said later. It wasn't meant as a distraction, but was simply the outcome of how he'd been taught to breathe on the court.

Still only 28, just two years removed from being ranked No.1 in the world for a record five consecutive times, Connors was nevertheless considered something of a veteran. In 1980, he had failed to reach a grand slam final for the second year in a row. But after toughing it out – and grunting as loudly as ever – on a scarred No.2 Court against Chris Lewis, taken to a tiebreak twice by the plucky New Zealander, he was bubbling with confidence. 'There is no age at which you can say, "I'm too old to win Wimbledon,"' he said.

His old ferociousness hadn't deserted him. 'No matter how it looks on the outside,' he said, 'I still keep a fire going inside.' Indeed, during the second set of a match in which the elastic broke in Connors's shorts – a woman in the packed crowd coming to his rescue by producing two safety pins – the player himself had nearly snapped too; the American queried a Lewis ace that he felt was out then mockingly bowed to the 'magic eye' machine when the umpire stuck to his decision. Connors wasn't happy. 'Jesus Christ, no wonder McEnroe gets upset with you guys,' he cried plaintively.

With a possible suspension hanging over him – another untoward incident and he was out the front gates in his white shorts – McEnroe was on virtual probation. In a quiet, polite match from beginning to end against Raul Ramirez, he kept a grip on his emotions (despite one blatantly bad line call; the Centre Court crowd applauding his restraint), but after struggling to outsmart the vastly knowledgeable Mexican in four sets, McEnroe admitted he'd found it 'a difficult experience', claiming that the threat of punitive action had dampened his spirits and his game.

The severe mauling of the seeds was perhaps at least something to give McEnroe cause for celebration, the No.2's opposition weakened further when Roscoe Tanner exited at the hands of extrovert Brazilian rock musician Carlos Kirmayr (who'd beaten McEnroe in a recent WCT tournament in New York). The two Brians whom McEnroe had seen off at the Queen's Club tournament, Gottfried (a straight-sets loser to 31-year-old Jeff Borowiak) and reigning Australian Open champion Teacher (beaten in five sets by Vijay Amritraj), also came to grief.

In the third round, Borg faced Rolf Gehring. Soon after their match in Brussels in March, Borg had opted out of tennis for seven weeks to rest his nagging shoulder injury, though Gehring dismissed rumours that the Swede lost because he wanted to get out of the tournament early. Ahead of their clash, the 25-year-old German wasn't that upbeat about repeating the feat. 'I would like to play someone else, anyone else,' he said. 'Borg is a different player in the major tournaments.'

If Borg was eyeing revenge then the score was settled reasonably swiftly, though the champion didn't have things all his own way. In a match affected by rain, Borg took the first set 6-4 but, with the cold and wind making it hard to return serve, the second set was an effort. When the Dusseldorf man broke in the eighth game of the set with a stinging passing shot to lead 5-3 then was 30-15 on service, it looked as though Borg's clean slate of sets would be ruined. Gehring's chance, however, was fleeting. With a blistering array of backhands and angled forehand passes, Borg broke back immediately. It was the first in a ten-game winning sequence that carried the No.1 seed to a 6-4, 7-5, 6-0 success. Gehring, wearing boxer's boots to protect a weak ankle, might have been better served by a pair of fighter's gloves.

Borg's two main rivals were also in convincing form. Connors crushed compatriot Tony Giammalva while McEnroe emphatically slammed doubles specialist Bob Lutz, whom he'd beaten in each of their five previous meetings. Remaining tight-lipped despite some doubtful calls, McEnroe's calm demeanour again drew more than one round of sympathetic applause from the audience. He had more bother with his cold hands – blowing on them to keep warm on a chilly afternoon on No.1 Court – than his hot head, though couldn't resist a stinging post-match jibe at one linesman he'd felt wronged by: 'I have played tennis for most of my life, so I should know and see better than an elderly guy with glasses.'

Meanwhile, with Lutz's doubles partner Stan Smith, now 34, serving and volleying soundly past No.15 seed, Balazs Taroczy, and ninth-seeded Luis Clerc, John Lloyd's vanquisher, finding the tall 26-year-old Australian Paul Kronk too powerful, the 16 original seeds were now down to six – not one was in McEnroe's half of the draw. (Fifth seed Gene Mayer had withdrawn with a wrist injury before the tournament began.)

Borg's fairly routine victory meant that he earned a fourth-round opponent but would lose a practice partner, as Vitas Gerulaitis, winner in five sets against Victor Amaya, was the next obstacle blocking his route to glory. From No.3 seed in 1978, the American, according to *The Times*'s Clive White, was 'now on the brink of oblivion at No.16'. But, having gone through several coaches while in a prolonged slump, Gerulaitis had brought along the venerated Australian coach Harry Hopman this year and had, Borg acknowledged, 'shown himself to be in good shape in our practices together'.

The Swede was relishing a testing encounter against his best friend. 'It is always good to have one hard match, providing you survive, before the final,' he said. As it was, the pair were locked in a two-hour-25-minute Centre Court duel. Borg edged his opponent 7-6 (7-4), 7-5, 7-6 (8-6) to score an 18th successive win over Gerulaitis but it was really only Borg's philosophy in tiebreaks – 'play pretty safe, taking no chances' – and his ability to navigate the important points better that separated him from the American.

As expected, McEnroe and Connors reached the quarter-finals, too, but in contrasting styles. While Connors zipped convincingly past Fibak, whom he'd been beaten by in their previous meeting at the US Pro Indoor earlier in the year, McEnroe found a tough customer in Stan Smith, overcoming some stiff early resistance to down the 34-year-old in four sets, his fifth straight success over the former champion.

Against Smith, who'd revived some fading memories of old glories with the upset over Taroczy, McEnroe often struggled to contain himself when shots and line calls went against him, especially when losing the second set 3-6. He yelled self-admonishments, and twice he shouted in irritation at ball boys. As Brian Glanville put it, 'the cloven hoof showed now and again'. Mostly, though, he appeared conscious of his 'bad boy' tag and behaved. After one line call, which he queried, was confirmed by the linesman, McEnroe even offered a courteous 'Thank you' before resuming play.

In the last eight, Borg was pitted against Peter McNamara, the tall, amiable Melbourne man. McNamara had triumphed at the prestigious West German Open in Hamburg the previous month, registering wins against Harold Solomon and Lendl before thrashing a brooding Connors in the final. At Wimbledon, seeded 12, he'd had an impressive run while using an oversized racket, polishing off some established figures – Heinz Peter Gunthardt, Sherwood Stewart and Andrew Pattison – before defeating the 78th-ranked but always dangerous Jeff Borowiak. He'd never before been beyond the second round.

In their five previous meetings McNamara had only ever taken one set off Borg, in the US Open of 1980, but since their only clash on grass, at Wimbledon in 1978, the 25-year-old had improved enormously, and was now advised by the Australian coach Bob Brett and the Davis Cup captain Neale Fraser. Every day for two weeks prior to The Championships he'd run four or five miles and had never been fitter in his life.

McNamara was another who felt that the Wimbledon committee was biased towards Borg: Centre Court was 'like his backyard now', McNamara said, and 'must be worth a game a set to him'. Still, he stressed that 'I have as much chance of beating him [Borg] as anyone', though he disliked going into a match with too many preconceived ideas. 'Maybe I'll go for a walk to Hyde Park Corner and ask one of the speakers how they would play Borg. They usually have all the answers,' he wisecracked.

He opened well. On a hard and dry No.1 Court that produced some irregular bounces in the early going, Borg seemed the player most affected. With McNamara, the defending doubles champion with his compatriot Paul McNamee, serving strongly and coming in effectively, Borg looked bound for an arduous afternoon. He struggled with the Australian's aggressive hustling tactics, losing points that normally he would have put away, and though he surprisingly broke in the third game, McNamara came back, taking Borg to deuce twice in the next game before breaking to level at 3-3.

Serving at 4-5, 30-all, the champion was two points away from losing the first set, but unleashed two service winners to restore parity. When a tiebreak ensued, however, McNamara virtually nullified his earlier good work. Having dropped only three points in four previous service games, the Australian, seemingly a little unnerved, double-faulted on the first point, slipped to 0-4 when Borg passed him down his forehand side off a short second service, then put a forehand wide as Borg sealed it 7-2.

From then on, Borg simply stepped up a gear and McNamara was unable to respond. His serve now in good running order and producing just about every shot in his repertoire, the Swede bolted to a 3-1 lead in the second set when he broke McNamara's service in the fourth game, losing only one point, and then took the set from 5-2 and deuce when the Australian was unfortunate netting a backhand then slipping on his approach to the net.

Borg could even afford a smile when, on the first point of that eighth game, McNamara fell but still managed an unanswerable half-volleyed drop shot while lying down. The Australian was also winning some friends with his humour. 'I'll give you £10 to call it out,' he quipped to a linesman, Fred Sore, when a Borg lob beat him and hit the baseline to take the score to 40-30.

McNamara had only spirit to keep his flagging challenge alive now. Borg opened the third set with one of the nine aces he produced during the contest, broke McNamara's serve in the sixth game, and though the Australian picked up his game for one last charge, taking Borg through two deuces in the seventh game, the end was nigh. After McNamara fought to hold serve for 5-3, and again took Borg to two deuces, Borg sewed up the match on a forehand cross-court pass and a McNamara error, chalking up a 7-6 6-2 6-3 victory in one hour 46 minutes. Even Borg was surprised by his awesome exhibition. 'I really didn't expect to play so well,' he said.

It meant yet another Wimbledon showdown with Connors. But only just. Unseeded Vijay Amritraj, who'd trounced one-time Queensland motel owner Paul Kronk, had won four of his nine meetings with Connors and, two sets to the good in their quarter-final, it looked like the lithe, smooth-stroking Indian had his opponent by the scruff of the neck. But elegance and beauty of shot weren't enough. Gutsy as ever, Connors – 'the notorious alley fighter' Will Grimsley called him – once more proved he hadn't lost his punch.

Rallying magnificently, his running forehand working like a dream, the American plugged away, dominating from the fifth game of the third set onwards after breaking to lead 3-2, eventually winning 2-6, 5-7, 6-4, 6-3, 6-2 in three and a half hours. The left-hander had reached his seventh semi-final in eight years. In 60 singles matches at Wimbledon, it was the first time he had recovered from such a position. 'I never rolled over and played dead before, and I'm not going to roll over now,' a defiant Connors stated afterwards.

McEnroe was talking and playing with assurance too. 'Some guy is going to have to play exceptionally well to beat me,' he'd declared after beating Smith. But, in their last-eight match, Johan Kriek wasn't that guy. The 22-year-old expatriate South African, now resident in Naples, Florida, renowned for his speed and tenacity, had ousted Mike Estep, Joakim Nystrom, Russell Simpson and Francisco Gonzalez but found the No.2 seed far too much to handle. McEnroe hammered him easily, as he had done in the WCT final in Dallas earlier in the year.

The other quarter-final threw up a clash between two players who'd attracted little attention: the tall, powerful 20-year-old, Tim Mayotte, from Springfield, Massachusetts, who'd only turned professional two weeks earlier, and the late-developing Australian, Rod Frawley. Mayotte, the American inter-collegiate champion and, like McEnroe, a product of Stanford University, was perhaps the big surprise. Bernie Mitton, Fancutt (Lendl's conqueror), John Sadri and Sandy Mayer (a first-round winner against Nastase) had all fallen to him.

But none of the experts had foreseen Frawley emerging from the pack, either. The 28-year-old, hampered by a persistent back injury, had only won five matches in 12 tournaments, was ranked 112th in the world, and scraped into the main draw by the skin of his teeth. At the Mecca of tennis, though, the sturdy Queenslander's solid serve-and-volley play had accounted for 17-year-old Thierry Tulasne (the world's top junior) and compatriot Cliff Letcher and, after seeing off Carlos Kirmayr, he'd reached the last eight having survived a traumatic battle with the 20-year-old South Australian, John Fitzgerald, that saw a series of midcourt arguments with the umpire Peter Smith and assistant referee Alan Mills.

And it was Frawley who, despite losing the first set to the American rookie, came through to reach the final four, Australia's first men's singles semi-finalist since 1975 when Tony Roche lost to Ashe. He hadn't faced a single seed en route, but wasn't complaining; a moustachioed John Newcombe lookalike with a mane of wavy hair, Frawley hadn't played his first Wimbledon until 1975, when he was 25, and then he'd appeared only in the doubles and, having never before won a singles match in his three previous visits, this was something of a dream come true. He was about to confront a living nightmare.

On the Wednesday evening before the semi-finals, McEnroe and his doubles partner Peter Fleming were involved in ugly scenes during a victory over brothers Vijay and Anand Amritraj. In a stormy fourth set, McEnroe blew up when one of his serves was called out by a veteran linesman, a Kenyan-born Sikh named Raghbir Mhajan. McEnroe called the turbaned linesman an 'Indian' and accused him of bias. He also protested to umpire Jeremy Shales that Mhajan standing up obstructed his vision, and that he talked too much during play. The American was later reported for abusing an official.

Perhaps it was unsurprising then that the New Yorker's irascibility carried over to the next day. McEnroe defeated Frawley, as he had in their two previous meetings, taking just over three hours to record a tedious straight-sets victory. But on Centre Court before a crowd that included Lady Di, the encounter was marked by clashes and arguments with umpire George Grime, who, at times, appeared more of a protagonist than Frawley. On an afternoon that should have been savoured, it left a sour note again.

Stalking around the court, head bowed, muttering to himself from the very start, McEnroe was a ticking time bomb likely to go off at any moment. It didn't take long. When a vehement dispute in the tenth game provoked him into first of all asking sarcastically of Mr Grime, 'Can you make another bad call for me?' then shouting from the baseline, 'I get screwed because of the umpires in this place', the No.2 seed received a public warning about his conduct plus a slow handclap from the crowd. Thereafter, the player described unflatteringly by Frank Keating as a 'podgy, pouting, red-faced third generation Irish-American' kept up an almost constant unintelligible monologue.

In the third set, though, there was little doubt what he said. At 4-4 and 40-30 to Frawley, McEnroe became so incensed after losing an argument over a line call, he screamed, 'You are a disgrace to mankind!' which the umpire interpreted as being aimed at him. When Grime, a dentist with the rank of Wing Commander in the RAF, announced a penalty point for unsportsmanlike behaviour, which gave Frawley the game, McEnroe stomped to the umpire's chair, insisting he had been yelling at himself, and repeatedly asked to see Fred Hoyles. The tournament referee, 'satisfied with the competency of the umpire', upheld Grime's decision. The match proceeded and McEnroe, made to battle for every point by the brave, determined Frawley, finally won 7-6, 6-4, 7-5. But his reputation had clearly suffered several more self-inflicted body blows.

He was still bristling afterwards. In the claustrophobic post-match interview room, McEnroe became involved in a series of caustic exchanges with reporters, triggered by a question from James Whittaker, a gossip columnist for the *Daily Star*, about whether he had split with his tennis-playing girlfriend, Stacy Margolin. (Some tabloids had persisted in writing of a tiff between the two.) 'It's none of your business, but the answer is "no",' he shouted. He then launched into a tirade against the British press, firing a volley of insults, accusing them of being 'liars', 'trash' and other less printable names.

McEnroe was understandably embittered. He believed he'd been given a rough time throughout the tournament – that journalists were turning fans against him. The previous Tuesday, several newspapers had carried a report that he'd been caught for speeding – it was Peter Fleming at the wheel of the car – when, as he protested at the time, 'I've never driven a car in England in my life.' As a further question on tennis was interrupted with yet another about the player's private life, McEnroe ended his diatribe by gathering his gear from the dais, and stalking out to the locker room. 'I'm through talking to you guys,' he snapped.

Stunned by his sudden departure, members of the press then began to bicker among themselves and there followed a comically inept fistfight – the *Daily Mirror*'s Nigel Clarke and Charlie Steiner, an over-patriotic American correspondent for RKO Radio in the States, rolling around on the ground – over the line of questioning directed at McEnroe.

Even so, the McEnroe episodes were ancient history and the interview room soon emptied when somebody brought news of the Borg semi-final, announcing that 'Connors won the first set, 6-0'. Shrugged off by the bookies – 'That's ridiculous!' he'd exclaimed incredulously on hearing the 12-1 odds against him at the tournament's start – virtually ignored by the media and forced to play most of his matches on outside courts ('treated like an unwanted stepchild by the august All England scheduling committee' wrote Will Grimsley), Connors had almost become the forgotten man of Wimbledon. Going into their semi-final, Borg now had a 13-8 lead in official head-to-heads against his once-upon-a-time chief antagonist. But statistics left Connors cold. 'We'll just go out and we'll try to kill each other,' he promised. 'That is what the public wants to see.' And that is precisely what the public got.

The American had said that, win, lose or draw, he couldn't ask for more if he played the last three sets as well as he did against Amritraj. Against Borg, if anything, he played even better. Using all of his furious energy, swarming about the court, a fully pumped-up Connors was like a man possessed. Right from the start he came out slugging and Borg was buried under an avalanche of early winners. The No.3 seed broke the Swede's first serve to 15 with a no-holds-barred forehand pass, and attacked relentlessly.

Borg, normally sure-footed, had trouble on a spongy surface made slick from early-evening dew but it was the irrepressible American who presented far greater problems. Belting the daylights out of every ball, Connors left the Swede hurried and harassed, almost shocked at the power of his opponent. As net cords bounced his way, the left-hander even had luck on his side. He swept through a sensational first set in only 24 minutes.

There was no let-up for the champion. Borg held his opening service game of the second set to finally register on the scoreboard but two games later, with Connors maintaining the pressure, he was broken. The two old adversaries were producing some glittering tennis now. An amazing eighth game took 19 minutes, lasted 24 points and went to nine deuces, Connors wasting six points to hold serve for 5-3, Borg needing five break points to hurtle back into the match at four-all. But the Swede faulted five of six first serves in the next game and dropped serve again. When Connors held for a two-set lead, his pre-tournament prediction that he would be the new Wimbledon champion seemed no idle threat.

Borg looked baffled but he wasn't beaten. Asserting his own quieter energy, he clawed his way back into the contest. After hitting as many shots as possible low to Borg's backhand, Connors began playing more to his rival's forehand, allowing Borg to increasingly come to the net. It was all the encouragement Borg needed. After losing serve from 40-0 in the second game of the third set, Connors broke back for 3-2, but a new pattern soon evolved: Borg, more forceful with his groundstrokes, adding pace and depth, found gaps in Connors's defence. The American, as though exhausted by his early brilliance, was no longer in full flow. Borg took the third set 6-3 – and 'it gave me a kick' he said later. Some kick! The Swede raced through the next set, winning it to love in just 28 minutes, granting Connors only 12 points. Connors now looked like a punter who'd stacked everything on winning in three sets and failed.

Both he and Borg upped the ante. 'The two players,' wrote Rex Bellamy, 'were like gamblers who had laid on the table the ultimate stake – their lives.' Neither was prepared to give an inch or drop the pace. Each had chances to break. But it was the Swede who always looked the stronger. For Connors each game became a backs-to-the-wall battle. But after coming from 0-40 to 30-40 in the seventh, the American, having saved nine break points already in the set, finally succumbed on Borg's tenth, driving a forehand long after changing his mind in mid-swing – he initially sought slice for the shot. That put Borg 4-3 ahead with his service game to come.

Yet it was still far from over. Connors had two points to break back immediately and only narrowly failed to win the second of them. Three aces eventually won the game for the Swede. A last fling in the ninth game saw Connors hold to love but when Borg served for the match, 5-4 ahead, in the dusky light Connors's valiant fight at last came to an end. Borg took charge of the final rally, pulled a tiring opponent wide, then beat him with a sharply angled volley to end the three-hour-18-minute tussle. The 0-6, 4-6, 6-3, 6-0, 6-4 victory, a 41st in a row for Borg at Wimbledon, was his 22nd in 26 five-set matches over his career. He'd come back from two sets down for the sixth time.

Of all the Swede's mammoth uphill struggles, arguably none could top it. Arthur Ashe rated it in the top five of Wimbledon Centre Court matches he'd ever witnessed. (Lady Di hadn't seen a stroke of it; she'd left after the second set of the opening semi-final, though it wasn't clear whether she'd had enough of McEnroe's complaints or been diplomatically ushered away to save her embarrassment.) Connors was nonplussed by all the excitement, though. 'I've played in lots of matches like that,' he said. 'It's part of the business.' Although it was 'nice that the public gets their money's worth', for the American there was no measure of pride in being part of such a memorable match. 'You win or you lose, that's it. None of the rest counts. But at least he had to play his best stuff to beat me.' Borg certainly had.

Asked for a forecast for the final, Connors joked: 'Cloudy, with some rain.' With John Patrick McEnroe Jr on court there was always a fair chance of the odd thunderstorm, as well. 'One thing is for sure,' Will Grimsley wrote in his preview, 'the curly-haired rebel from Douglaston, NY, will do something to electrify the galleries and get his own machine smoking. He may be cocky and boorish at times. He is never boring.'

In Thomas Boswell's view, the antics of McEnroe – 'the incredible sulk' – besides giving the tournament an extra dimension to previous ones, might actually have subconsciously been calculated. Wimbledon was 'Borg's shrine and McEnroe has been going around spitting on the stained-glass windows', Boswell wrote. 'Perhaps McEnroe knows he will only be loved here in the role of gallant loser to the superhero Borg, so he has chosen the only alternative – the role of heathen defiler.'

Was it inevitable that spectators would be pulling for Borg on the Saturday afternoon? Grimsley wasn't so sure. Borg might be 'Cool Hand Luke, beloved by the Wimbledon conservatives and cheered by America's teenage brigade', he suggested, but 'McEnroe, for all his whining, bickering and boorishness, is anti-establishment. That puts a lot of people in his corner.' Far from reducing his fan base, McEnroe's subversive attitude actually won him followers. He handled his racket, as Grimsley put it, 'with the command of a violin master with a Stradivarius' but showed the disdainful irreverence of a snarling punk rocker. There were fans at Wimbledon, arguably more knowledgeable about the game than anywhere else, who not only respected him for his rare gifts but loved him for his outspoken rebelliousness and revolt against authority.

Barry Lorge ventured that his countrymen felt much the same way as the British about the two stars – the vast majority of Americans would sooner see Borg win the title. 'The churl and the champ go at it again' ran one ungracious headline in an Oregon newspaper (Eugene *Register-Guard*) ahead of the final. 'When you weigh it up, it's not just winning a match that makes a man a champion,' said Lorge. 'In all sorts of ways Borg has proved himself most fitted for the role.' Arthur Ashe, as much as he loathed McEnroe's histrionics, had a slightly different take. 'It's a new world,' said the US Davis Cup captain. 'If everybody was like Stan Smith, Ken Rosewall and me, it would be a dull show.' The line between being colourful and being coarse was exceedingly thin, however, and McEnroe had stepped across it a few times too often.

The *Evening Times*'s Charles Graham – 'Scotland's most controversial writer' according to the paper – argued that 'Sport is enriched by characters, including bad characters. It is good for us to have people to hate as well as favourites to admire.' McEnroe might have made Nastase (whom American sports writer, Bob Rubin, amusingly dubbed 'Grandfather Brat') seem like 'quite a mannerly chap' but it all added to the drama. As much as television viewers watched for excellence and skill, they 'enjoy it, too, when someone slips up, when we see signs of human weakness and show off our prowess as armchair critics'.

'Seeing the ball ping-ponging about the court is fine,' Graham wrote, 'but it's when McEnroe has one of his fits that the whole family is screamingly summoned to the TV room.' Still, even Graham declared that he would prefer to put up with another year of Borg – 'the man who never says a word, except "thanks" for the trophy and the cheque' – winning again rather than see the title go to McEnroe 'until he has grown up and stopped behaving like a talking ape'.

Wherever the fans' loyalties lay, there was a clamour to see the clash. On the day of the final, when the All England Club gates were opened at noon, pandemonium broke out. Police barriers were knocked flying in the mad dash for free standing room on Centre Court. A number of fans were felled in the rush, though no one was hurt. Queues had begun the previous Saturday and by midday more than 3,000 fans without tickets were waiting outside the ground hoping for a precious place.

McEnroe went into the final with a title already to his name; on the Friday, he and Fleming defeated Lutz and Smith in the men's doubles final, 6-4, 6-4, 6-4, for their second success in three years. And, on a warm but heavily overcast afternoon, in a febrile atmosphere, it was the American who started with supreme confidence, surrendering just one point in his first two service games.

But if anyone wondered whether the after-effects of his titanic struggle with Connors might hinder Borg, the Swede soon provided an answer.

Striking the ball with fluency, power and perfect timing, he went out seemingly fixed on keeping McEnroe under control. The edgy uncertainty that characterised the first two sets of his semi-final was gone. In the fifth game, he made a crucial breakthrough. McEnroe, serving, fought back from 0-40 to deuce, but Borg fired a great return to take the advantage before McEnroe netted a backhand volley off the following service return to lose the game.

Borg was at his serving best. McEnroe mustered just two points in the Swede's first four service games. Nonetheless, at 5-4, Borg's supporters suffered some unwelcome palpitations. McEnroe held four break points in total, but two mistakes from the left-hander and two service winners from Borg came to the champion's salvation before he finally disposed of his challenger when McEnroe overhit a service return then Borg put away a forehand volley. Some 36 minutes after the first ball was hit, the Swede had claimed the first set 6-4.

He continued making life tough for the antsy American, but McEnroe was responding in kind. And remaining commendably calm. Even after the distraction of a spectator yelling out – in the first game of the second set, after McEnroe put a first service well wide, a voice blared: 'Why don't you get the referee, John?' – plus three questionable calls, he suppressed his testiness, eliciting sympathy from the crowd. At 30-40 in the fourth game when Borg's lashed forehand appeared to be out but was called good, a perturbed McEnroe stared at the brown spot beyond the sideline then slowly walked around in a circle visibly biting his lip to censor an outburst; as he settled to receive Borg's next serve, applause broke out for the unprecedented gesture, which McEnroe, standing and raising both arms to the crowd, acknowledged. He even smiled.

All through the set, both players produced some exhilarating exchanges with flowing strokes. At 4-3, the No.2 seed spurned two break points and after failing to convert several other chances to clinch the set – nine break points in all – games went to 6-6 and a tiebreak. Almost in the blink of an eye, McEnroe won it. While Borg had trouble getting his first serve in – allowing his opponent breathing space and the chance to attack – McEnroe's functioned immaculately, his express deliveries tipping the scales decisively. Borg was blitzed 7-1.

It was clearly now a dogfight. In the third set, Borg bit first. Coming out with renewed spirit, his groundstrokes were hit even harder; he went looking to follow his first serve in to the net. In the fourth game, when McEnroe double-faulted while trailing 30-40, the Swede achieved an important break to lead 3-1. It was soon 4-1, and McEnroe suddenly faced a psychological mountain. He climbed it. At 4-2 to Borg, the Swede's armour was pierced for the first time, McEnroe enjoying two huge slices of good fortune before reducing the deficit: at 15-all, he struck a backhand that touched the top of the net and trickled over, unplayable; at 30-40, after a long rally, Borg got a bad bounce on the wearing court when McEnroe hit a harmless-looking approach, the ball shooting under the top seed's racket as he swung at it.

In the next game, the New Yorker, even after double-faulting twice, squeaked by, levelling at 4-4 when a Borg service return flew long on the game's 12th point. But when Borg held to lead 5-4 and then, with the Swede 30-15 up in the tenth game following a beautiful running cross-court pass, a McEnroe volley landed on the baseline was called good, then overruled by umpire Bob Jenkins, the American with two set points against him faced yet another colossal test. Again, he passed it.

Containing his anger, McEnroe crouched down at the baseline, breathing deeply, before nodding with a sad look, and going back to the business of winning a tennis match. The only pyrotechnics came from his racket. McEnroe fired two huge serves at Borg to bring the score to deuce.

And though Borg had two more set points, McEnroe responded again by making his service tell, dominating at the net, eventually taking a game of six deuces when Borg sent an attempted forehand pass into the net.

Two games later, a second tiebreak ensued. And once more McEnroe's serve proved the deciding factor. After surging clear with a forehand angled pass then a backhand winner to lead 6-3, on his second set point, when Borg was forced wide to return, the left-hander, reaching acrobatically, volleyed into a vacant court. The Swede was now 0-3 in Wimbledon final tiebreaks, his losses all to McEnroe. The American would write years later that 'after I took the third set, I knew in my bones that I was going to win'.

In the fourth set, looking to secure his first title, McEnroe turned the screw tighter. Kept at full stretch, Borg clung on desperately to his crown. He had a break point in the third game, McEnroe two in the eighth. Neither could capitalise. Games were evenly poised but in the tenth, having served to move 5-4 ahead, McEnroe's big moment came. Borg, serving to save his title for a first time, went 30-love up but three successive unforced errors handed McEnroe Championship point. When a backhand volley off a poor return forced McEnroe into putting a pass yards out, the Swede saved it, and his fans breathed again.

On the next point, McEnroe attacked Borg's serve, volleyed deep and met Borg's scrambled return with a brave overhead smash. Another match point. This time he didn't let the defending champion loose. McEnroe closed in on Borg's weak second service, returned deep to the baseline and charged the net; Borg tried one last topspin pass but when McEnroe's crisp forehand volley down the line kicked up chalk deep in the forehand corner, with the Swede running in the opposite direction, that was it: at exactly 5.29pm, Borg's seeming lifetime lock on the men's singles title had been unpicked.

After the briefest moment when it seemed as though he could hardly believe victory was his, McEnroe, eyes closed, emitted a cry of jubilation, threw his arms in the air, and started to drop to his knees before, perhaps recalling Borg's prayerful ritual, deciding to stay on his feet. At the end of a tumultuous two weeks at loggerheads with the Wimbledon establishment, the umpires and the press, all the furore and feuding were forgotten in that instant.

As McEnroe received the trophy, Borg stood in obscurity in the loser's place behind the umpire's chair. But the cheers that rang out from the gallery for the runner-up were far louder than the reception given to the winner. The day belonged to McEnroe, though. It was a star-spangled Fourth of July, an afternoon on which, as Thomas Boswell put it, 'America's freedom fighter ... declared his independence from the King of Sweden.'

One of the most phenomenal streaks in sport had, Will Grimsley wrote, 'been broken on the taut gut strings of McEnroe's wooden racket'. 'Never has this 5ft 11in, left-handed blend of power and finesse given so fine a demonstration of proper grass-court techniques,' praised Boswell. But in Alan Trengove's view, McEnroe had liberated the crown because, most importantly, he'd harnessed the 'atom of self-control', showed that he could win without giving vent to his feelings. About what he called McEnroe's 'monstrous behaviour' throughout maybe the most turbulent of Wimbledon fortnights, a scathing American sports columnist, Milton Richman, had wondered 'if he ever uses his head for anything else but to put a sweatband around'. Against the Swede, McEnroe had employed his frizzy-haired loaf in the most effective manner, and the saying that tennis champions were made on a six-inch court – the width between a person's ears – had never been more appropriate.

As he had the year before, he'd kept his composure consciously, he revealed, because of the man across the net. 'It was respect for him [Borg] and the occasion,' he said. 'You have to give everything to beat him. You can't cope with other problems.' McEnroe *had* given everything, marshalling his gifts into an all-conquering whole. Having watched the Borg-Connors match on television, he'd made a mental note. 'It was like clay-court tennis on grass,' he said. 'They hit the hell out of the ball because that's the way they like to play. I was going out there to play a few shots softly and chip and dink and come in.' The plan worked.

Worried by his inconsistent serving before the final, McEnroe had also written a note to himself, which he deposited in his racket cover. It reminded him to keep his head up when serving, to throw the ball more towards the left instead of above his head. Although he served ten double faults to Borg's four, the American got in 62 per cent of first serves, while the Swede managed only 53, enabling him to move in swiftly and put away the volley. It was another significant factor. McEnroe, Borg acknowledged, had served too well for him, especially on the critical points in the third and fourth sets and in the two tiebreaks. Ever magnanimous, Borg called the outcome 'good for tennis'.

To reporters, McEnroe paid tribute to his opponent. 'I am glad to have beaten a guy who is one of the greatest players who ever lived,' he said. 'And I want to congratulate him because he's a great champion.' A great champion. It was debatable whether that same label could be attached to McEnroe. No player in Wimbledon's 104-year history had won a title in such disgrace. For all McEnroe's good sportsmanship in the final it was impossible to overlook what Geoffrey Miller termed the 'things that caused members of the highly respectable All England Club to splutter into their teacups'.

They were still spluttering. The American, quizzed post-match on whether his feuding with the club would stop, replied that 'I'm going to have a cup of tea with them later. The bottom line is winning the tournament. I couldn't be happier. Let's hope these problems don't happen anymore.' But it was a vain hope. The victory soon took on a bittersweet taste. Within one hour of his triumph, McEnroe was informed that the committee had recommended to the MIPTC a maximum £5,000 fine against him for bringing the game into disrepute during his semi-final (this was in addition to the committee's own fines for incidents in his first-round singles match and the doubles clash with the Amritraj brothers). He also faced an automatic 21-day suspension.

For the very first time the committee also went against tradition by refusing – 'due to McEnroe's poor behaviour and antics in the fortnight' – to make the new champion an honorary member immediately after his success. Not all of the members were satisfied that he deserved it. There might have been a cup of tea but there was no celebratory wine. To cap it all, later that evening the wayward genius further offended the Wimbledon chiefs by skipping the annual champions' dinner at the swank Savoy Hotel – his absence considered a blatant insult to his British hosts. Was it done in retaliation for his fines? 'I didn't go because nobody asked me,' he was quoted as saying (upon his return to America the following day). 'They didn't want me and, you know, it was fine with me.'

McEnroe claimed that, although he'd arranged a party for family and friends, he was willing to go and, as per custom, say a few words but said that his father was told that if McEnroe Jr didn't attend the whole dinner his invitation was rescinded. All England Club officials gave an alternative account. McEnroe, they countered, had informed them he couldn't be at the dinner until about 11pm but they'd asked him if he could get there around 10.15pm and it was left at that.

In the end it fell upon Chris Evert Lloyd*, the highly popular women's champion, to fill in. She gave one of the wittiest speeches heard by a champion in years. 'Sir Brian Burnett [chairman of the All England Club]

---

* In 1979, Chris Evert and John Lloyd enjoyed a marital matchup and she changed her name. The Wimbledon singles success in 1981 was her first since 1976, and would be her last at The Championships.

said, in John's absence, that I would have to make two speeches,' she told the guests. 'One for myself and one for you-know-who. Unfortunately, I can only make one because I do not have his vocabulary.' It brought the house down.

The 68-year-old Burnett, an Air Chief Marshall, said at the dinner that Borg's defeat ended an era. Previewing The Championships, David Irvine had asked, 'for how much longer can this imperturbable and immovable Swede resist the forces crowding at his heels? This year, next year, sometime certainly, a new ruler must be acclaimed. The leaders of the pack are closing in.' Centre Court did have a new king, and the player described by John Ballantine of the *Sunday Times* as 'a curious cross between a courtly English gentleman and a Swedish wolf' was now one of the chasing pack again.

But Borg was still only 25, the age at which many champions were just reaching their prime. With at least ten more years at the top a possibility for him, the pursuit of further Wimbledon titles would surely carry on. 'I'll keep coming back as long as I enjoy it,' he promised in the wake of his loss. It was a seemingly straightforward statement but one, though no one realised at the time, with a proviso whose significance would, before long, become all too apparent.

The Iceman Melts Away

TEN WEEKS after spoiling Bjorn Borg's summer on the Centre Court's chopped-up grass, John McEnroe, back home in his native Queens, New York, levelled a crowning blow to the Swede's dream of a first US title in ten times of trying, disposing of Borg in the final in four sets, again, as with his Wimbledon victory, coming back strongly after conceding the opening set. It was an oddly hollow performance from Borg this time, though. McEnroe would later record that 'it was almost as if he'd emotionally lost his edge, like he didn't want to be there'.

He certainly didn't stick around long after the loss. Commiserating with Borg to the 20,000 Flushing Meadows crowd as he accepted the winner's trophy (to polite applause) and a cheque for $66,000, McEnroe said, 'I think he's going to win this damn tournament someday but, hopefully, not when I'm here.' But Borg wasn't there to hear the consoling words. At the end of the match, surrounded by plainclothes policemen and security guards, he'd hurriedly left the court and made a hasty retreat to the dressing rooms. After showering quickly, he was rushed down a back stairway, past garbage from the concession stands and into a waiting car, a Volvo station wagon, which headed straight for Borg's luxurious home at

Sand Point, Long Island. Lennart Bergelin left with him. Mariana, who'd watched the final from the courtside, remained at the stadium.

Whether the unfailingly gracious loser had undergone a dramatic change of image and his fast exit was his own idea or the reason for the quick getaway was a telephoned death threat against Borg, delivered to the main switchboard at the National Tennis Center after the Swede took the first set – the second day in a row he had been threatened – stories post-match were conflicting. Regardless, while McEnroe was giving his speech, the vanquished Swede was heading out of the stadium.

Borg had insisted that, despite his wealth, his marriage and the numerous peaks he'd already scaled, his will to win had not diminished. To reach the US final, he'd out-toughed Tanner in the quarter-finals and Connors in the semi-finals. But after talking for two weeks of how the elusive title was his big goal in tennis – McEnroe felt Borg, in doing so, had put undue pressure on himself to win – in the final, Borg's great determination appeared to be missing. McEnroe, unlike the previous year's five-setter, had won with relative ease. It was McEnroe's third Open in a row on home soil, the first such streak since Bill Tilden won his sixth American championship in 1925. No player had won both the Wimbledon and US titles in the same year since Connors in 1974.

McEnroe, with his Wimbledon success, had already assumed the No.1 position in the computer rankings. He was a young man seemingly destined to keep stocking up his trophy cabinet. The 22-year-old hadn't ceased to appreciate Borg's artistry or status in the game; he just knew now that he had his number. 'A good deal of the time,' he said after the US triumph, 'I think I can read where he's going.' Though, following a difficult route reaching the final, McEnroe did acknowledge that he'd also now discovered what Borg had learned before him: 'It's a lot harder to stay on top than it is to get there.'

If the Wimbledon men's singles in the latter half of the 1970s would be remembered chiefly for the classic Borg-Connors confrontations, in the early 1980s the era-defining rivalry of not just The Championships in SW19 but tennis in general looked certain to be that of Borg-McEnroe. Will Grimsley – another writer to use the 'Western' analogy – envisaged an exciting head-to-head series between the two: 'It is the quiet "Shane" against the snarling man in black in a saloon shoot-out,' he wrote. Tennis was in for 'a great travelling roadshow – the two best players in the world, so close that a point or two can swing the pendulum either way – crossing oceans to battle each other like restless gladiators'. Their record now stood at seven victories apiece. 'The McEnroe-Borg globe-girdling circus,' Grimsley enthused, 'has all the ingredients of high drama and gripping suspense.'

Borg, however, had had all the drama and suspense he could cope with. At least for the foreseeable future. He needed a rest. A decent rest. After years without a break, he'd already decided that he just wanted to get away from tennis, so planned a five-month hiatus from the tour. After defeat in the States, he fulfilled obligations to play in Geneva (where, on his way to a 64th ATP title, he took down 17-year-old compatriot, Mats Wilander, the latest Swedish sensation who, the following year, would become the youngest-ever winner of the French Open) then a month later in Tokyo (where he was beaten by Tim Gullikson in the second round), but those were Borg's last tournaments of the season.

The following April when he returned to the Grand Prix circuit, playing in his own backyard at the Monte Carlo Country Club, Borg, although showing predictable signs of rustiness, made the quarter-finals, where he was comprehensively ground into the copper clay by Yannick Noah, 6-1, 6-2. Defeat was hardly surprising. Nor too dismaying: the young Frenchman had apparently heard Borg whistling merrily at the changeovers. What *was* strange, though, was that Borg had had to qualify to even make the field in the first place.

His presence in the qualifying rounds was a consequence of a refusal to comply with Rule 8 in the 1982 Grand Prix guide. A year earlier, on 30 April 1981, World Championship Tennis announced its withdrawal from the Volvo Grand Prix circuit, into which it had been incorporated since 1978, and the re-establishment of its own tour calendar for the 1982 season. The circuit was administered by the MIPTC, and to counter the threat of players leaving for WCT, the MIPTC introduced a mandatory commitment to play a minimum ten Grand Prix Super Series tournaments (between 4 January 1982 and 17 January 1983), the authorities decreeing that any top player who didn't agree would have to pre-qualify for all majors. There were no exemptions.

Borg chose to enter only seven tournaments. For a number of weeks after, he kicked against the rule. A request for a reprieve was considered. The player petitioned the MIPTC to alter their conditions, but they refused. So when, after a good deal of soul-searching, Wimbledon decided to back the Grand Prix, the Swede was now faced with the bizarre situation of being denied automatic entry for, amongst others, the tournament he'd dominated for so long; he would have to go through qualification with the other hopefuls at Roehampton the week before the 1982 Championships.

His fellow pros came out in support. 'He has the right to one year off or five years off if he wants to,' said Ivan Lendl, now the world No.2-ranked player. 'He has practised for four or five hours a day every day for ten years, so why can't he take a rest?' McEnroe thought it 'one big mistake' on the Wimbledon management's part. He called the Pro Council 'fools' for what they were doing. 'It's not only going to hurt him [Borg], or them, but us too,' McEnroe complained. Even Arthur Ashe, a member of the council who'd helped write the rule, agreed it was unjust.

In Monte Carlo, where he'd progressed from three qualifying matches, a compromise, via Sir Brian Burnett, was offered; the All England club would still permit Borg to enter its draw straightaway should he agree to play in ten tournaments between 1 April 1982 and 31 March 1983. Borg didn't accept. 'I am not helping them save face,' he commented. Two weeks later, in Tokyo (there to play in the $250,000 Suntory Cup tournament where, on a court built over the 1964 Olympic swimming pool, he thrashed Vilas in the final), Borg announced that he would sit out Wimbledon, along with the French Open and possibly the US Open, to protest the All England Club's stance. He was, he declared, only going to play exhibition matches the rest of the year.

Borg didn't believe he warranted special consideration. 'I really don't think it's fair that I must qualify,' he said, 'but not because I've won at Wimbledon five times – it has nothing to do with that. I don't think, if a player wants to get away from tennis for a while, or if he's injured for a long time, that he has to make up all the tournaments in order to qualify.' So, despite facing a fusillade of criticism from tennis's rulers, Borg, sticking firmly to his guns, became a voluntary exile from what he still regarded as 'the greatest tournament to play'.

On 21 June 1982, then, when McEnroe, as defending champion, had the honour of opening on Centre Court for the first time, the Swede who'd monopolised the traditional start to The Championships since 1977 was nowhere in sight. Most tennis aficionados supposed that McEnroe, once he took over from Borg as Wimbledon champion, would be just as difficult to depose. Lendl now appeared the major threat (though he was also missing this year). It was Connors who was seeded to meet McEnroe in the final, played officially on a Sunday for the first time – and the seeding worked out.

With Connors's age it was felt that his last realistic chance of another Wimbledon had passed. But any doubters foolishly failed to reckon with the American's supreme competitiveness. At his combative best, the 30-year-old had, since January of that year, charged back into the picture, significantly introducing more serve-and-volley into his game. And, after Connors defeated McEnroe 7-5, 6-3 in the final of the Stella Artois tournament at the Queen's Club, three weeks later, in the Wimbledon final for a fifth time, he outlasted his bitter rival 3-6, 6-3, 6-7 (2-7), 7-6 (7-5), 6-4 for a second (and what would be his last) title in SW19. Minutes after the four-hour-14-minute classic – then the longest men's singles final in Wimbledon history – the management committee of the All England Club announced that McEnroe had finally been rewarded with membership. Two months later, Connors went on to claim another US crown as well – overcoming Lendl (McEnroe's semi-final conqueror) in a four-set final – and by the end of the year had reclaimed the No.1 world ranking he'd lost to Borg in 1978.

Despite his disgruntlement with the game's governing bodies, Borg had reiterated that the plan was 'to come back to the top level'. As Yannick Noah had pointed out in Monte Carlo, when one is in the habit of winning it's far from easy to accept losing. On the face of it, he had at least four more years at the very summit. So when, on 23 January 1983, Borg revealed in an interview with *Kvallposten*, a newspaper in Malmo, that he'd decided to cancel his comeback once and for all after a layoff of some one and a half years from tournament competition and was retiring from the game, the announcement shook the tennis world. The Swede would complete his contractual obligations by playing at Monte Carlo and the Suntory Cup in Tokyo, but that was it.

The game was no longer enjoyable for him, Borg said. 'I have not got the right motivation,' the paper quoted him as saying. 'I cannot give 100 per cent, and if I cannot do that it would not be fair to myself to go on. Tennis has to be fun if you are to get to the top and I don't feel that way about it anymore.' Talking to Neil Amdur of the *New York Times*, the Swede elaborated. 'When you go out on the court, you should say "this is great, I'm going to hit the tennis ball, I'm going to try to win every point, and I like to make a good shot," he said. 'If you don't think and feel that, it's very difficult to play.'

In April, at Monte Carlo in the first outdoor tournament of the new European season, his last official outing attracted a top-class international line-up. Borg was knocked out in the second round by Frenchman, Henri Leconte. In the Suntory Cup, after beating McEnroe, he fell in the final to Connors. Borg left the court to a standing ovation, but said afterwards that he was glad everything was over. 'I don't really have any regrets,' he told reporters, 'but it would be more fun sitting here [after] winning the [US] Open, because I wanted to win that very badly. As long as you know you tried the best, there's not much more you can do about it.'

The interview all but amounted to a farewell speech. There were exhibition matches here and there in the months that followed, but essentially the career of the Borg that the world had come to know was finished.

In *Look-in* magazine, June 1979, it was suggested that the Swede might perhaps 'prove to be the last great champion. The financial bonanza that awaits any successful players these days could ultimately prove their downfall. After all, you need an extraordinary love for a sport that requires you to fulfil exhausting schedules, when you have enough money lying in your back account to enable you to head straight for the sunny Bahamas … and stay there!' At that time, Borg had his own 'sunny Bahamas' – a house in Cap Ferrat and a sumptuous apartment in the foothills of Monte Carlo; among the 11 islands that he owned, one, Kattilo, he could use as a hideaway haven – and an 'extraordinary love' for tennis had still existed. Even then, though, it was beginning to wither; Borg revealed he'd actually thought about calling it a day for a couple of years.

What he craved now was, if anything, a normalcy he'd been denied by his own devotion to the sport; to simply wake up in the morning knowing that he no longer had to practise, no longer had to adhere to the regularity and routine that had been his life for so long. It had been a constant slog, an endless treadmill. Over ten years of globetrotting travel and intense competition, from high-level tournaments during which he lived an almost monastic existence to lucrative but meaningless exhibitions (what Jack Kramer termed 'tinsel events'). Over ten years in which his life was mapped out almost hour by hour. The discipline required to cope with it all – the fame and adulation, the unvarying attention, the expectation that you should win every game you play – was immense. Whether he was injured or fatigued, the same level of excellence had to be maintained.

Borg once described it as a 'crazy life'. 'We [the players] see the court and hotel rooms,' he told Jay Teitel in 1978. 'And no seasons ... we have no idea of winter or summer.' There were maybe three or four weeks off a year, but even then, if Borg didn't practise for a day, he felt that he lost the rhythm of his game. And any drop in standards could prove fatal. There were commercial engagements, responsibilities to his sponsors. Even on supposed holidays, as evidenced during the filming of ITV's *Brian Moore Meets Bjorn Borg* documentary in 1980, Borg was often required to fulfil 'work' commitments – filming TV commercials, for example, or opening a tennis school. The demands were draining.

The rigours of the modern circuit had debilitating effects on his body too. Injuries became more frequent, as did the drugs taken for injuries. 'Four years ago, if I rested for two weeks, it took me one day to get back in shape,' he told Christopher Whipple of *Life* magazine in 1980. 'Now it takes me at least a week – and I'm only 24.' His wife suffered as well. 'When I was playing, Mariana was always nervous because she wanted the best for me,' Borg would say in October 1983. 'And I was nervous. Pressure. Always pressure. If I was getting mad, she was the one who got all the bad feelings from me.' As one of the world's most recognisable people, enjoying a 'real' life was nigh-on impossible. Time to themselves for the two was seldom easy. Meals out quickly became a confrontation with photographers and gossip seekers. Existing on 'a paradisiacal plateau', as Curry Kirkpatrick called it, was far from heavenly.

Inevitably, speculation as to Borg's reasons for quitting was rife but usually way wide of the mark. It was at Mariana's urging, some said. Stories circulated that she was ill; even dying from cancer. (She'd actually had treatment for kidney stones the year before.) The truth was, Mariana was as astonished as anyone by Borg's decision. She thought her husband was mad to give up the game. Bergelin was also stunned (though, according to Borg, his coach was once a player, so 'He knows about the day that comes when you have nothing more to give.'). Peter Worth, the agent assigned by Mark McCormack's IMG to take responsibility for Borg's affairs and who'd worked with the player for six years, just couldn't understand it.

Others dramatised the demoralising effect that individual matches had had. At Wimbledon in 1980, Borg had supposedly seen a foreshadowing of things to come and he'd confronted ghosts – a surrendering of his dominance, the sinking sensation he was no longer certain of winning. At the US Open final that year, according to J.A. Allen in the *Bleacher Report*, 'He looked across the net at the up-and-coming John McEnroe and felt his tennis future fading.' His Wimbledon defeat was allegedly crushing. Then, after the shut-out in the Big Apple, in Allen's words, 'His confidence was gone, as was his will to change and work harder.' Some harsher critics even cited his retiring as evidence of a lack of fight and fibre, a missing mental fortitude. Usurped by a young American upstart, the battler had become a bottler, they said.

Far from being crushed, when he lost the 1981 Wimbledon final, as Borg himself put it, 'what shocked me was I wasn't even upset'. McEnroe would later note that 'When we shook hands [at the end of the match], Bjorn looked oddly relieved.' As though a boulder on his rounded shoulders had shrunk to a pebble. The American had sensed during the actual match that Borg was 'not quite [as] hungry' as the previous year. The man who, according to Mariana, hated losing so much he normally 'wouldn't talk for at least three days' after a defeat had stopped feeling the pain.

Any endeavours to convince Borg to carry on failed. Borg was adamant. 'Absolutely nothing,' he promised, would get him to return. It wasn't strictly true. There was an appearance at the Stuttgart Outdoor tournament in July 1984 (where he again lost on clay to Leconte). In 1991, at the age of 34, after almost a decade of turmoil in his personal and business life, Borg made an abortive comeback to the regular tour, encouraged by a 79-year-old 'mind-body fitness guru', Welshman Ron Thatcher, whom Borg referred to as 'The Professor'. The ties with Bergelin had long been cut.

At the Monte Carlo Masters, wielding one of his old wooden Donnay rackets and sporting the same tight-fitting Fila outfit of his heyday, 'he bore as much resemblance to the player everyone remembered', Curry Kirkpatrick observed, 'as did the four guys up in the crowd wearing Borg wigs and Borg headbands.' A ghost of his former greatness, Borg fell to a little-known Spaniard, Jordi Arrese (using a graphite racket), and, soundly beaten in a succession of first-round ties over the next two years – he played and lost 12 matches – he once more withdrew. This time for good.

Of all Borg's leading rivals, it was definitely McEnroe who felt the Swede's absence the deepest. From their very first meeting, in Stockholm in 1978, Borg had offered the American support, something that was extremely important to McEnroe and later helped in his acceptance by other players in the locker room. Borg was, at that time, McEnroe's idol – as a youngster in Douglaston, the New Yorker had grown up with a Borg poster on his bedroom wall – but soon a friendship between the two developed. Their playing styles and on-court demeanours couldn't have been more contrasting but personality-wise they were closer than people realised. 'We had similar senses of humour, looked at things in the same way and were bemused by a lot,' McEnroe would reflect years later. A mutual respect was shared. On only one occasion did McEnroe ever go, in his own words, 'a little nutty' against Borg – during their third encounter, in New Orleans, in 1979; the Swede simply beckoned his opponent to the net and told him to 'just relax'.

McEnroe greeted the news of Borg's retirement with disbelief. 'It made absolutely no sense to me,' he said. Pleas for the Swede to reconsider fell on deaf ears. Tennis needed Borg, McEnroe told him. More to the point, the American needed him. They were making each other better players, he felt, and the sport in general more exciting. After the 1980 Wimbledon final, Mike Lupica wrote that all future finals would 'be measured against Borg versus McEnroe … This match is the standard now.' Their 1980 US Open final clash is commonly regarded as one of the finest ever. When what was building into one of the greatest matchups in tennis history was suddenly kicked over, it left McEnroe not just disappointed but bereft. The keen rivalry he'd enjoyed with the Swede, McEnroe would subsequently find, was never duplicated. For the rest of his career, he remained, he would later claim, 'in a kind of continued mourning for Borg'.

McEnroe won just three more grand slam titles. Two of those came at Wimbledon. He was men's singles champion again in 1983 (routing New Zealander Chris Lewis in straight sets) and 1984 (trouncing Connors for the loss of just four games). 'When I quit tennis,' he was quoted as saying during his notorious 1981 campaign, 'I want to be remembered as a tennis player, not as some jerk.' Borg had been adamant that the game should value the likes of the American, despite his constant railing at authority. 'It would be a very dull sport if everyone was as boring as me,' he said. But watching McEnroe, for all his sublime talent, was rarely a pleasurable experience. He had 'the look, posture and mannerisms of a man doing something he despises' wrote Bob Rubin in 1981. 'Total absence of joy.' Even if he had just cause for complaints about officiating, 'his means of expression', argued Rubin, '[made] everyone lose sight of whether he is right or wrong'.

In a *Radio Times* Wimbledon preview of 1970, Jack Warboys, the father of British tennis player, Stephen Warboys, while anxious for his son's career to take off, noted that 'Ultimate success depends on being successful at the sport and going down well with everybody. What's the use of being good at sport if people don't like you?' To win is one thing; to impart a universal goodwill in the doing is another. Unlike McEnroe, Borg undoubtedly achieved that – especially at Wimbledon.

In 1977, Frank Keating wrote of Borg: 'He is so self-contained, so coldly aloof that it's impossible to identify with him, to get so much as an inkling of what fiery inner turmoils he might be damping down.' After the final that same year, Ronald Atkin in *The Observer* described Borg's 'emotional boiling point' as 'about on a level with the Sphinx'. 'A typical Swedish personality,' Rex Bellamy called him, 'and I'm quoting from Henry Miller now – "His heart may be a gold mine, but it's at the bottom of a very deep shaft."'

But to those who inferred that Borg was missing the personal touch and thought him little more than what Will Grimsley called 'a veritable stroking machine', David Irvine supplied a corrective. 'The outward serenity betokens not a lack of imagination but the champion's greatest strength, an iron concentration,' he wrote of the Swede following his 1979 triumph. 'And if his technique seems mechanical, it is only because he has made the brilliant stroke such a common part of his racket's vocabulary.' It was not in spite of but because of these qualities that the Wimbledon-watching public warmed to him.

In a time of enormously inflated egos, surly tempers and inexcusable bad acting in tennis, Borg's Scandinavian gentleness and his natural modesty were attractive traits. There was no flash or flamboyancy. No fist-pumping, wiggles of the hips or waggling of a finger. His behaviour was beyond reproach. The respect for the institutions that made Wimbledon what it was, which didn't readily show itself in other top competitors, Borg displayed in abundance. Goliath never got too big for his tennis shoes. His 'pluck, gallantry and reserve … almost made him an honorary Briton', wrote Thomas Boswell. Borg, in John Barrett's words, 'showed us that chivalry had not died with the arrival of Open tennis. It was refreshing to discover that nice guys can still come first.'

In the *Radio Times* in 1980, ahead of Borg's quest for a fifth straight crown, Barrett wrote that 'At Wimbledon he [Borg] could write a new record this year that might never be equalled.' In the decades that followed, his 'new record' was equalled. Others were surpassed. Fresh rivalries emerged. Great Wimbledon champions came and went. After Borg's triumph that year, though, Fred Perry then with an overview of tennis that spanned half a century, insisted that it was 'impossible to cross age boundaries' and 'ludicrous' to make comparisons between players from different periods. 'You have to rate a man in the era in which he exists,' he stressed. There were too many significant changes, not just in equipment but in rules and conditions, to do otherwise. 'There is one champion for every era,' said Perry. Borg was the man of his.

The Swede would say that, of all the tournaments he played around the world, Wimbledon was the 'most special', the one that was and would always be deepest inside his heart. His early retirement brought to a close a story that might well have contained a few more glorious chapters. But one thing's for certain: what he left behind was a legacy to be cherished. Borg's triumphant run at the All England Club dwarfed all other achievements in modern times. He was the first tennis player ever to play through and win five consecutive Wimbledon Championships. No one in the 20th century held the men's singles title longer. 'The most incredible thing about Borg's streak,' said John McEnroe ahead of the 1981 Championships, 'is that I don't even look at him as a grass-court player.' The American wasn't the only one. Yet for 41 matches, for over half a decade, on a surface for which he seemingly wasn't suited, Borg remained unconquered. As the golden boy said himself, it was 'a pretty good record'. No one is ever likely to argue with that.

Acknowledgements

FIRST AND foremost, I would like to express enormous gratitude to Richard Whitehead, whose generous – in all senses of the word – supply of archive material from numerous British newspapers was a truly invaluable resource. He exposed me to the words of some of the finest writers about tennis there has ever been, many of which I've quoted within the text of this book. Big thanks, too, go to Paul and Jane Camillin at Pitch Publishing for offering me another opportunity to work with them. I'd also like to extend my appreciation to Duncan Olner for the superb book cover design, Katie Field and Andrea Dunn for their sterling editorial work, and David Snowdon, who kindly cast a keen eye over my manuscript. Last but not least, I shall remain eternally grateful for the love and support of my wife, Dianna, which keeps me chipping away however big the rock in front of me might sometimes appear.

Bibliography

Apsley, Brenda, *Bjorn Borg's Tennis Special* (World Distributors Limited, Manchester, 1978).

Barrett, John, *100 Wimbledon Championships: A Celebration* (Willow Books/Collins, 1986).

Borg, Bjorn and Scott, Gene, *My Life and Game* (Simon & Schuster, 1980).

Connors, Jimmy, *The Outsider: My Autobiography* (Bantam Press, 2013).

McEnroe, John, *Serious: The Autobiography* (Sphere, 2003).

Newspaper and magazine articles

Allen, J.A., 'Bjorn Borg: The Beginning of the End' (*Bleacher Report*, 26 September 2009).

Author unknown, 'The Million Dollar Man' (*Saab Scene*, Volume 3 No.2, July 1980).

Boswell, Thomas, 'Borg: Why He Keeps Winning at Wimbledon' (*Toledo Blade*, 1 July 1981).

Brasher, Christopher and Brasher, Shirley, 'Courtside at the Jimmy Connors Show' (*The Age*, 30 June 1975).

Deford, Frank, 'A Match Goes Down in History' (*Sports Illustrated*, 14 July 1980).

Grimsley, Will, 'Are Pro Tennis Players Really Snobs?' (*The Nashua Telegraph*, 1 July 1974).

Harris, Nick, 'How Bjorn Borg Won His First Wimbledon' (*Mail on Sunday*, 9 July 2016).

Jares, Joe, 'A Golden Week for a Lot of Golden Oldies' (*Sports Illustrated*, 20 May 1974).

Leavy, Jane, 'Bjorn Borg at 27: Retiring Early and Sleeping Well' (*The Washington Post*, 29 October 1983).

Lorge, Barry, 'Tennis Stars Believe in 'Faith Healing' (*The Washington Post*, 1 January 1978).

Lorge, Barry, 'Neither Wimbledon Nor July Weddings Can Perturb Borg' (*The Washington Post*, 23 June 1980).

McEnroe, John, 'McEnroe Remembers Bjorn Borg' (*The Telegraph*, 28 November 2015).

Musel, Robert, 'Wimbledon Sees History's First Noisy Tennis Fans as Girls Throng to See Swedish Prodigy Champion Bjorn Borg' (*Middlesboro Daily News*, 26 June 1974).

Ornauer, David, 'Angry Borg to Sit Out Wimbledon in Protest' (*Stars and Stripes*, 18 April 1982).

Richman, Milton, 'McEnroe: the Good, the Bad and the Ugly' (*The Bulletin*, 7 July 1981).

Segell, Michael, 'Jimmy Connors: The Games He Plays' (*Rolling Stone*, 4 September 1980).

Simpson, Anne, 'Wonder Boys of Wimbledon' (*The Glasgow Herald*, 21 June 1976).

Teitel, Jay, 'A Star Is Bjorn' (*The Windsor Star*, 30 June 1978).

Sports Illustrated articles by Curry Kirkpatrick:

AND IT WAS STILL THREE FOR ONE, 16 January 1978

BORG'S HOT HAND TOOK ALL THE TRICKS, 31 January 1977

HE MOWED BORG DOWN, 18 September 1978

HIS EARTH, HIS REALM, HIS ENGLAND, 13 July 1981

IT WAS A LIKE-HATE RELATIONSHIP, 17 May 1976

IT'S NICE WORK IF YOU QUALIFY FOR IT, 19 April 1982

SO YOUNG AND SO UNTENDER, 24 June 1974

THE BEARD HAS BEGUN, 22 June 1981

THE GRAND FINALE, 16 July 1979

TWO FEATS ON CLAY, 16 June 1980

UNBJORN, 6 May 1991

WIMBLEDON WAS NEVER BETTER, 11 July 1977

Websites:

www.menstennisforums.com

www.atptour.com

www.tennis-buzz.com

www.britishpathe.com

https://news.google.com/newspapers

https://genome.ch.bbc.co.uk